MODERN
MATTERS

PRINCIPLES
AND
PRACTICE IN
CONSERVING
RECENT
ARCHITECTURE

MODERN
MATTERS

PRINCIPLES
AND
PRACTICE IN
CONSERVING
RECENT
ARCHITECTURE

Edited by

Susan Macdonald

DONHEAD

First published in the United Kingdom 1996 by
Donhead Publishing
Lower Coombe
Donhead St Mary
Shaftesbury
Dorset SP7 9LY
Tel: (01747) 828422

ISBN 1 873394 23 3

A CIP catalogue record is available for this book
from the British Library

Typeset by GCS, Leighton Buzzard
Printed in Great Britain by The Bath Press, Bath

CONTENTS

LIST OF FIGURES

ACKNOWLEDGEMENTS

The papers reproduced in this book have been edited for publication from those originally given at the Modern Matters conference of 31 October - 1 November 1995. By its very nature as Proceedings this book is a collaborative effort and a large number of people were involved in organizing the event who deserve thanks. Firstly our contributors, who presented the talks at the conference reproduced here, and our chairpersons Bridget Cherry, Robert Thorne and John Fidler, who guided the lively and enthusiastic discussions that followed. We are particularly grateful to the international speakers who so willingly gave up their own time to travel to London for the conference. The staff of English Heritage deserve special thanks for their drive and determination to ensure that the importance of the architecture of the recent past is recognized and protected. Lastly we are indebted to Kate Macdonald, our consultant editor, for her efforts in pulling all the papers together and ensuring that the book reached the publishers.

A version of *Reconciling Authenticity and Repair in the Conservation of Modern Architecture*, by Susan Macdonald, previously appeared in the March 1996 issue of *The Architects' Journal*, 2, (1). *Reinforced Concrete: Principles of its Deterioration and Repair* by Gareth Glass and Nick Buenfeld is adapted from course notes on concrete repair technology funded by the European Community Programme on cooperation between universities and industry regarding training in the field of technology (COMETT).

Photographs are reproduced by agreement, and the copyright holders of each are acknowledged in the captions.

AUTHOR BIOGRAPHIES

John Allan, Avanti Architects

A director of Avanti Architects since 1983, John Allan has had experience with Irvine New Town Development Corporation, Scotland, the GLC Department of Architecture and Civic Design and Shepheard Epstein & Hunter. His work at Avanti has included community and medical projects, and a range of restoration projects for modern movement buildings including the Penguin Pool, Highpoint, the Gorilla House and Finsbury Health Centre by Lubetkin, The White House by Amyas Connell and Willow Road, Hampstead by Goldfinger. He is the author of *Berthold Lubetkin: Architecture and the Tradition of Progress*, RIBA Publications (1992) and 'The Conservation of Modern Buildings' in *Building Maintenance and Preservation*, Butterworth-Heinemann (1994).

Adam Brown, Troughton McAslan

Adam Brown studied at Edinburgh University, obtaining an MA in Architecture in 1988 and Diploma in Architecture in 1989. Since 1991 he has worked with John McAslan as project leader on a number of Troughton McAslan's restoration-based projects including Florida Southern College, the De La Warr Pavilion, Isokon Flats, the Royal Society of Arts and the Commonwealth Institute.

Martin Cherry, English Heritage

After teaching history at the Universities of Exeter, St Andrews and Leicester for eight years, Martin Cherry moved into the area of historic buildings in the early 1980s. Working successively as a field-worker on the accelerated listing survey in Devon, as an investigator for the RCHME and as Conservation Officer for Leicestershire County Council, he joined English Heritage where he is now Head of Listings.

Catherine Croft, English Heritage

Catherine Croft was the English Heritage case-work officer for Alexandra Road and currently works as an Inspector of Historic Buildings for the East Midlands Region. She has been an Architectural Advisor for the Victorian Society and is on the committee of the Twentieth-Century Society. She has a BA in Architecture (Cambridge), an MA from the University of Delaware and a Diploma in Conservation from the Architectural Association.

Edward Diestelkamp, The National Trust

Born in St. Louis, Missouri, Edward Diestelkamp received a BSc in Architecture from the University of Southern California (1973) and a PhD from University College London (1982). He worked as an Architectural Assistant for the Louis de Soissons Partnership before moving to the UK. He worked for the National Trust as the Assistant Historic Buildings Representative of North and South Wales and is now Assistant to the Trust's Historic Buildings Secretary.

John Figg, Ove Arup & Partners

John Figg is a Chartered Chemist and an Associate Director with Arup Research and Development, Ove Arup & Partners, London. He has more than 40 years experience in the construction industry and is the author of over 50 publications on the chemistry and performance of building materials.

Gareth Glass, University College London

Gareth Glass studied chemistry and physics at the University of Cape Town, South Africa. Between 1980 and 1984 he completed his MSc and PhD at the Corrosion and Protection Centre, UMIST, Manchester. He has undertaken research in corrosion, mainly on steel in concrete, at the Building Research Institute, CSI in South Africa and at the Department of Civil Engineering, Aston University, and at Taywood Engineering Ltd and Concrete Repairs Ltd, working on the electrochemical protection of steel reinforcement. He now works as a Research Fellow in the Department of Civil Engineering at Imperial College, London, and current research projects include an examination of innovative repair techniques and chloride ingress into concrete.

Elain Harwood, English Heritage

Elain Harwood is an English Heritage historian, specializing in twentieth-century buildings, and has been involved in English Heritage's post-war research and listings programme. She studied building conservation at the Architectural Association (1984-6) and is on the committee of the Twentieth Century Society.

David Heath, English Heritage

David Heath trained as an architect at Cambridge University, and after fifteen years in private practice joined English Heritage in 1987 where he is now Chief Architect.

Wessel de Jonge, DOCOMOMO International

Wessel de Jonge graduated in architecture at Delft University of Technology in 1985, and founded DOCOMOMO International, The International Working Party for Documentation and Conservation of buildings, sites and neighbourhoods of the Modern Movement, with H.J.Henket in 1988. He has been Secretary General since 1990 and is the editor-in-chief of the DOCOMOMO Journal. He was in charge of the recent restoration of the Netherland Pavilion at the Biennale in Venice, Italy (Gerrit Rietveld, 1953-4), and in cooperation with Henket Architects he is currently engaged in the complete restoration and rehabilitation of the former sanatorium Zonnestraal in Hilversum (Duiker and Bijvoet, 1926-31).

Peter Johnson, OCS Group Ltd

Peter Johnson has spent the last 27 years working on many aspects of building facades. As a Director of the OCS Group, one of the UK's largest property maintenance organizations, he has been involved in the practical aspects of cleaning, maintaining and restoring many different types of facade materials. A former President of the Steel Window Association, he has particular experience in the maintenance and replication of windows in steel and other materials. He is Chairman of OCS West Leigh and of the Cotswold Casement Company.

Bob Kindred, Association of Conservation Officers

Bob Kindred has been the Ipswich Borough Conservation Officer since 1987. He has served on the National Executive of the Association of Conservation Officers since 1985 and is the Editor of its professional journal *Context*. He is a National Committee member of the Association of Preservation Trusts and of the Victorian Society and a Heritage Advisor to the Association of District Councils.

John McAslan, Troughton McAslan

John McAslan obtained an MA (1977) and a Diploma (1978) in Architecture from the University of Edinburgh. He worked in the USA with RTKL in Baltimore and Cambridge Seven Associates in Boston in 1975 and 1978-79 before joining Richard Rogers and Partners in 1979, where he was a project architect. In 1983 he established Troughton McAslan with Jamie Troughton. He is principally involved with design and has a specialist interest in the restoration of twentieth-century buildings.

Susan Macdonald, English Heritage

Susan Macdonald graduated as an architect from the University of Sydney and completed her conservation training at ICCROM, Rome. Before joining English Heritage Susan worked in private practice in Sydney and the UK, most recently at Peter Inskip & Peter Jenkins Architects. She currently works in the Architectural Conservation branch of English Heritage, and is secretary of DOCOMOMO UK.

Richard Morrice, English Heritage

Richard Morrice works for English Heritage as the Inspector of Historic Buildings for Kent and Sussex. Currently the Secretary of the Association of Conservation Officers, he teaches on the RICS Conservation course and is working on *The Regency Architecture of Hastings*.

Peter Pullar-Strecker

Peter Pullar-Strecker provides specialist consultancy advice on concrete problems. His work ranges from investigating durability failures, to providing expert witness in arbitration and litigation. He has worked for clients from Africa to Abu Dhabi and currently co-ordinates UK input to the forthcoming Eurocode on concrete repair. He spent many years commissioning and managing research for the Construction Industry Research and Information Association (CIRIA) where he became Deputy Director General. He continues to manage research and co-ordinates LINK programmes for the Department of the Environment and the Engineering and Physical Sciences Research Council. He graduated in Engineering Science at Oxford and is a Fellow of the Institutions of Structural and Civil Engineers.

Andrew Saint, University of Cambridge

Andrew Saint is a Professor of Architecture at the University of Cambridge. He worked for the GLC's Historic Buildings Division between 1974 and 1986 and for English Heritage between 1986 and 1995, and is the author of several books.

John Streeter, Bickerdike Allen Partners

John Streeter has a Diploma in Architecture from Thames Polytechnic School of Architecture and Landscape. He is a Registered Chartered Architect, a member of the Royal Institute of British Architects and of the Association of Planning Supervisors. He has some 30 years of architectural experience, working on new-build and refurbishment projects for public authorities, private building owners and commercial developers. He joined Bickerdike Allen Partners in 1981 and became an Associate of the practice in 1987. He advises architects, contractors and buildings owners on general construction technology issues, arising at all stages of the design and construction process, and has acted for loss adjustors and other legal advisors in the assessment of technical issues arising out of storm damage or personal injury claims.

Jadwiga Urbanik, Wroclaw Technology University, Poland

Jadwiga studied architecture at the Technical University of Wroclaw, specializing in the conservation of monuments. Since 1979 she has worked at the Institute of Architecture, Arts and Technology, Technical University of Wroclaw, taking part in the research work carried out by the Institute and lectures and seminars on town planning, garden history and conservation of the urban and architectonic heritage. Since 1992 she has been involved with the conservation supervision of the hotel by Hans Scharoun in Wroclaw.

H. John Yates, English Heritage

H. John Yates is the English Heritage Inspector of Historic Buildings for the Western Midlands Region. He read Fine Arts at the University of East Anglia and then spent three years as an assistant to Erno Goldfinger. He worked in the GLC Historic Buildings Division from 1978-86. His present work involves negotiating on adaptation and use of all types and periods of historic buildings, but industrial buildings are his specialism.

FOREWORD

As the twentieth century draws to a close we find ourselves examining its history, aspirations and achievements with greater interest. The statutory protection of pre-, inter- and post-war buildings and the formation of interest groups such as the Twentieth Century Society in Britain and DOCOMOMO International are indicative of a greater recognition of architectural contributions to our cultural heritage from this century. The inclusion of twentieth-century masterpieces such as Gaudí's Casa Milá and the heroic structures of Brasilia on the World Heritage List confirm the international interest in conserving the best of our more recent past. With growing appreciation of the value of this century's cultural achievements comes a wish to cherish and celebrate them. Our role at English Heritage is to champion this cause.

The importance of the architectural icons of the early twentieth century, the works of Mackintosh or Lutyens, or the early works of Le Corbusier, Gropius or Lubetkin, are now widely appreciated. Although the early modernists were associated with the 'new', the avant garde, a machine age and new forms of social organization, their buildings are indicative of a former age. The meticulous craftsmanship of their houses is rare today, as are their spartan kitchens with accommodation for servants replaced by our appliances and gadgetry. We are now beginning to accept that Modern belongs to a bygone era, a now distant past for most of us.

Cultural heritage encompasses all our past. However, the statutory protection of historic buildings in England holds the past at bay with the 'Thirty Year Rule'. This remains the case for all buildings apart from those younger buildings at risk which are of exceptional architectural interest and are at least 10 years old, which may be 'spot' listed (used for emergency cases). The controversy for listing pre- and inter-war buildings has abated, and it is now the buildings of the post-war era which are struggling for recognition, and are the focus of much media attention.

As English Heritage is here to promote, listing is about managing change, not freezing the past in time. Conservation is about learning to manage change. Statutory protection brings with it new issues which need our urgent attention. The history of the buildings and the society that shaped their context have yet to be comprehensively recorded and assessed, and we are only just beginning to understand their technology, the construction methods and materials.

The English Heritage conference *Modern Matters* on 31 October - 1 November 1995 attempted to examine the philosophical, methodological and practical problems associated with conserving our recent past. The conference sought to establish what progress had been made in the protection and care of twentieth-century buildings, to share this information and to determine where the gaps in our knowledge lie in order to best direct our future efforts.

Our century has been one of inexorable change, particularly since World War II. The huge rise in population, the effects of world-scale industrialization and increasingly sophisticated technological advances have put new pressures on architecture and construction to provide quicker, cheaper and more varied responses than ever before. As a result the twentieth century embraces a number of architectural themes or styles, the expression of which boasts a vast array of materials and techniques which exploit the newest technological advances. The buildings which have been carefully listed, amid resistance and controversy, represent the extraordinary, or the very best of their time. In the future, as twentieth-century buildings become rarer, those achieving protected status will no doubt include the ordinary as well, just as today there is an interest in the humbler Georgian or Victorian buildings. As heritage values change to be more representative of the full depth and breadth of our most recent history and culture, what we protect will also change.

At this time we are dealing with the most innovative, often the most experimental twentieth-century exemplars, and with this come the most difficult problems. Polarized opinions on values and approach, new technical challenges and, in the case of high-rise or large housing schemes, the largest scale of conservation we have yet had to face, are just some of the challenges to be met. The philosophical and methodical issues now concern post-war buildings, but as the papers in this volume show practical questions have been dealt with more slowly. The problems of conserving pre- and inter-war buildings are only now attracting solutions, while those of post-war structures are on the frontier of research.

This conference chose to start with the most urgent problems, the most frequently-encountered difficulties with our listed building stock. In this respect the papers discussing examples from the first half of this century are perhaps biased towards Modernism rather than mainstream architecture. This is simply a reflection of the fact that it is the buildings which fall within the international Modernist idiom which demand knowledge and experience that we are only beginning to develop to enable us to deal with the specific planning and technical issues their conservation requires. Modernity has a variety of expressions, and some of the more traditional expressions have their own pressing problems. However with our present knowledge of traditional materials and construction methods there are better established parameters for the repair of these types of buildings (those which use new materials but traditional construction techniques and vice versa). By addressing the more technically innovative buildings which experimented with materials and methods which would become mainstream today, we are able to combine this information with our knowledge of traditional materials to deal with the problems of the mainstream building. It is proposed in future conferences to widen the discourse to encompass the full richness of our twentieth-century cultural heritage by exploring a wider range of styles and materials.

The papers in this book attempt to consolidate some of the pioneering work in this area of conservation. Part I discusses philosophy, protection and management, focusing on efforts in the UK. The case studies provide examples of the difficulties and show how strategies can be determined in response to specific concerns. Part II seeks to determine what progress has been made in dealing with the practical problems associated with the conservation and care of modern buildings. Concrete, the most widely used modern material in Britain today, is given due attention. Metal windows are another of the most important characteristics of modern architecture and their loss usually incurs major design alterations to listed buildings. The case studies were selected to draw on experiences from both the UK and abroad to illustrate the range of technical problems associated with concrete, metal windows and other common materials. While the care and consideration associated with any of the case studies examined is exemplary, the conclusion can be drawn that we still have a long way to go to develop economically-viable repair options for dealing with large-scale concrete repairs, or to deal with visually acceptable repairs for fair-faced concrete buildings of the post-war era. There is a multitude of material and technical issues which we have yet to come to grips with if we are to care for the full range of architectural treatments used by the architects of the twentieth century.

The bibliography will provide a useful reference for further reading within the themes of the conference. Names and addresses of useful organizations actively involved in twentieth-century conservation and the repair process have also been included. English Heritage is continually updating its information and resources, and will be interested to hear of texts which have been found useful by others. Please write to Architectural Conservation, English Heritage, 429 Oxford Street, London W1R 2HD.

English Heritage was established to advance the understanding and care of historic buildings. By publishing the proceedings of this conference we seek to disseminate knowledge about the value, conservation and care of our twentieth-century buildings. The conference was useful in establishing the current level of understanding and thus identifying which challenges need to be pursued in the future. Work must now be done to focus research to ensure we are equal to those challenges.

Susan Macdonald
March 1996

CHAPTER 1
INTRODUCTION
Chris Green

It is quite remarkable that we can be just 1,521 days away from the end of the twentieth century with public and media opinion still uncertain about this century's achievements in its built heritage. In 1,522 days we shall be talking about the 'heritage of the last century' and I predict that only then will nostalgia at last set in for twentieth-century buildings. The task of this book is to lead public opinion in preparing the ground for this conversion in the belief that Modern does Matter.

I am aware of an awakening interest in modern architecture, and not just in our more traditional pre-war heritage. This reflects considerable credit on the dogged perseverance of both the Twentieth Century Society and of DOCOMOMO in attracting interest, knowledge and funding to this great cause.

Every generation has undervalued recent architecture while overpraising older work. The Victorians attacked the very Georgian buildings that are now listed grade I a century later. I cannot believe that our generation can wish to leave no contemporary heritage behind for the interest of future generations. Public debate over post-war buildings in particular has tended to focus quite wrongly on facile attempts to judge contemporary buildings as ugly or beautiful.

You will be relieved to know that the 1983 Heritage Acts offer a more intelligent set of criteria based on identifying the best of our heritage on the basis of architectural interest and/ or historic interest. These criteria are intended to reduce emotive debate on fashions in architectural beauty and to create a more analytical debate on the selection of the buildings which will be of the greatest value to future generations.

You will be pleased to know that English Heritage is involved in a thematic study of all post-war buildings to ensure that a representative group of buildings are recommended to the Secretary of State for final listing. About 155 post-war buildings are listed at present, and we hope to see this number increase significantly over the next five years.

It is, however, one thing to list a modern building and quite another to ensure its long-term survival. It is not just what we want to preserve: this book is also about how we should do it.

I do not belong to the school that claims that all post-war buildings have been built for a short life and should be allowed to expire peacefully within a generation or two. This may be true of some buildings but it is certainly not true of the whole stock. Our twentieth-century buildings did not arrive from Mars: they were built by and for humans and their construction is well documented. Early experience on buildings such as the modern Coventry Cathedral has already shown that fundamental repairs to preserve life are both feasible and affordable.

This is a worldwide challenge and we should note that Chicago has already run its second conference on the restoration of modern buildings. At our first conference in the UK, the proceedings from which are presented here, were papers from Poland and Holland as well as project experience from the USA. The purpose of this book is to create a wider interest and respect for the preservation of the best of our twentieth-century buildings. I would like to introduce the papers with an assurance that English Heritage is totally committed to the identification and conservation of modern buildings from our lifetime. We recognize the long-term vision of allowing future generations to experience the best of our own architecture. We need to identify effective conservation methods for twentieth-century buildings. Above all we want this book to kill the myth that all modern buildings are unrepairable.

English Heritage most certainly agrees that Modern Matters.

31 October 1995

PART ONE

CURRENT
PHILOSOPHY,
LEGISLATION
AND
PRACTICE

CHAPTER 2

LISTING TWENTIETH-CENTURY BUILDINGS: THE PRESENT SITUATION

Martin Cherry

Listing on new frontiers

The essays in this book are concerned with the philosophical and practical challenges of conserving the most interesting buildings of the recent past. The underlying assumption is that the best are worthy of protection. Listing is the procedure most often used to accomplish this objective and this paper discusses some of the problems and principles of this core activity. Listing is not designed to fossilize buildings as museum pieces for all time whatever the cost. It provides the opportunity to explore all possible means of maintaining an historic building in viable use without compromising its historical and architectural character. With care, resources and imagination this can normally be achieved, although some change is likely if a building is to continue serving the needs of its occupants.

If conservation is to be successful, it must command a consensus. Listing enjoys a wide degree of support. A recent opinion poll indicated that a majority of respondents felt that not enough was being done to protect our historic environment[1], but certain areas remain problematical. The listing of inter-war buildings is now well-established and generally non-contentious. The first fifty, selected under the guidance of Niklaus Pevsner and his colleagues on the Historic Buildings Council, were identified in 1970, and there are currently about 600 buildings from this period listed in England.

The listing of post-war buildings, on the other hand, does not yet appear to enjoy universal favour. At present, 154 post-war buildings are listed, ranging from widely-acknowledged masterpieces such as Coventry Cathedral to less well-known structures such as the railway stations at Coventry and Oxford Road, Manchester and at Birmingham New Street Station (Figure 2.1). The issue of post-war listing has generated a degree of interest out of all proportion to the actual numbers involved: these remain small, and for some time to come will continue to be considerably less than 0.1% of the total stock of listed buildings. Widespread interest has been stimulated by the Secretary of State's decision to open up post-war listing to public consultation. Greater openness is entirely desirable but presents a challenge to those responsible for conserving the recent past. Because the serious study of recent architecture is

Figure 2.1   Birmingham New Street Station, Signal Box on Navigation Street, listed grade II, 1964, by Bicknell & Hamilton (English Heritage)

a relatively new departure research findings are not easily accessible and current specialist thinking has not yet, in the main, found a voice that is either intelligible or persuasive to lay thinking. This gulf needs to be bridged if modern buildings are to gain a place in the affections of the public.

In order to do this, we need first to understand the principal objections to listing, both in general terms and when raised in the context of twentieth-century and, especially, post-war architecture. We then need to take stock of the debate to date. This paper looks at both these areas. But, until we have a much clearer idea how people feel about these questions, we will be proceeding at best in the half-gloom. We urgently need more hard data on public attitudes if we are to present arguments in favour of conservation to best effect.

The listing issues

Much of the controversy results from the widely-held misconception, often fuelled by ill-informed and sometimes mischievous press coverage, that listing 'freezes' buildings.

Nothing could be further from the truth. If we look just at the small number of post-war listed buildings[2], one of them has been demolished and another (Keeling House) appears at the time of writing to be facing a similar fate. Significant alterations have been made, for instance, to the Trades Union Congress HQ and the Smithsons' Economist Building, and major new work has transformed Richardson's Bracken House (the first post-war building to be listed). Outside London, changes have taken place at the Gollins Melvin Ward Partnership's Sheffield University Arts Tower and the situation at Sir Basil Spence's University of Sussex is discussed in detail elsewhere in this volume. All these interventions have been carried out with listed building consent.

Listing was introduced in the 1940s as part of the Town and Country planning legislation and is concerned about managing change rather than fossilizing buildings. It is an inherently flexible system which flags the architectural and historic character of buildings in order to ensure that this is taken fully into account when changes or demolition are proposed. The situation was carefully defined in November 1993 by the then Secretary of State for National Heritage, Peter Brooke, when he announced the listing of Sir Denys Lasdun's 1955 high-rise cluster block, Keeling House in London's East End (Figure 2.2). It is worth quoting fully:

Figure 2.2   Sir Denys Lasdun's Keeling House, Claredale Road, London, 1954, currently under threat of demolition (English Heritage)

I am aware of the structural and technical problems associated with [this building], and the various estimates of the costs of repairing it. But the legislation requires that I list buildings which I consider to be of special architectural or historic interest. Once I consider a building to have such interest, then I may not take into account the costs of repair or the consequences of listing in other ways.

Listing clearly creates a presumption in favour of a building's preservation, but it does not necessarily mean that a building must be preserved whatever the cost; its main purpose is to ensure that care is taken over decisions concerning its future. If an application were made for consent to demolish Keeling House, the listed building consent procedure would permit the special interest of the building to be weighed against other arguments which may point in favour of demolition.[3]

Opposition to listing revolves around four principal premisses. None can be dismissed lightly although all are underpinned (and thereby undermined) by the assumption that listing freezes buildings. The first objection has run through the history of the state protection of historic sites ever since Sir John Lubbock steered the first legislation through the House of Commons in the 1880s. It is that statutory protection unreasonably erodes private property (and commercial) rights. Closely related to this is the question of accountability, the assumption that listing is inherently anti-democratic. The fact that the decision to list a building lies with the (elected and accountable) Secretary of State is often overlooked and the reaction to listing decisions coming 'out of the blue' can be fiery.

Stephen Dorrell's speech to *The Architects' Journal* centenary dinner in February 1995 indicated some official sympathy for the view that the listing procedures needed to be opened up. When announcing his intention to introduce public consultation for certain sorts of listing cases he said:

> *In my view it is no longer tolerable, in a society committed to openness and respect for the rights of the individual, that the first that many owners learn of listing is when an official letter drops on the door mat announcing a fait accompli. I have decided that the wider public should have a greater opportunity to comment on listing recommendations put to me. It is, after all, they and not only the experts who have to live with the buildings I decide to list.*[4]

The third objection to listing is that it inhibits much-needed development, a point to which I will return. Fourthly, there are those who fear terminal decline and the creation of a museum culture serviced by the heritage industry. Post-war planners were inclined not to let old buildings stand in the way of establishing the brave new world, and some people now see listing, conceived in those same heady post-war years, 'as a pathetic attempt by a former world power to stop time in its tracks'.[5]

All these viewpoints resonate through the current debate about the listing of twentieth-century (and particularly post-war) buildings. But the protection of recent buildings raises further specific issues. The first concerns objectivity and distance. Are we really far enough away from the period in question to assess the buildings dispassionately? While there will always be disagreement about how long a 'cooling-off period' is needed, the 'Thirty Year Rule', a convention that excludes buildings of between ten and thirty years from listing unless they are of exceptional importance, that is, of grade I or II* standard, and clearly under threat, probably provides an adequate amount of time for a cool and detached assessment to be made. Such an assessment depends on the availability of sound research which can help the public, politicians, planners and specialists place buildings firmly in their context and justify the selection of individual cases for listing. The role of English Heritage's research-based post-war listing programme, designed to meet this need, is discussed below.

Popular public perceptions are more difficult to gauge. Do people use the concept of 'heritage' as a means of distinguishing the past from the present? If so, will modern buildings ever be widely accepted as precious cultural products worthy of protection? Or are people generally more tolerant of an environment that includes buildings that they themselves once reacted to with hostility? These are difficult questions to answer and more focused research on public opinion is needed before we can be sure how informed, concerned or indifferent people really are and, consequent upon this, how those responsible for enhancing the public's enjoyment and understanding of historic buildings should best move forward.

More technical concerns about the listing of recent buildings centre on their intrinsic character and use of materials. In a thoughtful article published in October 1993, Robert Thorne drew attention to the peculiar problems of conserving non-traditional modern buildings which were:

> ... executed in a fundamentally different manner. In the use of new materials, from reinforced concrete to aluminium and plastics, in new jointing systems, and new combinations of structure and finish, they constitute a revolutionary change in building form. [6]

The likelihood is (argues Thorne) that where repair treatment is required for modern buildings conceived of as 'flawless objects', it would need to be radical since a conventional SPAB-inspired patching strategy would run entirely counter to the objectives of the architect. In some cases high-class replicas in proven materials carried out to high specifications by reliable operatives might be the most honest solution.

In any case, for 'radical' read 'very expensive'. This dilemma runs throughout the essays in this book. The heavy repair costs for the Roman Catholic Metropolitan Cathedral of Christ the King at Liverpool (which attracted a £1.5 million grant from English Heritage), like those for Lasdun's Keeling House (which failed to win public funding), may be seen as challenges to conservation policy-makers: should post-war buildings of this kind be treated as special cases deserving a larger slice of a diminishing budget? Or should prohibitive repair costs render buildings like this ineligible for listing? Or should they be placed in a category where demolition is an easier option? But before yielding to the temptation of dealing with 'problem buildings' of this period as a special case, it needs to be remembered that not all twentieth-century (or post-war) buildings fall into this non-traditional category, and not all traditional repair jobs to older historic buildings come cheap. John Carr's The Crescent, Buxton, of the 1770s and listed grade I, has cost the public purse in excess of £1 million (purchase and repair). And, as Catherine Croft points out in her essay on the Alexandra Road housing development (listed in response to an unsatisfactory concrete patching programme), small-scale craftsmanlike repairs can be both practicable and effective even on the most 'flawlessly' conceived building where the original standards of workmanship and materials were of a high order.

A third objection to the listing of certain post-war buildings is the apparent contradiction between the need for maximum flexibility (where this was central to the original design brief) and the notion of conservation. Sir Andrew Derbyshire has frequently raised this issue with special reference to his York University buildings which were designed 'for uncertainty' with the possibility of radical change an integral part of the concept.

Listing can live comfortably with change, the underlying premise both of the legislation and the practice being, after all, the management of change, but problems arise when the concept of designed-in obsolescence enters the equation. Some twentieth-century buildings were clearly designed with a short life-span in mind, although many of these, such as prefabs and Nissen huts, have proved stubbornly long-lived, and Andrew Saint explores further the deeper issues of renewal with special reference to post-war schools in his paper elsewhere in this volume. But many categories of building, even the most flexible and including the first post-war generations of commercial and industrial buildings, were not conceived by either architects or patrons as being temporary in any sense.

Radical critiques question the value of any form of protection for post-war buildings. But even if protection is seen as justified, it does not follow that listing is the most appropriate designation to adopt. Many buildings, such as housing in the New Towns, for instance, where their importance lies more in their overall planning and setting than in their intrinsic design and detailing, might be more effectively managed through Conservation Area controls (perhaps with Article 4 Directions to provide additional protection for specified details). Similarly, listing may not always be appropriate for buildings made up of large numbers of repetitive and identical units (such as much high-density public housing), where it is neither necessary or desirable to extend conservation controls into the interiors of people's homes.

Recent developments

The 1946 guidelines for listing (*Instructions to Investigators*) anticipated hardly any post-1914 buildings being placed on the statutory lists.[7] By 1970, as we have seen, a small number of (mainly classic modern) buildings of the inter-war period were recommended, followed by a further and more catholic selection of 150 in 1981. Almost a generation, and over 600 listed buildings, later objections are rarely made when buildings of this period are added to the list and, when these occur, it is invariably in response to the perceived high-handedness and undemocratic nature of the listing system, rather than a challenge to the intrinsic merits of the buildings themselves.

Post-war listing has had a rather more tempestuous ride. In 1988 ministers accepted in principle that buildings of this period were eligible for listing. However, because they were still considered to be subject to fierce controversy 52 out of 70 candidates put forward for listing by the Historic Buildings Council were rejected, although a number have been listed since. The problem was not simply the contentious nature of the proposals. The lack of a coherent and consolidated body of research work on these buildings made it difficult for ministers or members of the public to place them securely in context.

The nettle was finally grasped by the Minister of State, Lady Blatch, who, in 1991, asked English Heritage to embark on a three-year programme of research and assessment which would result in a number of firmly contextualized recommendations for listing that could also set a standard for post-war listing decisions in the future. It was decided to tackle the complex subject by building type, and English Heritage's first batch of recommendations, for schools and universities, was accepted in its entirety by Peter Brooke in March 1993.

The listing of these educational buildings stimulated considerable interest and elicited a number of carefully considered features in the specialist press. Some of the decisions were positively welcomed and objections, where they occurred, were muted. One commentator suggested that this may have been the result of the fragmented nature of educational (especially schools) management which militated against a co-ordinated response.[8]

Public interest in the issue of post-war listing was kept on the boil by a number of high-profile spot-listing (or emergency) cases. The debates over Liverpool Cathedral and Keeling House (referred to above), for instance, were concerned mainly with the costs and justification of repairing buildings that used untried materials or failed to meet the architect's specifications. The likelihood that Coventry's Lower Precinct would be listed raised the spectre of freezing development, that of Alexandra Road in Camden questioned the reasonableness of imposing conservation controls over an entire community: both of these cases focused attention on the relative merits of listing or Conservation Area designation for large-scale urban megastructures. A theme common to all these situations was a lack of consensus about the intrinsic quality of the buildings: was it justifiable to value them as one would a Jacobean house or a Georgian church?

Public opinion was never subjected to scientific analysis. The debate about the Coventry Precinct in the columns of the local press, however, indicated a much stronger attachment to the building on the part of local people than opponents to listing had bargained for, and unsolicited letters from residents of some of the public housing developments being considered for listing elsewhere revealed similar levels of support.

During these months, however, a stronger and more powerful head of steam was building up. Commercial and landowning interests were mobilizing and directed their attack against both the 'undemocratic' nature of listing and its apparent lack of realism, its failure to respond to the realities of contemporary economic life. The Country Landowners Association called for greater openness to remove the 'academic mystique' surrounding listing decisions; an *Economist* article took up the theme of other-worldly boffins with no knowledge of the real world making decisions that had a direct effect on livelihoods and profit margins. The *Chartered Surveyors' Monthly* ran a campaign to extend the listing selection criteria, currently solely concerned with the 'special architectural and historic interest' of a building, to include aspects such as economic viability and structural condition.

As we have seen, the Secretary of State for National Heritage responded dramatically to the issue of openness by announcing that he would consult with owners and the general public on a number of listing cases starting with post-war commercial, industrial and railway buildings, a batch of recommendations from English Heritage that his office had been considering for some time. Mr Dorrell also recognized other areas of concern which he promised to look into further in a Green Paper, including the appropriateness of extending listing controls to interiors in all cases, the relative merits of listing and conservation area controls in towns and villages, the question of whether the general listing criteria should be revised and the virtues of a special category for post-war buildings of special interest.

Public debate and the thrust of most of the detailed responses to the first post-war listing consultation exercise centred on questions of economic viability. Should not the wider consequences of listing be taken into account at the time of listing? Views were informed more by gut reaction and hunch than empirical research. What research there is on the subject, and it is far too little at present, was commissioned by English Heritage and the Royal Institution of Chartered Surveyors. *The Investment Performance of Listed Buildings* showed that the long-term economic performance of listed commercial buildings can equal (and in certain circumstances exceed) that of unlisted ones. Other research confirms that listing may adversely affect a building's value at the point of listing,[9] but this is normally a temporary blip in its longer-term commercial history. There is clearly an inherent conflict between the interests of those investors and developers who are seeking short-term returns and those operating the listing system who have to take the longer view, but listing is by no means intrinsically inimical to the interests of responsible commercial institutions.

As the Secretary of State makes clear in the passage quoted earlier, the listed building consent procedures provide the best means of balancing the interests of the owner (questions of economic viability and the costs of repairs, for instance) and the wider community (the cultural value of the historic building, for example, and the environmental and ecological gains of conservation over demolition and rebuild). These interests are not necessarily competing ones, and over 90% of listed building consent applications are granted.

One further problem about addressing all the issues at the point of listing, rather than at the consent stage, is that listing does not necessarily (or even normally) occur at a time when there are proposals for change. Viability and structural assessments carried out then would quickly become out of date and no reliance could be placed upon them when owners later wished to make changes. It would be difficult to justify the additional costs to the public purse that such wider surveys would entail.

Future trends

There are three main ingredients in a successful conservation policy. First, it must ensure that the selection of buildings for protection is safe and sound, based on rigorous research, and that the designation (for example listing and Conservation Area status) is appropriate. Second, that public support must be secured through debate and education, and third, that the planning environment must facilitate sound management and reduce unecessary delay and uncertainty.

The main thrust of English Heritage's listing survey work is the programme of research-based assessments based on specific building types. These are concerned primarily with those areas that have been overlooked or under-researched in the past: the post-war project is one example of this initiative, work on textile mills and industrial buildings generally, another. [10] Only by providing an academically watertight basis for our recommendations for ministers will they feel able to take our advice. This is particularly important with unfamiliar or contentious buildings, and this thematic approach to listing will continue to characterize our strategy for some years to come.

The government's decision to open up these areas of work to greater public scrutiny will help reduce the mystique that many people feel surrounds listing. The first attempts made by English Heritage to open up the debate on post-war listing, through the media of exhibitions, conferences and publications (for example, *A Change of Heart* in 1992 and *The Age of Optimism* in 1993[11]) were frustrated by the then current convention of confidentiality that made it impossible to discuss openly any individual buildings that were being considered for listing. The conference and exhibitions supporting the public post-war listing consultation exercise carried out during 1996, *Something Worth Keeping?*, were not constrained in this way.

Public confidence can only be assured if the full facts are known. The criteria for selecting the post-war buildings for listing have been outlined in an English Heritage leaflet[12] and a new publication on the period will follow.[13] But there are many other aspects that need further work. Following on from the research on the economic performance of listed buildings referred to above, English Heritage has commissioned investigations into the wider (and less easily quantifiable) social benefits of maintaining and enhancing valued historic environments and on the whole complex issue of their sustainability.

Finally, there is the question of management. The most frequently voiced complaint levelled against listing is the delay and uncertainty it can cause. The recently published English Heritage discussion paper, *Agreements for the Management of Listed Buildings*,[14] explores ways of expediting the listed building consent procedures especially in relation to the larger and more complex sites. While streamlining procedures remains a desirable objective, no sound management decisions can be taken without fully understanding the building in question, its special historic interest and character and the nature of its construction. Researching construction techniques and the performance of the materials used, especially those pioneered in the twentieth century, is a central and urgent requirement. It is one of the central concerns of the essays in this book. If, by widening the debate on the management and conservation of modern buildings, this book (and the conference on which the papers are based) helps build a more viable future for the best of them, its main objective will have been accomplished.

References

1   English Heritage press release 414/994 (1994), 'Poll reveals growing support for heritage'.

2   At 1 January 1996 there were 189 listed post-war items on 111 sites.

3   Department of National Heritage press release 166/93 (1993), 'Peter Brooke announces listing of Keeling House'.

4   Stephen Dorrell's speech to the Architectural Journal (9 March 1995, p7).

5   Popham, P. (27 November 1995), 'Grade I, grade II...but does making the Grade stunt our cities' growth?', *The Independent*.

6   Thorne, R. (1993), 'The right conservation policy for post-war listed buildings', *The Architects' Journal*, **198**, (13 October), 21.

7   Ministry of Housing and Local Government (1944), *Instructions to Investigators,* London: unpublished document.

8   Bell, S. (1994), 'The listing of post-1939 educational buildings: burden or blessing?', *Chartered Surveyor Monthly*, **3**, (6), 16-17.

9   Scanlon, K., Edge, A. and Wilmot, T (1994), *The Economy of Listed Buildings*, Discussion Paper **43**, Cambridge: University of Cambridge Department of Land Economy.

10   Cherry, M. (1995), 'Protecting Industrial Buildings: The Role of Listing', in M. Palmer and P. Neaverson (eds), *Managing the Industrial Heritage,* Leicester: Leicester Archaeological Monographs.

11   Saint, A. (1994), *A Change of Heart*, London: RCHME, and ibid (1995) *The Age of Optimism*, London: English Heritage.

12   English Heritage (1996), *Understanding Listing: Post-War Architecture*, leaflet.

13   Harwood, E. (ed) (forthcoming), *England's Post-War Building*, London: Yale University Press with the Paul Mellon Foundation.

14   English Heritage, (1995), *Agreements for the Management of Listed Buildings*, London: English Heritage.

CHAPTER 3
PHILOSOPHICAL PRINCIPLES OF MODERN CONSERVATION

Andrew Saint

'Philosophical principles' is a portentous phrase. In preparation for this paper I therefore cast my net into the ocean of conservation philosophy to see what I could trawl up that might be most pertinent to the care and conservation of modern buildings. I looked at Ruskin and Morris, I consulted the Venice and Burra Charters governing international conservation principles and action, I perused A. R. Powys's classic statement of the SPAB's creed, *The Repair of Ancient Buildings* (1929, 1981), and I read a neglected book called *Conservation of Buildings* (1972) by that fine elder statesman of English conservation, John Harvey. They all had pointers to give. But on the whole I felt disturbingly alone. It is a feeling which seems to be widely shared when it comes to principles for the conservation of modern buildings.

Why is this? The main reason, I believe, is that the guidance in principle which we need today for the care and the future of modern listed buildings usually falls somewhere in the middle between outright conservation philosophy on the one hand, and restoration philosophy on the other. By outright conservation philosophy I mean the matter you find in the charters. Typically, this is couched as a framework of broad generalization. The Burra Charter, for instance, defines the concept of cultural significance, and then breaks this down into the kinds of value that this may embody, aesthetic, historic, scientific or social. Later, it goes on to set out the various steps to be followed in adopting and implementing a conservation policy. I could spend the rest of this paper playing the part of a native of the planet ICOMOS and suggesting ways in which these successive values and steps can be satisfied in respect of twentieth-century buildings. Most of us would probably agree that these general values and steps are as valid for the twentieth century as they are for earlier periods, and indeed that the fundamental emotive responses identified by Ruskin, Morris, Harvey and many other authorities that make people want to preserve the material culture of the past remain the same for all periods. But for just these reasons, I am not convinced that at the end of such an investigation we would feel that the process of reaffirming those values, those steps and those responses for the twentieth century had got us further forward.

By restoration philosophy I mean the kind of thinking represented by Powys's *The Repair of Ancient Buildings* and other manuals down to Christopher Brereton's *The Repair of Historic*

Buildings, published by English Heritage in 1991. Taken as statements of principles for technique and repair, these manuals are proud, practical and often thought-provoking stuff. Only the most recent deal with questions and methods of repairing modern buildings, whose radical differences in material and technique are bound to feed back into issues of principle. But there is a more general point about restoration philosophy. This is that it tends to collapse so speedily into empirical particularities that we seldom find much ground on which to philosophize at all. Each case, almost all the restoration experts and manuals stress, has to be judged and validated on its merits, character and context. Judgement is everything: a general mode of conduct is as hard to prescribe as in architectural design itself. You only have to read about any specific restoration, ancient or modern, to be reminded that there are almost no rules, only applications of sound judgement, experience and sensitivity.

So it is between the Scylla of resounding, charter-like generalization and the Charybdis of self-referring specificity that I launch my frail philosophical bark, with two plain questions as my map to guide me. What is it, if anything, that makes modern buildings, twentieth-century buildings, differ from those of previous centuries? And, if we can establish that, what implications does this have for the way we treat the best of them? Let us establish some clear lines of thinking in response to these questions.

There are six basic ways, it seems to me, in which modern buildings may differ from older ones:

1.   number
2.   technique
3.   intention
4.   performance
5.   viability
6.   appeal

For the rest of this paper I shall simply explore each of these categories or factors in turn, trying to keep them apart for the sake of clarity but increasingly failing to do so because, of course, they all act and react upon one another.

Number

The first of my categories is number. It is a self-evident truth that we have more recent buildings than older ones. A great deal of the existing official conservation system is geared not towards beauty, or towards historical significance in the simple and ordinary understanding of that phrase ('Queen Elizabeth slept here'), but towards sheer rarity. The sliding scale which governs the listing and scheduling processes means that a tiny lump of Roman ruin will be protected, whereas most complete twentieth-century buildings won't.

This quality of being common won't, of course, last forever. It is only temporarily attached to twentieth-century buildings and will in the fullness of time dissolve. In this respect, modern buildings are more like Victorian buildings than Georgian ones, and indeed it is not so long since there were more Victorian than twentieth-century buildings in this country.

In its operation, the sliding scale rule certainly creates peculiarities and anomalies. The lump of Roman ruin is sometimes damnably raw, not to say downright ugly, and technically less sophisticated than most things built today. In London, the plethoric terrace houses of the 1820s, mostly sparse in design terms and without much interior interest, are generally listed because they are 'Georgian', whereas their grander Kensington and Bayswater descendants of the Victorian period are often not listed. Nevertheless the principle of protecting more as we go back in time and buildings become rarer, protecting less as we approach the fertility of the present day, commands pretty general agreement in principle. The sliding scale operates at two levels: not just at the level of designation or listing, but at the level of the treatment meted out to buildings, listed or unlisted. All things being equal, when it comes to change the modern building or structure is going to get the rougher treatment because it has more sisters and cousins of its own age. It may even have exact copies or equivalents, in which case, powerful arguments about its popularity or beauty or practicality or symbolism are going to have to be adduced to prevent it being taken down or altered. Such arguments were made, for instance, in the case of the telephone box controversy a few years ago.

Precisely because there are so many recent buildings, the Darwinian argument for a process of natural selection, for the survival of the fittest and the luckiest without the intervention of the state to protect weaklings or obsolescent specimens that stand in the way of younger, thrusting new species, is an attractive one. (It is also one that holds particular attractions for builders and architects, the natural parents of up-and-coming contenders in the guise of new buildings.) Rarity can hardly yet be pleaded for the products of twentieth-century architecture as a whole (Figure 3.1). Sometimes someone will plead that a building is the world's only bootcamp by Bloggs the celebrated brutalist, or the first example of a prestressed bridge in Barsetshire. When you think about it, these are really special cases of pleading for significance by reason of technique or artistic intention, not examples of overall rarity. If one of the main emotive arguments for conservation is that of preserving testaments to different phases of regional, national or international culture, we can for the moment rest pretty secure that for the twentieth century there will be plenty of such testaments left when the ball and chain have ceased to swing.

The question about numbers, then, seems to be a simple one, and one that is well understood. We list fewer modern buildings, we preserve fewer of them, and we bear less hard on alterations intended to be made to them, unless some other criterion comes into play. There is no real difficulty about this because the principle is accepted for earlier periods. In this sense the difference between modern and older buildings is contingent, not necessary, to use the language of the philosophers.

Technique

Technique comes next. Technique raises its head as a philosophical issue because the pace and manner of change in twentieth-century building have rendered much old-style conservation thinking irrelevant. It is a matter of common observation that architecture,

Figure 3.1   Panorama of housing at Gleadless Valley, Sheffield, 1955 onwards. The extent and repetitive house types of this splendidly landscaped development preclude the possibility of listing, although means must be found for its protection (Andrew Saint)

construction and servicing are very different animals than they were a century ago. These changes cause particular difficulties of adjustment for the English conservation tradition, with its Arts-and-Crafts pedigree and its SPAB-style stress on the material significance of buildings and therefore on fidelity to structure, craft and texture. At the head of that tradition stands Ruskin. With his passionate emphasis on the value inherent in the worked surface and ornament of a structure because it represents and honours the sweat and skill of those who laboured on it, Ruskin gave a powerful and original twist to this view of conservation that remains peculiarly English. It is, of course, a philosophy which has succeeded splendidly for long-life masonry structures and high-class interiors of buildings with long-term institutional stability in use.

Two plain points are worth making about the relationship between conservation and changes in twentieth-century building technique. Firstly, rapid though those changes have been and continue to be, it is a matter of historical fact that they have been evolutionary, not revolutionary. We are not talking about an utterly new and separate class of buildings distinguishable in some self-evident material way from those of the past. Nor, as all the better recent historians remind us, can we arbitrarily start the clock and say modern architecture began at a certain point. Not the least absorbing conclusion of the research carried out by

English Heritage on modern buildings in connection with the listing programme has been to reinforce and remind us of the fact that fine traditional architecture has gone on throughout the twentieth century and never really collapsed. Not only that, but the distinction between modern and traditional architecture will not often hold water, as a study of structural technique shows in particular. There are fine, progressive-looking buildings with old-fashioned structures and old-fashioned-looking buildings hiding or incorporating technical novelties (Figures 3.2 and 3.3).

The other thing to remember about technique and conservation philosophy is that the old SPAB approach was evolved for a specific kind of indigenous architecture. It never fitted the whole international gamut of historic building techniques as well. Once we look beyond masonry buildings, whether to the mud or straw huts of tropical and subtropical cultures or even to the traditional framed buildings of so much of Northern Europe and Northern America, the game is different and the rules change. When we worry about twentieth-century

Figure 3.2   The Royal Horticultural Halls, London. Easton and Robertson, architects, with Oscar Faber, engineer, 1926-8. An elegant academic front hides a concrete-arched interior of different character but equal value (English Heritage)

Figure 3.3   Concrete-arched interior of the Royal Horticultural Halls, London. (English Heritage).

buildings which cannot survive unless their internal structure is reinforced, or unless they are radically replanned or reclad or refenestrated with materials different from those originally used because the old cladding or windows are no longer available or have proved faulty, we should feel reassured that these are not such new issues as all that. Any timber-framed building that has been moved or partitioned or clad in tiles or weather-boarding has been through some of these processes.

The question we ask when changes of this nature are contemplated to a historic building of any date is always the same one: will the building after the changes remain a structure of architectural and historic interest? So far as technique is concerned, the answer is going to lie in the gap between present appearance and construction on the one hand and original intention on the other. It is in such a context, I believe, that we have to locate the search for 'authenticity', the nebulous word that has crept into modern restoration philosophy in place of older, simpler concepts like 'truth to materials'.

Intention

An authentic restoration, it may be ventured, is not just one in which all the parts, visible or otherwise, are repaired or replaced on a like-for-like basis, but one also in which the original priorities of the building's authors (all the building's authors) are critically heeded. And thus we come on to the third of my concepts for examination, that of the intentions behind twentieth-century buildings. Do they differ from those of earlier centuries, and if so, how? On the face of it, this question seems so monstrous and all-embracing that it can hardly be worth posing. Nevertheless it lies at the heart of the matter and it seems to me that some progress can be made with it.

The first thing to be said on this score is that where modern buildings are concerned, the authors' intentions are often (though by no means always) accessible, if only we take the trouble to look into them. This may seem self-evident, but it is certainly worth saying because a tradition of rigorous and objective research into these matters can by no means be taken for granted. We have to know not only what we are dealing with and by whom, but what the architects, engineers, builders and clients (I stressed all the building's authors) were trying to achieve. This may not turn out to be the deciding factor in conservation decisions, but it is a prerequisite. Sometimes it will throw up surprising, even unpalatable results. It may turn out that we are tempted to make a shibboleth of a building's structure when its authors were indifferent as to how the building stood up, or we may have grown fond of its surface texture when, as in many post-war examples, the architects would dearly have liked to use better cladding had it been available. Having found out the answer, we are not obliged to respect original intentions, but it cannot be good conservation philosophy to disregard them altogether. They must count for something.

Intention in architecture should not be confined to a mere idea or concept; it must extend also to the quality and execution of a design. But in the case of twentieth-century buildings, a distinction which has implications for practical conservation may sometimes need to be made between those in which the original primary care and enthusiasm went into the concept of the design itself, and those in which quality of design and quality of execution went hand in hand. In assessing architect-designed buildings of any age, some kind of evaluative balance has to be struck between these factors, between the value we attach to the original idea and to the existing structure we have before us. What makes many modern buildings practically problematic for conservationists is a growing tendency, both among architects themselves and in the value system of art history, to attach greater significance to the idea and the image than to the building itself.

The many reasons for this can only be alluded to in so short a paper as this one. The twentieth-century severing of design skills from technology and construction, the increasing availability of buildings in the guise of published images and the ever-faster rate of change which buildings in use undergo are the main factors which encourage people to value concept over fabric. We are entitled to do so, if we like. But it is as well to remember that the logical conclusion of the conceptualist approach to conservation is to say that a record of the idea is enough, whether in the form of pictures, drawings, models or 'virtual reality'. On this reading, the material presence of the building in feeling, performance, use and as it has evolved over time loses all value. This, whatever the intentions of the original authors, can surely only be acceptable in conservation practice as a last resort, where the gap between design and execution is extreme.

One way in which some twentieth-century buildings differ from the kinds of earlier buildings that British conservationists typically deal with and think about is in their life cycle. The life cycle of modern architecture can be conceived of in two ways, the life cycle which architects and others anticipate for their buildings, which has to do with intentions, and the life cycle the buildings actually experience, which has to do with my next subject, performance in use. There has been a lot of confusion recently about intentions, some people claiming that modernist architects built for a shorter life cycle than formerly, others that this was not the case. The fact of the matter is that you can not make an overall generalization, though for most individual cases you can find out what you need to know. Common sense is also helpful. The Royal College of Physicians was evidently built as a monument, the prefabs and the immediate post-war schools were built for shortish life cycles until (as people then thought) we could all come up with something better.

In the cases of modern buildings with short life cycles, the determining factor was not only what architects and clients wanted, which at its most utopian was that they did not want to saddle future generations with costly, obsolescent buildings of the type from which they felt their generation had suffered, but also, and perhaps more often, the loan repayment period for the capital borrowed for constructing the building. This factor is not a new one. It determined the intended life cycle of the urban terrace house, for instance. But institutionalization at the heart of modern construction is one of the great and critical changes in twentieth-century architecture, and we have to take note of it if we wish to influence the future of modern buildings.

Performance

And so, on to the question of performance in use – what happens to buildings over time? Irrespective of intentions, some buildings do enjoy a much longer life cycle than was ever intended for them, while others have a shorter one. The overall pattern of change is towards a shorter life cycle, for logical, if not ecological, reasons. The pace of change is simply too fast for us to expect people to build more than the occasional building on the long-term monumental pattern of the past. Rising expectations, together with the ever-growing proportion of the cost of each building that consists of ephemeral finishes and services rather than structure and envelope, mean that it becomes increasingly unrealistic to expect architects and investment managers to build consistently for permanence in the old way.

All this has implications for viability. It suggests that conservationists may have to spend more and more money propping up more and more naturally obsolescent structures. We could, of course, decide only to conserve those buildings which were built more or less on the monumental principle. But I do not think we would feel that such a decision was an adequate reflection of cultural significance in the twentieth century. In this respect, every time we prop up a cheaply structured building we are imposing new values and may be going against the authors' intentions. That is all right, so long as we are conscious about what we are doing, and examine rigorously the value we attach to these buildings.

Buildings fall out of date faster than they used to as a consequence of the so-called functionalist movement in modern architecture, whereby everything in buildings, structure, plan and equipment, was to be fitted to a specific, practical purpose. Taking this philosophy on its own terms and setting aside any emotional or artistic limitations it may have, the problem is that when needs change, the finely tuned building is metamorphosed from racehorse into dinosaur. It would be too superficial a reading of this issue to suggest that the inflexibility of so many modern buildings was due to an architectural theory. Rather, it was the other way round. Architecture reflects demands and expectations, in this case the forceful, definite and immediate ones of modern materialist culture. Then when the demands and expectations alter, the architecture gets into difficulty and has to be changed. In this respect, to use the current cliché, the conservation of twentieth-century buildings has indeed to be about 'the management of change'.

One attempted answer to this on the part of architects has been the so-called 'long-life, loose-fit, flexible' building, in which partitions move around and the structure stays the same. The difficulty with this architect-designed solution to prolonging building life is that the designer is obliged to second-guess the future about the nature of the changes that are likely to occur. The really flexible building tends to be the vernacular type that has evolved gradually through adaptive use down the centuries and is the invention not of designers but of a whole historical process. One way to describe this is to say that vernacular types of building characteristically fulfil the criterion of performance in use very well, at the expense of the criterion of intention: they are void of architectural ambition. Modern buildings of interest tend to be the other way round; they are full of conscious architectural feature and meaning, but because of the nature of our century´s technology and culture they have too often proved fragile or unsatisfactory in performance over a fairly short time.

The moral of this part of the story, so far as I can see, is this. Unless there is a specially powerful artistic intention allied to successful technical performance in use, we must ready ourselves as far as the interiors of many types of modern buildings go for a fairly radical degree of adaptive reuse, because they were nearly always designed to a highly specific brief and the expectation of almost all new briefs is going to be just as specific again. This is not a licence to disregard what is there: the mode and style of that adaptation must always take original intention into account, even if ultimately to set it aside.

The relationship between intention and performance in use seems to pose particular problems for the proper evaluation and conservation of modern architecture. In theory, intention and performance can be separated, in practice, they often coalesce. Thus for instance, the process whereby post-war buildings have been assessed for listing in English Heritage´s recent programme has largely been based on evaluating their architectural merit, conceived in terms of intention, quality of design plus original execution. As a rule, performance comes into the picture during listing only in so far as a building must be examined to see whether the degree of alteration it has undergone since its construction has damaged the original concept to the point which may debar it from the lists. Here is a clear, comprehensible and familiar criterion. Yet the intentions of much modern architecture go more clearly beyond aesthetics than they do for earlier periods, to embrace technical and social ends. So the corresponding task that has to be performed when such a building is assessed for listing may also have to stray over into these complex areas as well. In such a case intention and performance begin to run together.

At first sight, the same ought to be true for earlier periods. A bridge has got to be very old or technically very special if we list it when it is having difficulties in standing up, likewise, a Manchester mill should have fulfilled its function successfully as well as looking imposing if it is to get on the lists. But the Darwinian process of self-selection to which I referred earlier when talking about numbers prevents this being so serious an issue with old buildings as it is with recent ones. The nearer we get to the present day, the less 'natural selection' will have occurred, the more proof we need of successful performance in use, and the harder it becomes to disentangle the techniques with which buildings were built or the social programmes they hoped to fulfil from their aesthetic intentions. Often enough, the aesthetic intentions have not been matched by technical or social performance (sometimes the reverse is true).

The obvious instance in modern British architecture in which intention and performance cry out to be addressed together is that of the many buildings that derive their defining characteristics from the dynamic but risky experimentalism with structure and materials that grew out of the building booms of the 1950s and 60s. We still hear much anxiety and breast-beating about the technical shortcomings and failures associated with that period. Such failures are not unique, I would argue. After enough time has passed building failures become, like ancient murders, almost comic: think of John Nash and the 1820s. They also provide wonderful testing grounds for the extension of conservation techniques. So technical failures are not all bad. But they are still for the moment a grave practical and psychological obstacle to ensuring the future of many interesting modern buildings.

There are two ways of facing this difficulty. One is to argue that before modern buildings are listed, they should receive a full evaluation in which intention and performance in use are explicitly linked together. The other is to stick to the line traditional in official British conservation policy, and insist that the record or performance of a building, like its future economic viability and physical capabilities for adaptive reuse, are practical matters to be looked into when its future is in question. It hardly matters which approach is taken as long as there is clarity and consistency, which in the case of modern listing have been in some danger of erosion. My own view is that it is sensible and reasonable to consider performance in use when we evaluate modern buildings for listing. But that is quite different in principle from considering viability, the issue of what kind of future a building may have in use, at that stage. Performance is a reasonable criterion for listing or not listing, because it is about the past, viability is not a reasonable criterion, because it is about the future. Viability becomes of the essence when we have to deal with the practical future of buildings, which is the next stage along the road once their merit and value have been determined.

Viability

Viability is my penultimate topic for discussion, and I shall be very brief about it. That is partly because much of what needs to be said under this heading has been stated or implied above under intention and performance in use, and partly because I see no clear general way in which modern buildings differ from older ones in terms of their future viability. In so far as twentieth-century buildings were built to fulfil fairly recent needs, they were built to fulfil specific briefs or for a limited life cycle, they can be hard and costly to adapt to new needs and the temptation to scrap them and start again increases, as I said above. Generalization on viability is hazardous, because it depends on so many unpredictable, specific circumstances, economic and political as well as architectural. Nor, so far as I know, has a consistent history of adaptability in buildings down the ages ever been attempted. It would make interesting reading and might throw some light on the subject.

All practical conservation decisions involve some conscious separation and then reintegration of the factors of intention, performance and viability. The trouble we seem often to have with modern buildings is in distinguishing between the total gamut of original intention and performance on the one hand, which should be a matter of objective assessment, and future viability on the other hand, which is a matter of practical judgement. In each case the ingredients need first to be sorted out and then put together to make a slightly different cocktail.

Take two cases by way of illustration. First, the fraught but honourably handled case of the Brynmawr Rubber Factory. Here, as so often occurs, a listing decision had to be made at crisis point. The factory was undoubtedly listed on aesthetic grounds, as a celebrated building that had been published in all the British architectural journals at a time when there was precious little to publish. Had the CADW inspector known fully quite what a disaster the factory had always been in terms of economic performance, should he have considered that in making his listing decision? I believe he should, because the highly rigid plan form of the factory was in part responsible for a certain number (by no means all) of its difficulties in use from the beginning. In this case, most of us would still say the merits of the architecture outweigh its failings in performance. We then come to viability. The poor planning officers who have been grappling with this factory for the past ten years have found that the possibilities for reuse, already problematic because of the sheer size of the structure in so poor a community, have been compounded by that record of poor performance and rigidity. As scheme succeeds scheme, an increasing proportion of the fabric becomes a bargaining counter so that the most aesthetically remarkable features, the great domes at the centre and probably the view from the lake, survive. At the time of writing it seems as if the whole building will finally have to go. If that is what happens, the merits of sheer artistic intention will have been tested against viability to the point of destruction: Darwin will have won (Figure 3.4).

Take now Park Hill in Sheffield, another post-war heritage hot potato. Here the intentions behind this deck-access housing estate are highly important to understand, because some aspects of the design were controversial from the start, whereas others commanded general acceptance but have since become controversial. To that extent the task of those who wish to conserve and extend the estate's life has to begin with honest and accurate history. Public housing was not controversial when Park Hill was built, but is now. We have to persuade the public and the decision makers, national and local, that the intentions of the architects and clients were validated at the time and must be respected at the start of the conservation process, even if we end up with a different system of management or even use at the end of it. Deck-access housing, on the other hand, has been controversial from the start and is generally condemned today. Park Hill, however, has worked rather well, and there has been study after not quite conclusive study to discover why, when other similar schemes even in Sheffield have failed, this estate has been, as these things go, popular. So here we have an encouraging measure of success in performance, and in this case English Heritage was drawn into these questions before a listing recommendation was made, in my view rightly.

But there are, of course, other questions of performance. The concrete balconies on Park Hill are beginning to crumble, and the structure is pretty good but is going to need something doing to it in the medium term. Nor, successful though the estate has largely been, has its drab detail even been popularly appreciated, a kind of failure of performance, if you like. We then come to viability. What is going to happen to Park Hill with its near thousand units of housing? In addressing that grave question, we must constantly balance performance with intention. Thus, for instance, experimental replacement balconies in steel have been designed for the estate, radically different from the original design but safe, colourful and easy to erect. If these balconies are proceeded with throughout Park Hill, they may well prove popular with tenants. But too much of the original intention will have been lost for most people interested in architecture to stomach. From the conservation point of view, Sheffield might as well start again or reclad the whole thing. Yet radicalism of a different kind may very well be reasonable at Park Hill, perhaps a change of use (student housing?), or a change of internal plan, or a reordering of the landscape.

Both at Park Hill and at Brynmawr, the juggling of intention, performance and viability should end in our coming back to a clear and familiar principle of conservation: identifying where the architectural and historic interest of a building is concentrated, going straight for

Figure 3.4   Interior of the Brynmawr Rubber Factory, by the Architects Cooperative Partnership, 1948-52. Now faced with almost certain demolition after years of effort to find it a new use (National Monuments Record for Wales)

that and endeavouring not to get distracted by side issues along the way. If we do not sanction and even encourage a fairly radical approach to many of these buildings, we shall not have them much longer. But the radicalism must proceed from serious study and understanding.

Appeal

My last category of the ways in which twentieth-century buildings differ from their predecessors is appeal. In some ways this is like my first category, numbers. There are lots of modern buildings around because, for example, they were built so recently. Modern architecture is not popular because there is so much of it around that it does not seem special to most people. That is a starting point, but the issue cuts much deeper. We cannot deny the fact that in some fundamental way much twentieth-century architecture, notably 'modernist' architecture, remains unpopular. Does this matter? There is a historically sanctioned argument that it does not, and that we should not worry over-much about the fact that politicians, planners and the populace at large are still not comfortable with the aims and aesthetics of modern design. It is perfectly reasonable to recall that the Georgian and Regency periods were once scorned, that Victorian architecture used to be mocked and to anticipate that given time, education and a few more pushes the Modern Movement too will be wholly rehabilitated. The protection of any period of buildings never begins in a climate of acceptance when the subject has settled down. That is because if the buildings are not considered before then, many of them will not survive. This certainly is what has happened in the case of the post-war period.

I confess to being imperfectly convinced that things even out for twentieth-century buildings, or at least Modern Movement buildings, exactly as they have before. This is because the aesthetic, technical and social intentions of those producing modernist buildings seem to me often to have been, and continue to be, too dissociated from the ideas and ideals both of the British establishment and of the population at large for them to be readily comprehended, accepted and appreciated. Elites have always, of course, built in different ways from ordinary people. When Inigo Jones was building the Banqueting House, timber-framed farmhouses were still going up all over the country, so the 'dissociation of sensibility' is nothing new. The difference is that the professional elites who designed the buildings of the 1930-70 period were not just building for a small and politically dominant class of people or for one another, as was Inigo Jones, but for the country at large. Often they did so with a high measure of idealism and responsibility, but their access to power and influence proved ephemeral. To use plainer language: architects are unpopular and there is no present sign of that changing. It is improbable that the conservation officer who advocates the restoration of a deck-access housing estate to his or her planning committee or the architect who commends the retention of an elegant but redundant factory to an international corporation will be talking to people who think that way at all. I do not say persuasion, publicity and education won't work; they must be practised, and where the quality of the building and the effort of the advocate are first rate, they will succeed. But it is likely to be an uphill struggle for many years to come.

What will the outcome of all the effort to protect modern buildings depend on? Better intellectual and historical appreciation of our century and its aims, certainly. But there is something else which is basic and without which any conservation philosophy is sunk. That is the sheer emotional appeal of any building, without which it has no creative future. This emotional appeal seems to go in waves: a powerful peak when a building is first designed and built, among the professional and chattering classes chiefly. We call this appeal fashion. Then it goes down, and it is not until a building emerges from that trough, normally a good deal more than thirty years after it was built, that we begin to see whether its emotional appeal will revive. That is still a big problem with recent buildings. Some, like the Festival Hall, seem to have come out on the other side: others, like the Lloyds Building, have not yet entered the period of being out of vogue, though they are almost bound to do so. Will Lloyds pass through the tough test of performance in use and continue to move people in thirty years' time? We shall simply have to see. Philosophical we may need to be, but we shall only succeed in ensuring a future for the modern architectural heritage when we can be sure not just that its buildings move us, but that others can be moved by them too.

CHAPTER 4
MANAGEMENT ISSUES AND WILLIS CORROON
Bob Kindred

Introduction

Although mechanisms for the day-to-day management of change to historic buildings may seem a prosaic issue, at some point all proposals for material alterations and partial or total demolitions will require applications for consent from the local planning authority. This paper discusses some of the general issues, but with particular reference to the Willis Corroon building (Sir Norman Foster 1975, listed grade I) which was the first listed building to be the subject of management guidelines (Fig 4.1).

With the listing of buildings from the post-war era (particularly recent large-scale and complex developments), it is emerging that in any decision on such applications a balance has to be struck not only between two long-established factors, recognition of the special architectural and historic interest of the building and the framing of the current listed building legislation, but between two more recent, but no less important considerations: respect for its original design philosophy and the day-to-day needs of the owner. Listing carries with it certain cultural and communal as well as statutory responsibilities, but this has to be tempered by practical considerations about the present-day (and likely future) functioning of modern buildings, particularly complex, large or specialized ones in the service industries, technological manufacturing and research.

Users continually make adjustments to their buildings to suit their day-to-day requirements, such as the upgrading or maintenance of services and plant or by minor adjustments to internal layouts. From time to time more substantial changes are also required. Where modern listed buildings are involved, such minor incremental changes may seem (and indeed may be) unobjectionable when taken singly but cumulatively they can be quite damaging to the special architectural and historic interest. This can be compounded if such changes are also carried out to an indifferent standard. This process is sometimes known as the salami principle, that is, sub-dividing any contentious issue into thin enough slices in an attempt to make their acceptance more palatable. Managing change to listed buildings in this incremental way is unlikely to be acceptable, is always undesirable and this is recognized and discouraged by the Secretaries of State (of Environment and National

Heritage) in their helpful advice in paragraph 3.13 of Planning Policy Guidance Note 15 (PPG15).

Assisting owners

What owners and operators of large and complex modern listed buildings want above all else is a reasonable degree of certainty about the limits of what they may be able to do, or at least clarity about the statutory planning framework within which they must operate. They need to be reasonably confident that minor routine alterations can be carried out without necessarily falling foul of the historic building legislation, particularly when the time from registration to decision can take between 7 and 15 weeks. The speed of the current processes (as they see it) is not conducive to the rapidly changing business climate they operate in. A degree of discretion by way of informal agreement with the local planning authority (and where necessary English Heritage) is likely to be more acceptable to historic building owners and in contentious listing cases less likely to bring the current legislation into disrepute. Management guidelines cannot be forced upon owners. Once the building is listed, if the need for planning consent is not clear-cut the local planning authority should decide if some additional guidance is appropriate.

Not only do guidelines need to be framed with the responsibilities of conservation officers in mind (where they are employed), but also those of the planning officers operating the development control system. Development control staff's priorities and work pressures, and therefore their response to, and the operation of, such guidelines, may be different and this needs to be taken into consideration.

Informing owners, engendering cooperation

The recent debate about the listing of modern buildings has focused on the extent to which an owner should be involved in the discussions about its architectural and historic interest before the decision is reached about its listing. This clearly breaks with a practice which stretches back almost 50 years and it will be interesting to see what the Department of National Heritage proposes in its forthcoming Green Paper on the subject. One important influence upon this debate has been the well publicized and unfavourable reactions of a minority of unsuspecting owners when served with the Department of National Heritage Notification of Listing. This has usually been their first inkling that their freedom of action may have been curtailed.

Few owners of modern buildings seem to have greeted listing with much enthusiasm. This is often based on misapprehensions about the effect of the listed building legislation, sometimes ignorance of the significance of the special architectural and historic interest of the building in its wider context and occasionally it is a reaction to inaccurate or outdated professional advice given to the owner.

In the Willis Corroon case, spot-listing followed incautious remarks from a director acting for the company who was quoted in a local newspaper as stating that the swimming pool on

Figure 4.1   The Willis Corroon Building, Ipswich, was the first modern listed building in Britain to be the subject of management guidelines. The organic shape of the building reflected a footprint which grew during the design stage as additional sites were acquired (English Heritage)

the ground floor was to be 'filled in'. The phraseology used was important because (irrespective of the company's actual intentions), the perception this conjured up, a threat to the integrity of the design, was ultimately responsible for the formal protection of the building. In that case, a short and intensive lobbying campaign against the proposal was mounted by local architects and a variety of organizations including the (then) Thirties Society, *The Architects' Journal* and the *Architectural Review*, all of whom claimed some credit for the subsequent spot-listing decision. I don't think that Willis Corroon thought for one moment during the lobbying (conducted almost exclusively in the specialist architectural press) that the building would be listed.

Once it was listed grade I, the company were initially (and unsurprisingly) hostile to the decision as they felt it would seriously compromise their day-to-day business operations. They then appealed to the Secretary of State, but this was (also, unsurprisingly) unsuccessful. The present legislative framework inevitably creates a potential for this climate of hostility aimed against the local authority (which serves one copy of the Notification of Listing), the Department of National Heritage (which serves the other) and English Heritage, assuming of course, that the owner can distinguish the separate roles of each, as many owners fail to appreciate the responsibilities of each of these bodies. Furthermore, in my experience, many owners seem to see the local planning authority's involvement in listing as purely administrative, that is, after the fact, but they often assume that the final decision has been taken by English Heritage (rather than the Secretary of State). The local authority can therefore be regarded as an 'honest broker' offering ameliorating guidelines while the owner blames English Heritage or the Secretary of State for their predicament.

Understanding and defining special character

Guidelines can define, within the scope of the planning legislation, what the special character of the building amounts to, what changes are likely to be possible without that special character being affected and therefore what is not likely to require listed building consent. I have referred earlier to the need for certainty about the scope for change but if guidelines also foster a better understanding of the special architectural and historic interest of the building and its context by the owners and users, it is likely to be better appreciated, particularly where the owner's initial reaction to listing has been unfavourable. Furthermore, from the local planning authority's point of view an informed analysis will almost certainly help it in the efficiency with which it makes a decision on any works which may subsequently require consent.

Of course, a clear and succinct definition of character is not necessarily the same as a list description, the primary purpose of which is identification of the building. What can be guaranteed to irritate an owner are obvious discrepancies between the list description and the physical evidence of the building. This can get negotiations about guidelines off to a bad start. This is not to criticize either English Heritage or the Department of National Heritage. Under the present arrangements, it seems to me that during the compilation of a list description in spot-listing cases without the benefit of prior consultations with the owner, where direct access to the building may not be possible or even desirable, it is almost inevitable that a description will have to be based on the evidence submitted by outside proponents of the building's special merit. In the Willis Corroon case, evidence for urgent spot-listing was partly based on coverage in the architectural press dating from 1975, but the list description issued in 1991 referred, for example, to floor finishes which had been replaced in 1986. If the evidence on which a list description is based has been superseded by physical changes to the building by the time the description is issued, any guidelines will have to be explicit about those differences. Even when it is possible to identify and define special architectural character to the satisfaction of the local planning authority and English Heritage, the evaluation may cut no ice with the owner.

Long before Willis Corroon was listed (but for several years after it was first occupied), the management would say somewhat self-consciously (and reverentially) that they were still learning about the subtleties of the Foster design, the ways in which the building could be adapted to their changing needs and how they were coming to appreciate and understand the architect's original intentions. If an appreciation of the subtleties of some large modern buildings can take years to develop, it follows that the local planning authority (often needing to develop guidelines quickly) may not get it right first time, especially when it may only have the list description as a starting point.

Documentation concerning the architect's philosophy of approach, the evolution of the design and the relationship between client and architect is not usually readily available to the planning authority, which is unfortunate since this material can greatly aid an understanding of the building if it is available, if for no other reason than to form a point of departure for discussions about further changes. In the Willis Corroon case, the building design process is particularly well documented in contemporary architectural publications. For those unfamiliar with the building, its organic shape reflected a footprint which grew during the design stage as additional sites were acquired. Foster was also concerned about his design's effect on the immediately adjacent Unitarian Meeting House of 1699 (also listed grade I), widely regarded as the finest timberframed nonconformist chapel of its date in England.

The Willis Corroon building showed the architect's concern for bringing social architecture into the business environment. A swimming pool for the employees was included on the ground floor (Figure 4.2), the open-plan offices did not differentiate between senior managers and other employees and a rooftop restaurant and garden were provided. Such considerations were new when incorporated in this building on completion in 1975 although they are quite commonplace today. There were also marked constructional

Figure 4.2   The swimming pool on the ground floor at Willis Corroon, prior to the alteration proposals. The preceived threat to the pool was ultimately responsible for the formal protection of the building (Bob Kindred)

Figure 4.3   Marked constructional innovations included the use of curtain wall glazing suspended from the roof deck. Changes to the pattern and type of glazing (and screening by blinds) are part of the management guidelines (Bob Kindred)

innovations in the use of curtain wall glazing, the appearance of which was much copied, but without the same technical bravura (Figure 4.3). All this resulted in the building receiving numerous architectural honours, culminating in 1990 in the award of the first Trustees Medal of the RIBA, with the citation that it was 'the finest building in the world designed by a British architect within the last 25 years'.

Guidelines for management

The Willis Corroon guidelines of 1991–92 seem to have been the first of their kind. It was perhaps inevitable that such guidance would be initiated by the local authority in conjunction with English Heritage, as a response to a seemingly unique situation and the alarm of the company. It did not occur to me at the time that it might set a precedent, merely that it seemed a sensible thing to do.

The initial draft was written in about two hours and was then refined in collaboration with the building owners. Before the guidelines were finalized by all three parties, discussions were held with the company's lawyers and property advisors: this stage may now be less necessary as the principles are becoming better established and other models are available. Externalizing the analysis of the building's character and making assumptions and principles more explicit for the purposes of operating the listed building legislation is crucial to the success of any guidelines.

A further, unique aspect is the possibility that the original architectural practice is still being employed. At the *Spirit of Optimism* conference on the listing of modern commercial buildings in February 1994, Paul Finch, the editor of *Building Design* magazine, suggested that had Sir Norman Foster been employed to draw up the controversial alterations to the swimming pool at Willis Corroon there might never have been pressure to list it.

Assuming that a practice is still in existence is it important that the original architects continue to be employed on further works to the building in the event that it is listed? Is it appropriate for the local planning authority to consult them over changes proposed by other architects? Architects are often fiercely protective of their designs and it would not be the first time that an architect had asked the Department of National Heritage for one of his own designs to be listed to protect the integrity of his concept from the depredations of someone else.

Disseminating guidelines to decision makers

The development of guidelines is equally important in instances where the commissioning client may no longer be the owner or user of the building or its day-to-day management may be the responsibility of those indifferent to its special interest. Guidelines should be disseminated to property or site managers and services staff as well as to senior management. All need to understand the significance and intended purpose of the document, who within the local planning authority they can contact for clarification or further advice and who else has copies (such as the local authority's building control staff and the officers of the local fire authority).

An interesting example of establishing acceptance of new design guidance from the world of corporate design has been given by Wolf Ollins who, some years ago, designed a new corporate image for British Oxygen. One of the ways in which he viewed its success was that long after its implementation, local site managers (who had initially been sceptical about the concept of corporate identity) were still giving pride of place at their sites to the posters he had produced explaining his scheme and were still enthusiastically following it. If guidelines are going to work they must be accepted with more than grudging acquiescence. If some enthusiasm can be engendered effective guidelines may become self-reinforcing. The alternative, in planning terms, is for owners to seek a written opinion on whether any proposed works are likely to require consent. This is hardly an efficient procedure bearing in mind there is no *de minimus* provision in the historic buildings legislation for works of demolition or alteration to a listed building and no statutory procedure to make an application for determination of what works require consent.

Advice from a local authority that works do not require listed building consent does not bind the authority, but failure to obtain it is potentially an offence. Clearly, while guidelines can be neither definitive nor binding, in listed building terms what they can provide is clarity and explicitness and their objectivity can be open to scrutiny. Over time, the appreciation of the special architectural and historic interest of a building will change. Perception of the impact of alterations will also change. As the value of the historic environment and the loss of original fabric becomes a matter of greater and greater concern, so many of the minor works which would have been routinely approved 20 years ago would be considered unsympathetic today. This is the salami principle at work again.

Scope

Written guidelines must not be considered as binding agreements under current legislation. They can define what is important and if possible they should be explicit about what is not. In law, they cannot override the statutory requirement for consent, but in practice they will either be processed speedily or the guidelines will obviate the need for consent for certain clearly defined categories of works. A standard format is unlikely to be appropriate but I have already touched on some of the issues likely to be important. Having decided that guidelines would be likely to assist the process of managing change, from the local planning authority point of view, guidelines are likely to include some or all of the following points:

- the status of the document, who has prepared it, who has agreed it, who can be contacted about it and who else might need to be aware of its contents
- the definition of special interest, and what is considered to be not of interest
- an analysis of the design philosophy, and context, plan form, structure and materials, internal and external treatment, the decorative schemes and finishes, any fixed integral machinery and fixed original art works
- future intentions in significant programmes of demolitions, alterations, extensions and any schedule for the modification or replacement of machinery
- the legal position
- what will be likely to require listed building consent and what is likely to be acceptable
- any matters likely to require separate planning permission
- any departures from the list description or significant changes between the list description and the guidelines
- clear delineation of curtilage and any associated structures
- a timetable for review of the document

Two final examples of these aspects are given by way of illustration. Firstly, it will be important with large and complex buildings to have a full understanding not only of the design, history, structure and fabric but also (if necessary) decorative finishes if they are an important part of the architectural character. Seemingly small details may take on a disproportionately greater significance. For example, at Willis Corroon, the colours of the decorative finishes (primarily yellow walls and green floors) are covered in the list description. These colours are precisely specified and made up specially. They are also precisely defined in the management guidelines and listed building consent would be required if the shade were proposed to be significantly varied or the colour changed. One might speculate about whether this might mean that the building must remain painted yellow and green in perpetuity (surely not the purpose of the process?) and at what point the present colours become a historic decorative scheme.

Secondly, the replacement or enlargement of external plant (or internal plant if it is a clear architectural element within the building) may need to be the subject of an understanding about the need for replacement within a rolling programme. At Willis Corroon these are subject to a detailed long-term schedule of their estimated life and phased replacement. They are annexed to the guidelines and kept separately under review every three years. One small unexpected consequence, following the adoption of the guidelines (but not anticipated in them), occurred when large items of plant and associated ducting were replaced under the schedule in the externally visible plant rooms. At the initiative of the company's services engineer, the redecoration of these areas was carried out to Foster's original 'historic' colours.

CHAPTER 5
INTERIORS AND EXTERIORS: ACQUIRING MODERN BUILDINGS FOR THE NATION

Edward Diestelkamp

The National Trust's first modern property is to open to the public in 1996. The acquisition of 2 Willow Road in Hampstead was completed in July 1994. Following a programme of repair and preparation for public viewing, it will be possible for visitors to enjoy the interiors of this house designed by Ernö Goldfinger in 1937-8 for himself and his family.

Goldfinger was born in Budapest in 1902, and moved to Paris while still in his teens. He studied architecture at the École des Beaux Arts and in 1925 joined the breakaway atelier of Auguste Perret, the French rationalist who promoted and pioneered the architectural use of reinforced concrete during the early years of this century.

During the 1920s and the early 30s, Goldfinger met and became friends with many avant-garde artists, moving in Parisian artistic circles. In 1931 he met Ursula Blackwell, an English art student studying in the studio of Amédée Ozenfant. They were married in 1933 and the following year moved to London. In 1935 they leased a flat in Highpoint I, the apartment block designed by Berthold Lubetkin and Tecton, and they soon began planning and thinking about building their first home.[1] The site they acquired on Willow Road had four small two-storey terraced houses which were demolished to make way for the three-storey terrace of three houses that Goldfinger had designed. Construction began in 1938 and was completed the next year, just before war broke out. Built of reinforced concrete and faced in red brick, the terrace overlooked the southern slopes of Hampstead Heath, with generous glazing north and south to the first floor living rooms (Figure 5.1). The ground floor street elevation was given over to the entrances to the houses and to garages for cars. No. 2, the largest of the three, occupied the centre and had a garage on either side of the entrance door, showing Goldfinger's passion for automobiles.

In January 1991 an article in the Astragal column of *The Architects' Journal* drew attention to the recent death of Ursula Goldfinger, who had recently completed the transfer of her late husband's drawings to the RIBA Drawings Collection and had redecorated the interiors of 2 Willow Road to their original colour scheme. The writer regretted the threatened loss of the contents within the house, that 'constitute a fine document of Modern taste amassed over a period of 70 years.[2]

Figure 5.1   The Living Room of 2 Willow Road in 1940, by Ernö Goldfinger (Architectural Review)

Following an approach by the National Trust, the Goldfinger family responded with enthusiasm to the notion that the house might be preserved together with its contents and collection of works of art. The house itself was transferred to the National Trust through the Treasury in lieu of Inheritance Tax, while the contents were a gift of the family and the works of art were placed on a long-term loan, to remain in the house permanently with the intention that their ownership should pass to the Trust in lieu of tax in the future. The question of merit and the cost of long-term preservation of 2 Willow Road were considered by the committees of the National Trust in 1991, following an extensive structural survey carried out by Avanti Architects. This report considered the required repairs, the works needed to open the house to visitors and various options for the showing and letting of parts of the house. The public response to the Trust's inevitable need for money to endow the house and to carry out the repairs was very difficult to predict early in the summer of 1991 when interest and excitement in the possibility was growing. As the Trust, and indeed no other preservation body in Britain, had ever appealed for public support to acquire such a building, the prospect entailed many unknowns. How would such an acquisition be perceived by the members and generous supporters of the Trust? It was thought that the traditional sources of support might not be interested in a project such as this, given that it was so different to anything that the Trust had ever appealed for in the past.

To help establish the interest that such a proposal might attract, and to help identify possible areas of new support, a feasibility study by Mark Jefferies of Craigmyle and Co. Ltd. was carried out. Influential architects, designers and people interested in modern art, architecture and design were approached for their advice and impressions on the potential success of such a proposal. The response received from those consulted was largely very enthusiastic, to the extent that the committees of the Trust agreed to a public fundraising campaign in the autumn of 1992, with the condition that a minimum amount of £200,000 was to be raised by Christmas of that year and with the understanding that, if this amount was not raised, the proposal would be abandoned and the Goldfinger family told that the Trust could not proceed with the proposed acquisition. An important consideration in the strategy of the proposal was establishing the threshold or maximum cost of the project. The question 'how much does it cost' was to recur time and time again. To reduce the high cost of endowment, the possibility of creating a flat on part of the ground and basement floors was considered with the object of raising income to offset running costs. This arrangement was adopted with the result that the overall sum needed for the endowment was significantly reduced to an amount that was thought to be considered realistic and achievable by public appeal.

The most important and influential promises of support came from the Trustees of the National Heritage Memorial Fund and from the Trustees of the Henry Moore Foundation in the earliest days of discussion. This did much to encourage optimism and launch the public appeal. The Trust was also supported with great enthusiasm by the Twentieth Century Society, many of its members helping in different ways by publicizing the appeal in newspapers, journals and on television, distributing information and appeal leaflets, and assisting in the opening of the house to the public during a series of open days held in October and November 1992.

Through the generous support of many individuals, charitable trusts, bequests and a grant from the National Heritage Memorial Fund, the appeal succeeded in the last few days before the deadline. Not only was the required sum raised but the entire amount needed to acquire, endow and repair the house was secured by Christmas, and the Trust was able to confirm to the Goldfinger family that it would like to proceed with the acquisition.

The consideration of 2 Willow Road, with its contents and collection of works of art, was judged by the committees of the Trust in the same respect as previous acquisitions, looking in particular at its quality and merit in terms of historical importance, in both a local sense and on a national scale, and also taking into consideration the threat to the long-term survival of the property if it were not acquired by the Trust for permanent preservation. Of particular importance and relevance was the collection of art by artists such as Max Ernst, Amédée Ozenfant, Hans Arp, Marcel Duchamp, Man Ray, Robert Delaunay, Henry Moore, Roland Penrose, Stanley William Hayter and Prunella Clough. Equally important was the fact that much of the furniture had been designed by Goldfinger, some of it specifically for the house

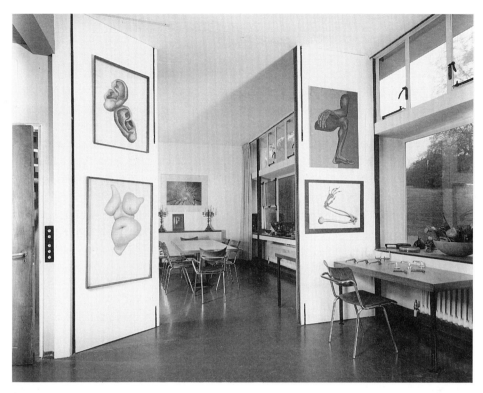

Figure 5.2   2 Willow Road, view of the Dining Room (The National Trust)

(Figure 5.2). In the case of 2 Willow Road it was recognized that the continued survival of the contents and works of art within the house would not have been possible, whereas the house itself would have been protected by historic building legislation. However, it was also recognized that the interior decoration and retention of contemporary fitted fixtures, an important characteristic of houses of this period, might be difficult features to protect in spite of existing legislation, particularly if the property fell into the hands of an unsympathetic owner in future.

Certainly for the Trust and for the Trustees of the National Heritage Memorial Fund, it was the totality of 2 Willow Road together with its collections and contents that made the prospective acquisition so appealing. House, furniture, works of art, library and archive together represented the modern artistic taste of their creator owners. Furthermore, with the exception of the sale of certain works of art in the 1970s by the Goldfingers themselves, the collection of art they had assembled from their time in Paris throughout their lives remained intact. The additional fact that all of Ernö Goldfinger's drawings and professional correspondence were deposited in the British Architectural Library lent further support to the argument that the preservation of their house with its contents would provide future generations with a unique record of a modern architect's life and work in twentieth-century Britain.

Both of the Goldfingers lived at their house in Willow Road until their deaths and so the house together with its contents is a record not only of their modern taste in the thirties but also of that throughout the rest of their lives and, to a lesser extent, that of their children and grandchildren as well. This record of generations assembled over five decades was considered as important as the initial concept of the house and this precept has guided policy and decisions on the conservation programme for the house and its contents, as well as showing arrangements for the public. One option for showing the house considered a return of the interiors to their appearance in 1939 as seen in the evocative black and white photographs taken by Dell and Wainwright for the article which appeared in the Architectural Review, but such a decision would have excluded and made irrelevant later very important acquisitions of furniture and works of art.[3] Over half the works of art on show in the house date from the 1960s on, as does a large portion of the furniture. While it was recognized that the house was much more sparsely furnished in the 1940s, corresponding more to the clean, bare modern interiors recorded in the early photographs, and that this presentation would have doubtless been instructive as well as popular, the possibility of presenting this appearance of the interiors could still be achieved in the guidebook and through the exhibition of photographs and on film.

Unlike the Rietveld Schröder house in Utrecht, where it was decided not to show the house with contents but instead to restore the interiors to their early form and to retain the incomplete contents, archive and library in the Central Museum, Utrecht, at 2 Willow Road this was not an objective nor a realistic possibility as the house was filled with many things, and there was nowhere for them to be stored off the site. The two houses form an interesting comparison as their presentation is so different.

The Schröder house underwent a major restoration in three phases between 1974 and 1987, unlike 2 Willow Road which was in good condition for the most part and only required repairs, though some on a major scale, particularly the renewal of the flat asphalt roof and repair of the parapet wall. Many of the contents of the Schröder house were not acquired by the Rietveld Schröder House Foundation and an arrangement of the interiors as they were at the end of Mrs Schröder's life was neither her nor the Foundation's objective. Another significant difference between the two houses is in their size. Even though 2 Willow Road is an urban terrace house in London, the Schröder house is on a much smaller and intimate scale, with much smaller interiors and the absolute minimum of circulation space. A second important difference is the status of the two houses. The Schröder house is a widely-recognized monument of twentieth-century architecture and a place of pilgrimage for architects and students from all over the world, and therefore attracts many people throughout the year to the extent that it has been necessary to have a booking system for tickets.

The amount of public interest in the forthcoming opening of 2 Willow Road is difficult to predict. The house will be open to the public on three afternoons a week, with special arrangements made for pre-booked parties. Timed tickets will be issued at the door and visitors encouraged to look at other sites of interest in the area while they wait for the admission time on their ticket. This arrangement may need to be adjusted to suit demand in time and with further experience.

The understanding of the way of life at 2 Willow Road was considered an important aspect to explain to visitors who are to see a house that is no longer lived in, particularly given the Goldfingers' creative personalities. It is hoped that the lifestyle, the character of the inhabitants and family friends and events surrounding 2 Willow Road will be evoked through film. Goldfinger took cine film of his family from the mid-1930s through the 1970s, including scenes of the house under construction, and this archive has much good material that will provide an emotive and moving visual link for visitors to the house. The making of the film and conversion of one of the garages into a small viewing room has been made possible through a grant from the National Lottery Fund distributed by the Arts Council and a donation from the John Ellerman Foundation. Goldfinger's professional career as an architect and the varied range of his designs for interiors, furniture, children's toys, posters and graphic design will also be of interest to visitors. A small changing exhibition of photographs and other objects from the archive at the house is to be displayed in the nursery, which visitors will see at the end of their visit.

At the moment it is proposed that the house will be shown by guided tour. The rooms are not large and groups will need to be limited to 12 people. The guided tours of the Schröder house were considered particularly effective and informative for visitors where the guide directed attention to the construction of the building and to features of the interior that otherwise might easily have gone unnoticed, and demonstrated the moving partitions and fixtures to show the changing spatial qualities that can be created. Guided tours also provide a time structure which is important when the number of visitors must be limited. It would be difficult to allow every visitor to open cupboards and drawers at 2 Willow Road, but it is recognized that these fitted fixtures are particularly interesting and enjoyable for visitors to see so it is intended that guides will demonstrate how these fixtures work. To prevent damage to floors, most of which still have the original finish surfaces, visitors will be asked to wear non-slip protective shoe covers. Other options to protect the floor surfaces such as druggets and ropes would be a serious intrusion within the domestic scale of the interiors. The experience of the curators at the Schröder house in Utrecht has helped the Trust to identify possible solutions to some problems of showing the house which are appropriate to the scale of the interiors and the character of the house.

In 1993, during the acquisition of 2 Willow Road, the Trust was told of the intention of Patrick Gwynne, the architect, to leave his modern house, The Homewood in Esher, Surrey, to the National Trust for permanent preservation (Figure 5.3). Like 2 Willow Road, The Homewood was designed in 1937-8 and was built in 1938-9, being completed just before the outbreak of war.[4] Designed for his parents while Patrick Gwynne was working in the office of Wells Coates, it replaced a Victorian villa set within a ten-acre wooded site west of the old Esher-Portsmouth Road.[5] Both the country setting and the scale of the house are in contrast to Goldfinger's urban terrace in Willow Road. The Homewood is a substantial house on two floors with an extended plan in three distinct blocks, one for sleeping, another for living and the third a service wing. The main living rooms are raised on the first floor with extensive views

Figure 5.3   The Homewood, Esher, Surrey, designed by Patrick Gwynne, 1937-8 and built 1938-9 (Architectural Review)

out over the wooded landscape setting. With the exception of the years during the war, The Homewood has been continuously lived in by its designer and owner, Patrick Gwynne, who decided to move there and establish his architectural practice after the death of his parents.

Before the prospective acquisition of The Homewood was presented to the Trust's committees, the opinion of experts in twentieth-century architecture, interiors, furniture design and landscape was sought during a series of visits to the house. The merit of the house and landscape was recognized and approved by the majority of those canvassed, although there were some that did not think that The Homewood was worthy of preservation by the Trust. In the minds of Trust staff, this potential acquisition raised the question of how many other buildings there were of this type and period, and this was asked by many people who visited the house.

Alan Powers had predicted this enquiry in his assessment of the importance of the house, which included a comparative table of twenty modern houses built before the war. This considered four factors, which included external condition, internal condition, setting and listed status. Comments under these general headings indicated that The Homewood was in good condition, that there had been slight alterations, that the interiors were still largely in their original condition, that the original setting had not been altered and that it was listed grade II. Comments on the condition of other houses indicated that only 7 out of 20 houses considered were still in what was described as good condition. More telling was the column listing internal condition which showed that none of the other houses still contained their original contents (2 Willow Road was not included on this list). The setting of eight of the houses was not considered to be of interest and in some cases these had been damaged by later changes, most notably by the sub-division of the original plots and the erection of more houses. The most significant finding of the comparison showed that apart from 2 Willow Road, The Homewood was the only Modern Movement house to have been continuously inhabited and to have retained its original contents. It was also observed that all of the houses included within the study were properties of high commercial value which could only come to the Trust as the result of a major benefaction, which there was no reason to expect in any of the other cases.

Alan Powers agreed to extend the scope of his survey, and to look more closely at a wider range of factors. This extended assessment considered 11 different criteria, which included the survival of the house as built, the survival of the interiors as built, the originality of design, the quality of execution, the standing of the architect, the influence which the design had on other architects, the quality of the interiors and contents, the quality of the garden and landscape, the survival of the setting, and finally, an indication or assessment of the arrangement of spaces of the plan as an indicator of the house as a realization of a social idea. The assessment was preceded by a table listing all the houses and giving numerical values for the criteria under consideration. This was followed by a written analysis of each house, explaining the reasons for the numerical values that were given. The Homewood scored high over all the other houses in two important categories, the survival of original contents and the survival of the original setting.

The paper prepared for the Trust's committees took Powers' findings into account to explain the broader context in which the prospective acquisition might be considered. Like the paper prepared for 2 Willow Road, the one for The Homewood considered the architectural and historic interest of the property on a national level, as well as the importance of the designed landscape. The rarity of The Homewood was established through the findings of the assessment, and as with 2 Willow Road, the recognized threat to the long-term survival of the house was the possible loss of the contents in the future, many of which were original, and the possible breaking up of the integral landscape setting. The paper emphasized important differences between the Goldfinger house and The Homewood. The difference in architectural character is significant, The Homewood exemplifying a more English synthesis of modern ideas with acknowledged references to modern masters such as Le Corbusier and Mies van der Rohe and also to modern works in Britain by Wells Coates and to Highpoint I by Lubetkin and Tecton. The relationship of the house to the landscape setting represents an English interest in the picturesque, extending the living areas into the garden by means of the terrace beneath the main living rooms of the house. In contrast to 2 Willow Road, the collection of works of art is not of the same stature and does not contain works by such distinguished artists. However, the works are more directly related to the arrangement of the interiors rather than independent works of art in their own right. The decoration of the interiors of The Homewood has been altered over time by Patrick Gwynne. Wall coverings, carpets and curtain have been changed as old ones have worn out. New pieces of furniture designed by Patrick Gwynne have been introduced beside original furnishings, so the interiors reflect his taste of the 1960s and 70s as well as the 1930s (Figure 5.4).

The greatest difference between the two houses is their relationship with their setting. The urban setting of the Willow Road terrace required the design to conform with established building lines, while the fenestration of the north and south elevations responds to the admission of light and requirements for privacy. The rural woodland site of The Homewood allowed much more freedom in the response to the natural setting. The landscape garden was an integral aspect of the design of the house and aspects of the garden were completed even before the house was finished. The garden has been developed over the past 50 years and is now a mature landscape that still retains its carefully designed relationship with the house.

These differences between 2 Willow Road and The Homewood can be seen as complementary and support the prospective acquisition of the latter by the Trust. From an educational point of view, both properties provide great potential, illustrating different aspects of the Modern Movement in Britain, the continental influence and the national synthesis of ideas. It is the entity of both houses with their contents and collections, and in the case of The

Figure 5.4   The Homewood, Esher, Surrey, view of the Living Room (Architectural Review)

Homewood its integral relationship with its landscape setting, that make both such appropriate acquisitions for preservation.

In 1994 the committees of the National Trust approved 'on merit' the proposed acquisition of The Homewood and recommended the acceptance of the proposed devise by Patrick Gwynne on condition that a financial arrangement for the long-term preservation of the house and landscape is approved by the Finance Committee. A detailed survey of the building has been carried out by Avanti Architects to look at the necessary repairs. Reports and estimates by the Trust's conservation advisers have been compiled. The funding required, which has yet to be secured, would enable repairs to be carried out to the house and garden in three phases over a ten-year period, improvements and facilities to be provided for visitors to the property and a programme of conservation to contents, fixtures and fittings.

References

1   Jackson-Stops, G. (1991), '2 Willow Road, Hampstead', *Country Life*, **185**, (37), 146-9.

2   Astragal (1991), 'Last Memories', *Architect's Journal*, **193**, (5), 7.

3   anon (1940), 'Three Houses at Willow Road, Hampstead, Ernö Goldfinger, Architect', *Architectural Review*, **88**, (89), 126-130 and 149-153.

4   anon (1939), 'House at Esher, Surrey', *Architectural Review*, **87**, (88), 103-116.

5   Bingham, N. (1993), 'The Homewood, Surrey', *Country Life*, **187**, (29), 84-7.

CHAPTER 6

ALEXANDRA ROAD, LONDON

Catherine Croft

The Alexandra Road Estate has provoked controversy since its conception in 1968. Camden Council's proposal to erect a large concrete council estate to house over five hundred families on a site adjacent to affluent St John's Wood met with predictable local opposition. When finally completed in 1978, the architectural confidence and technical innovation of the buildings ensured that the estate attracted enthusiastic favourable attention from the professional press. It was the most impressive of a series of distinguished, low-rise, high-density buildings by a highly talented in-house architects' department and established the international reputation of the young project architect, Neave Brown (Figure 6.1).

However, accusations of financial mismanagement resulting from construction delays and a massive overspend (the original tender figure was just under five million pounds but the final cost was close to nineteen million), gave the project a less welcome reputation. In addition, government policy on housing had by then switched to favour rehabilitation and much lower densities. Despite extensive debate, no clear conclusion emerged. Opinions were divided between those who thought the estate was a triumphant architectural masterpiece and those who saw it as a monument to misguided, grandiose attempts at social manipulation with little regard for the real values and ambitions of those destined to live there.

Many residents believe that since completion Camden has done its best to forget about the estate and has carried out very minimal maintenance. Many of the alterations which are cumulatively eroding the quality of the estate are far more a reaction to a perceived lack of care and the failure of the housing department to enforce tenancy agreements, than a positive symbol of self-expression.

By 1993 the council's poor handling of a major repairs programme had led preservation bodies and some residents to lobby for the estate to be listed. (This repair work is funded by an Estate Action Programme, financed by the DoE through the Regional Government Office for London, GOL). Major concerns included surface-mounted lighting and conduits replacing recessed lighting, poorly matched concrete repairs and the threat of replacement PVCu windows. Residents involved DOCOMOMO who sought letters of support from Richard Rogers, Philip Powell and the Royal Fine Art Commission. It was argued that the estate was both an

Figure 6.1   Looking towards Block A on the Alexandra Road Estate, London, from underneath the community centre (English Heritage)

outstanding architectural achievement, an exemplar of ambitious, humane modernism on a scale that was unlikely to be to repeated and a historically important record of a period when a generously-funded socialist housing policy could produce a distinctive architectural form and style.

Contrary to many expectations, Alexandra Road was listed at grade II* in August 1993. (It is worth noting that a closely-related work, the Brunswick Centre by Patrick Hodgkinson, was granted a certificate of immunity from listing by the Department of National Heritage shortly afterwards.) The listing occurred before the wider review of post-war public housing for which Andrew Saint has recently completed his research. Alexandra Road was the youngest building ever listed, arguably the largest 'building' to be listed and the first post-war housing estate to be listed. (Apart from Lasdun's Keeling House it is still the only example of listed post-war public housing.) It was also an unusual case in that its original architect was still alive and the estate had recently undergone a change of management and was controlled by a cooperative. In addition there were technical problems, most notably concrete repair problems, which English Heritage had almost no experience of dealing with.

Age

Because the estate was less than thirty years old it had to be considered for listing under the 'Ten Year Rule' and could only be listed if it met two criteria, it had to be of outstanding national interest, and had to be shown to be at risk of demolition or damaging alteration. Because of the first of these criteria only those portions of the estate which were considered to be of grade II* quality could be listed. There are some buildings which although probably of grade II standard are not eligible for listing until they reach 30 years of age. It was not very clear from the list description issued when the estate was first listed exactly which parts were listed, and the situation was further complicated because by definition post-war listed buildings cannot have detached curtilage structures (because these have to have been built before 1948). A row of storage buildings therefore unintentionally remain unlisted. Additionally a school building on the estate was eventually determined not to be listed as it was not 'ancillary' or subordinate to the estate, although it ran underneath the Community Hall, which was specifically mentioned in the list description. The play centre which is attached to (listed) walls in the park is ancillary to the estate as a whole, therefore English Heritage have argued that it is listed. However, two buildings by Tom Kay and two by Evans and Shalev which form part of a second phase of development are not listed because they are of grade II standard and therefore not of 'outstanding interest'. They will only become eligible when they are 30 years old. The second criteria (being at risk) meant that initial requests for listing were deferred until the full extent of the effect of the repairs could be seen on site. Therefore English Heritage became involved on the statutory side when works were already in progress but when the full extent of the listing remained ambiguous, and some key buildings definitely had no protection at all.

Size

Because of the size of the buildings and the resource implications of adding over 500 dwellings to the total of listed buildings in Camden, it was clear that English Heritage needed to have a strategic approach to managing change at Alexandra Road. English Heritage has recently published guidelines on management agreements aimed in part specifically at large post-war buildings. Because the repair works were already in progress the strategy had to be developed while English Heritage was also dealing with day-to-day questions about repair-led changes that seemed to have been given little consideration before awarding the repairs contract. It was essential that the strategy should increase appreciation of the architectural quality and the historic importance of the estate, but should also demonstrate that English Heritage was sympathetic to individual residents' desires to personalize their own homes. Additionally it had to recognize the complex ownership structure of the estate. The situation was more complicated than at the Willis Faber building where this approach had first been tried.

The Alexandra Road Estate is owned by Camden Council. The housing department is responsible for capital repairs but it had recently devolved responsibility for rent collection, day-to-day management and maintenance repairs to a newly formed cooperative, the South Hampstead Housing Cooperative. The cooperative had been set up in line with central government policy because the tenants were dissatisfied with the way that repairs were being managed by the housing department. (It is technically a Tenants Management Committee or TMC.) The residents (tenants and a small minority who had recently opted to become right-to-buy leaseholders) had understood that they would gain full control over the DoE Estate Action money, but subsequently discovered that the housing department would remain the client for these major works. This emerged after the cooperative had held interviews with architects on the basis that they would appoint their chosen consultant. The residents favoured a very appropriate combination of practices: Avanti, who had recently completed the Penguin Pool restoration, and Architype, who specialize in work with cooperatives. The housing department decided to use their own in-house Building Design Services team (BDS) to design and supervise work. BDS had been responsible for maintenance before the cooperative was set up and did not have a good reputation with residents. When English Heritage became involved the residents felt that they had been promised autonomy once and failed to get it. Some welcomed listing as an alternative way to curb BDS's power, while some thought that they were being further marginalized in the decision-making process by the need to comply with listed building consent. Initially there was a lot of ill-feeling and many people felt that they had been treated in a patronizing or even underhand way. English Heritage decided that it would be a good idea to reinforce the listing by designating a Conservation Area.

Ideally, for simplicity, the aim should be to protect large estates either by listing with management agreements to make controls less cumbersome, or by Conservation Area status enhanced by Article 4 agreements. In the case of Alexandra Road the quality and innovative form of the interiors merit listing, but Conservation Area status is needed in addition for several reasons. Usually Conservation Areas are designated by local authorities, but it is possible, in London only, for English Heritage to make designations, provided that it has specific authority to do so from the Department of National Heritage. The Secretary of State was approached to arrange this for Alexandra Road in 1994. It was hoped that taking this action would encourage Camden to make the designation of an Alexandra Road Estate Conservation Area a priority. The advantages of Conservation Area designation would be threefold:

1. It would offer protection to the unlisted buildings which form an important part of the estate and would safeguard the setting of the listed buildings and the quality of the landscaping.
2. The local authority would have a duty to formulate and publish proposals for the Conservation Area's preservation and enhancement and submit them to public consultation, which was felt could be a very positive exercise.
3. It would allow for the possibility of future funding through a Conservation Area Partnership (CAP) scheme.

One of the reasons for pursuing designation was that shortly after listing there was an application for planning permission for the redevelopment of 48 Boundary Road, the Evans and Shalev home for the disabled (Figure 6.2). This was referred to English Heritage by Camden Council Planning Department as a development affecting the setting of a grade II* building and objections were made. The case also prompted considerable support in the architectural press. English Heritage asked the Department of the Environment to serve an Article 14 direction on the application because it was felt that Camden Council, as owner of the building, was likely to place too high a priority on maximizing the site value and might not give sufficient weight to the wider conservation issues. However, demolition alone (that is, not linked to proposals for a new building on the site) would not have required any consent at all. Once the site was within a Conservation Area, Conservation Area consent would be needed for demolition and appropriate conservation criteria would have to be considered when determining planning applications.

The future of 48 Boundary Road now looks more secure. The costs of relocating an underground fuel tank beneath the building but serving the estate proved prohibitive and the building is now being looked at by a potential purchaser who wants to convert it to sheltered housing. Because 48 Boundary Road, like most on the estate, makes complex use of the cross-section it is not a very flexible building or an easy one to convert to a new use. Student housing or a nursing home where communal facilities would be needed would require the least alteration.

The need to publish proposals for the future of the Conservation Area would offer an opportunity to put together a document presenting conservation as having a more positive and constructive role than the crisis-management imposition of this particular listing. This could focus on identifying popular and successful aspects of the buildings and promote reinforcement of the strengths of the original design as a key to successful regeneration of the estate. It would also need to give clear guidance on which alterations would need Conservation Area consent and would reiterate the provisions of a management agreement identifying what would need listed building consent. It would formulate policies on frequently-requested

Figure 6.2   48 Boundary Road, Alexandra Road Estate, London (English Heritage)

proposals and give specific design advice covering works that would be carried out by Camden Council's Housing Department, works that the cooperative would be in charge of and alterations that individual residents (either tenants or leaseholders) might want to make. It would include landscape works in the park.

The degree of control imposed on interior alterations is very often a controversial issue where post-war buildings are concerned. The first draft of the management agreements document drawn up in 1994 pointed out the importance of the ply and dowel stairs and the sliding screens that allow flexible use of the living areas (which are on the upper level of each of the two-storey apartments and have full-width windows on to roof terraces). It was felt important and reasonable to require retention of these, but it was made clear that listed building consent would not be needed for new kitchen fittings or new bathrooms. Externally, satellite dishes which are not allowed under tenancy or leasehold agreements in any case would be prohibited. (Cable television is being installed so the demand for satellite dishes on the estate may cease.) The park raised several specific points. Play equipment was clearly ephemeral, but it was agreed that the basic structure of walls and planned enclosures were important.

Lighting throughout the estate has been a highly controversial issue. The tenants are concerned about personal safety and damage to property and there is a difficult balance to be achieved between their right to be and feel safe and conservation concerns (shared by many residents) over the visual impact of new lights. The park is one area where lighting has not yet been resolved, but because there are safe routes to all destinations without going through the park it could be possible to preserve its rural nature by keeping lighting out of the core area.

Public consultation on the estate's Conservation Area designation started with evening meetings held on the estate in autumn 1994, but because of staff changes and a lack of resources at both English Heritage and Camden Council the initial impetus was not maintained and designation has still to be finalized. In retrospect, more effort should have been made to win the support and enthusiasm of the residents. Specialist public relations advice should have been taken and more emphasis placed on the benefits of conservation and the importance of the estate before detailing the restrictions of the listing and requirements for Conservation Area and listed building consents. To have any impact on an estate where residents are regularly swamped with information on building repairs and alterations the residents' imagination and enthusiasm needs to be captured. There appears to be enough interest in an evening where some of the original architects would talk about their involvement on the estate's design, and several of them, who can speak on their subject with great energy and passion, have said that they would be willing to do so.

Involving the original architects in conservation issues is obviously an unprecedented opportunity and a useful one. Many of the original consultants involved at Alexandra Road have been generous with their time and helpful in providing information to help understand the buildings more fully. Reading Neave Brown's articles on housing and discussing his objectives with him was useful in developing a broader understanding of the estate. He lectured to English Heritage about the development of his design and thus helped create a broader understanding of its importance and a wider recognition of the issues raised. He was involved with Christopher Dean of DOCOMOMO in the initial listing request and, perhaps surprisingly, was particularly concerned by the alterations to the roof edge details where he felt very strongly that the proposed new detail which wraps the waterproof membrane over the edge was too clumsy. It is possible that his interest in this particular aspect diffused the overall argument and deflected attention from more clearly damaging proposals. English Heritage encouraged Camden Council to employ Neave Brown on a limited basis as a consultant to identify how certain aspects of the project were originally designed to work, including the complex drainage systems from the larger blocks. Theoretically Camden hold all original contract drawings and specifications (BDS are the direct descendants of the original design team) but the records are not in a coherent or accessible state. Given the past history of the estate, and in particular residual bitterness as a result of a 1972 inquiry into the original overspend, Camden Council were, not surprisingly, wary of employing Neave Brown even in this limited capacity. It should be stressed that it was not suggested that he should be employed to sort out any shortcomings of his original design: refurbishment of post-war buildings, just like the conservation of buildings of any period, is a very different specialization to designing new buildings.

The services engineer Max Fordham was also helpful. He was able to point out that the wiring conduits were PVC when it was claimed that they could not be reused because they were completely rusted. Janet Jacks, the landscape architect responsible for the park, and Tom Kay, architect of two of the later phase buildings, were both helpful and provided information for inclusion in the character assessment for the Conservation Area.

However, some of those originally involved in the design of the estate undoubtedly had over-optimistic views of what listing could achieve. They shared what is probably a widespread public assumption that listing could force Camden Council to reinstate elements that had been lost and redo the roofworks and concrete repairs that had been poorly done before listing. It was also thought that listing could and should prevent any future change. This inevitably means that their objectives are unlikely to ever fully coincide with the philosophy of managed change which must be especially crucial to the conservation of this type of building.

Concrete repair

Concrete repair is covered in detail elsewhere in this volume so is mentioned only briefly here. Alexandra Road has very carefully detailed, white *in situ* concrete which is board marked. At the Brunswick Centre it was always intended that the concrete would be painted, but here this was not the case and the aggregate was very carefully selected for its aesthetic qualities. Most of the repairs to the two northerly blocks were carried out before listing and they are very dark grey patch repairs. Figure 6.3 shows a section of wall where trials had been carried out, showing how the dark grey mix had been compared to a much better colour, but because it was not available as a standard factory-mixed product and would not be covered by the manufacturers' guarantee it was rejected and the dark grey used instead. It seems very unlikely that this guarantee (and various others discussed in relation to other materials) would be of any value as the level of site supervision would be likely to hamper any claim against the manufacturers, but this argument was used to support the use of many different types of product. The cooperative felt that dark grey patches were a base coat and that there was a commitment to providing a better-matching top coat, but the initial repairs were left flush with the surface and could only have been intended to be painted, either just overpainting the patches or all-over painting. English Heritage felt very strongly that all-over painting would be a mistake as the subtlety of the carefully selected aggregates would be lost and, more importantly, there would be a long-term maintenance problem. A compromise has been worked out and it has been agreed that the larger patches will be cut back and resurfaced, while the smaller ones will be painted over.

This is clearly not a satisfactory way to approach concrete repair with problems arising because all the damaging cutting-out was carried out and the works largely completed before listing. Similar problems are faced by the Nottingham Playhouse Theatre (Peter Moro 1959-64) but because this was listed before repair works started it was possible to ensure that proper assessment took place and it is hoped that a suitable repair strategy will be adopted. The assessment included a cover metre survey, carbonation tests and accurate mapping of areas of damage which can be compared to the original reinforcement layout drawings. Re-alkalization followed by limited patch repair seems likely to prove the best way forward at Nottingham and this would probably have been the case at Alexandra Road too.

Figure 6.3   Poorly matched concrete repairs carried out on the Alexandra Road Estate before listing (Catherine Croft)

Lessons to be learnt

As Alexandra Road was the first building of its type to be listed, many of the problems raised had not been addressed before. Many lessons have been learnt which could be applied to the conservation of post-war housing estates listed in the future.

- It is essential to understand what is architecturally and historically important about the building. Information from contemporary articles and possibly from the original architect will be crucial, but it may be hard to maintain a critical distance.
- The technical specification of the building must be understood, and here the original architect may be invaluable. It will be important to understand the properties and failings of proprietary products and components which may no longer be available.
- It is important to learn about repair techniques for modern materials such as concrete and to make sure this information is drawn together and is easily accessible.
- The structure of public housing management, and who is responsible for what, must be understood. Where funding comes through regional government offices there needs to be close liaison between English Heritage and the regional government office. All local authority listed building consent applications have to be referred to the Department of the Environment for the Secretary of State's approval, and it may present real problems if English Heritage advises the planning part of a government office that a scheme financed through one of the funding schemes they administer is not acceptable.
- It is essential that the timescales drawn up for funding bids allow enough time to gain necessary consents and that the design work is carried out thoroughly with a clear understanding of the particular merits of the building. There may need to be a greater level

Figure 6.4   Rowley Way and residents of the Alexandra Road Estate, London (Catherine Croft)

of preparatory design work and specification clauses such as 'to meet manufacturers' guarantee requirements' should not be included.

■ It is important to seek only the minimum level of legislative control necessary. Formal management agreements and/or formally-adopted Conservation Area analyses and proposals should be agreed as soon as possible after listing or preferably at the time of listing. Also, residents need to be convinced that it is to their advantage to be listed or in a conservation area, preferably not by offering grants but by selling them the benefits of controls which are widely recognized by many private householders living in the planned private sector mass housing of previous centuries (Figure 6.4).

CHAPTER 7

TECTON BUILDINGS, DUDLEY ZOO

David Heath

Introduction

Dudley Zoo originally opened in 1937. On Castle Hill, on steeply-sloping wooded ground, 13 new reinforced concrete structures had been created to the designs of Berthold Lubetkin. Between about 1930 and the outbreak of the Second World War there was a brief English flowering of the International Style of the Modern Movement. Relatively few buildings were actually erected, certainly by comparison with continental experience, and even fewer were grouped together in anything like such a homogenous group as those at Dudley. This alone makes the Tecton Buildings of particular importance. There was a pioneer spirit, a hopefulness, even a recklessness in the approach which did not survive the war years, or, if it did, became something different, more earnest and more austere (Figure 7.1).

History

Dudley Castle, a roofless ruin and scheduled ancient monument, stands at the top of Castle Hill, a limestone outcrop in the Black Country. This geological resource has had considerable economic importance and has been ruthlessly exploited, first as the source of lime for building mortars and then for fluxes used in the production of iron and steel. The hill is full of the evidence of surface working, but less obvious and of significance to the zoo design team were and are the large underground caverns and tunnels, including a canal tunnel, under the site. There has been a history of collapses and partial collapses right up to the present time. This post-medieval history helps explain why the site was not considered suitable for development before 1935.

The idea of a zoo was first mooted in 1935 by the Earl of Dudley (owner of the Castle Hill), Ernest Marsh (director of Marsh and Baxter, a local meat producer) and Captain Frank Cooper (director of the jams and marmalade manufacturer of Oxford). Captain Cooper was already owner of Oxford Zoo, and apparently he wanted to dispose of his animal collection. The Dudley Zoological Society was formed, with these three as directors, and appointed Dr Geoffrey Vevers, Superintendent at London Zoo, as Advisor.

*Figure 7.1   The entrance to Dudley Zoo in 1937, designed by Tecton
(British Architectural Library)*

The Tecton Partnership, formed in 1932, had already handled several projects for the Zoological Society at London Zoo. The Gorilla House was completed in 1934 and the Penguin Pool in 1935. It was through this connection that they were appointed at Dudley. The design and construction period was rapid, and took place from late 1935. The zoo opened on 6th May 1937, when an estimated 250,000 people crowded around Castle Hill but only 50,000 managed to get in. This day still forms part of an important folk memory in Dudley and its importance should not be underestimated.

The contractors were J.L. Kier and Co., for whom Ove Arup was working at this time. The resident site engineer was Michael Sheldrake, and the job architect was Francis Skinner, who made weekly trips from London. The major design input was Berthold Lubetkin's, but in the development of a range of standardized details, for instance hand rails and parapets cast in serrated formwork, there was an opportunity to make some alterations on site based on ground conditions. Another local contractor was brought in to help out late in the project. There was considerable client pressure to get everything ready for the 1937 season, to get, as Lubetkin recalled, 'as many goods as possible in the shop window'.[1] The budget was limited and appears to have been about £40,000, which did not include the animals.

The Zoo was initially an enormous success. The post-war years, however, have seen changes in ownership, maintenance and setting. The 12 remaining Tecton structures (six now listed grade II* and six listed grade II: one has been demolished) now form only a relatively small proportion of the over 90 structures now on the site. There have also been considerable changes in the zoological standards for the display and care of captive animals, and also changes in the public perception of zoos.

The debate has polarized between those who feel that the zoo function is of great importance (there is considerable civic pride concerning Dudley Zoo and the keeping of large wild animals on Castle Hill), and those who argue that the zoo must close. The former group contend that the Tecton Buildings are too expensive to repair and adapt and should be demolished and replaced with new, and the latter implicitly contend that all the buildings should be demolished. Somewhere in the middle English Heritage is arguing about the importance of the listed buildings and the need for their proper care and maintenance. English Heritage grant aid has been made available for some repairs, but cannot be made available for alterations or improvements or changes in their landscape context, and yet these are clearly desirable.

There are zoological problems in continuing to use the Tecton Buildings for their primary purpose. To some extent these problems are technical: the lack of a filtration system in either the polar bear pool or the sea lion pool means that these have to be drained and refilled by manual labour. Some problems were obvious almost from the outset and uses were changed. For example, the building known as the aviary, apparently designed for tropical birds, is

Figure 7.2   The Tropical Bird House in its setting of mature trees (RCHME)

virtually uninsulated, and has a central oculus in the dished roof open to the external air. It ceased to be used for the display of tropical birds many years ago but other problems have never been satisfactorily redressed (Figure 7.2).

It must be admitted that some of the problems relate to the concept of the design. From the turn of the century there had been a move towards the display of animals in a simulated natural habitat. Lubetkin did not agree: 'This conception has two main faults', he wrote. 'It allowed the very shy animals to hide themselves from public gaze, almost indefinitely, while those with a taste for publicity were not able to indulge it to their best advantage'.[2] The polar bear complex contains a round central enclosure for the polar bears which was clearly designed as a performance space. It is now recognized that polar bears did not respond well to this environment, and they are no longer kept at the zoo (Figure 7.3). Only six of the Tecton Buildings are animal enclosures. Three are cafes, two are kiosks and the sixth is the

Figure 7.3   The Polar Bear Pit at Dudley Zoo. The concrete is already beginning to show signs of weathering in this early photograph (British Architectural Library)

entrance. They all seem to be designed for an outdoor lifestyle based on a climate only intermittently found in the Black Country, and yet they need a year-round use (Figure 7.4). There have been a number of brutal alterations. Part of one of the cafes is now a nightclub unconnected with the zoo.

The Tecton Buildings have not benefited from constantly changing management regimes and priorities. The zoo is now owned by Dudley Metropolitan Borough Council, and it was hoped that this would result in a clear strategy for their future. Unfortunately this has not yet emerged. In 1990 English Heritage jointly funded a feasibility study for the restoration and reuse of the Tecton Buildings at Dudley Zoo. This was prepared by a number of consultants, including zoological consultants, led by Avanti Architects (who were responsible for repairs and improvements at the London Penguin Pool, and who are currently repairing the Finsbury Health Centre). To date, few, if any, of their recommendations have been implemented. The Tecton Buildings therefore present problems both of repair and of adaptive reuse. Either, or both, will involve substantial expenditure.

There have been two phases of grant-aided repairs in the 1980s, neither of which have proved particularly satisfactory, and no further major repair projects are currently planned. From the client' point of view the repairs were very expensive, the cost control was poor, the zoological use of the buildings has not been greatly enhanced (the proposed improvements were cut to pay for the increased cost of repairs) and few, if any, additional visitors have been attracted. From the conservation point of view, there have also been numerous difficulties.

Figure 7.4   One of the kiosks designed for an outdoor lifestyle unfortunately not compatible with the local climate (British Architectural Library)

Observations on repairs

Reinforced concrete seems to have been regarded by the designers and builders as a material that would last forever. The concrete cover to the reinforcing bars (rebars) is often minimal. The cantilevers are daring and the sections are thin, and there are often numerous rebars overlapping. One problem of this is aesthetic as we do not (yet?) regard rusting rebars as pleasing decay, and another is technical in that it does not (yet?) seem possible to repair such buildings without extensively removing and replacing the concrete. At the London Penguin Pool, what has been 'conserved' are the rebars of the interlocking ramps, all the rest is new, and it has been much the same at Dudley. The surface is finished with a modern epoxy-modified mortar, and modern high-performance paints, neither available in the 1930s nor then considered to be necessary. This both looks different, and weathers differently to the original appearance. One has to ask whether the cultural meaning of a building conserved in this manner has not been altered by such drastic introduction of materials and techniques not available at the time of their construction.

The best conservation is that where the life of original material has been extended without any major aesthetic modifications and when it is hard to see where the money has been spent. The repair work so far undertaken at Dudley Zoo does not fall into these categories.

Part of the problem has been in the nature of the repair contracts. Concrete repair is a specialized field, and is at present often essentially contractor-led. The contractor has a range of specialized proprietary products which he recommends where to apply. The role of the supervising officer can be reduced to agreement with the contractors' proposals. This is unlike the process of appropriate repair of older historic buildings, where the sympathy and understanding of the repair architect is critical.

Many conservation architects experienced in the repair of historic buildings are inherently antipathetic to the aims and aspirations of the Modern Movement: they are not interested in repairing such buildings. On the other hand, many architects whose careers have been based on the principles of modernism recognize the iconographic significance of early buildings such as those at Dudley Zoo, but they have little conservation experience and the primary design idea is important to them rather than the weathered and possibly altered fabric. They want to make such buildings appear again as they would have done when built, to 'restore them to their former glory', rather than to recognize that these buildings are nearly 60 years old and need to show their age.

The landscape context

The major loss of Dudley has been the design context of the Tecton Buildings. At the time the zoo was designed the castle was already a scheduled ancient monument. The Ministry of Works was involved in approving the designs of what was, in effect, an enabling development to continue the use and repair of the castle ruins. Certain design parameters were set, and responded to, concerning protecting the visible skyline of the castle, respecting the moat and approach axes and the use of natural materials facing the castle. The zoo buildings themselves were originally shown illustrated in sylvan glades. Every effort was made to retain existing trees and to respond to the natural environment. It is this context which is now so altered by tree loss, municipal planting beds and subsequent development. Unless and until this context is itself recognized and repaired the future of the Tecton Buildings seem bleak.

The Tecton Buildings at Dudley Zoo have few friends. Most parties would be prepared to demolish them: the zoo authorities as inefficient, zoo antagonists as symbols of oppression, modernists as flawed fabric needing to be replaced as new. The general public seems indifferent at best. English Heritage, arguing the case on behalf of the cultural importance of the buildings, is ploughing a lonely furrow.

References

1   anon, (1937), 'Dudley Zoo, Worcestershire II: Architects: Tecton', *Architecture and Building News*, **152**, (12 November), 201-207.

2   anon, (1937), 'The Zoo at Dudley: Tecton Architects', *Architecture Review*, **82**, (October), 167-86.

CHAPTER 8
FAILURE AND SUCCESS IN THE SEVERN VALLEY

H. John Yates

This is a tale of two twentieth-century concrete structures in Shropshire. It is a tale of public perception. It is also a tale of buildings in their contexts, and how those contexts have influenced priorities and decisions.

The buildings concerned are the Free Bridge at Jackfield in the Ironbridge Gorge, and Oldbury Wells School at Bridgnorth. Both became grade II listed historic buildings in recognition of their pioneering design and construction. But the school survives, while the bridge doesn't.

In the early twentieth century the Ironbridge Gorge had passed its industrial heyday as a centre of ironmaking, but it was still a very busy place, particularly in the ceramic industries. In the gorge itself the Severn was spanned by Darby and Prichard's famous Iron Bridge of 1779 (Figure 8.1), Telford's Buildwas Bridge of 1795 stood two miles upstream and the Coalport Bridge of 1799 stood two miles downstream. These three virtuoso iron structures spanned a difficult river, subject to violent floods and running between unstable banks. The bridge promoters levied tolls, so ferries survived at several traditional crossing points, reached by steep and winding roads.

One of these crossings was the Adams Ferry at Jackfield, about half a mile downstream from the Iron Bridge. This was the site of the Free Bridge, built in 1909 after a campaign of fundraising and public subscription.

The Hennebique Mouchel system of reinforced concrete construction was adopted to produce an economical structure that would cause the least possible obstruction to floods. The bridge consisted of two parallel arched ribs spanning between free-standing piled piers, with similar half-arches connecting the piers to the banks. The spandrels were open except for vertical struts from the arch ribs to the deck. The ribbed construction of the deck cantilevered beyond the arches to a slightly greater width. It is believed to have been the 44th bridge built in Britain to this system, the earliest dating from 1901.

By the 1930s the Free Bridge was already giving trouble, with spalling of the concrete exposing the reinforcement. This became a continuous problem, treated first by mortar repairs, then from 1937 by cutting back and spraying concrete (the Gunite technique) to a greater

Figure 8.1   The Iron Bridge, Ironbridge Gorge (English Heritage)

thickness on an extra layer of mesh. These failures appear to have been caused by a combination of factors. The cover-over reinforcement was inadequate, concrete quality was variable in the first place, but carbonation and chloride attack set in early, worsened by overloading of this slender structure as vehicle weights increased. In 1937 a weight limit of 12 tons was imposed, but often flouted. The major failure of a spandrel strut in 1969 was repaired with resin-modified concrete.

Local industries declined as the century wore on, but by the 1980s the pressure was on, literally. The Ironbridge Gorge stood at the forefront of the heritage industry, while the new town of Telford was growing up next to it. The Iron Bridge itself had been closed to traffic in 1934. The Free Bridge was not only structurally poor, but its single carriageway caused serious traffic jams as visitors flocked in. The weight limit was further reduced to 3 tons in 1986, then the parapets were demolished and a bailey bridge was placed over the failing structure.

In 1988 Shropshire County Council proposed to build a new road bridge at Ladywood, between the Free Bridge and Iron Bridge. By this time the Iron Bridge and the nearby Bedlam Furnaces were scheduled ancient monuments, the Free Bridge was a grade II listed building and the gorge was both a conservation area and a world heritage site. The new bridge would have been clearly visible from the Iron Bridge and damaging to its setting. The bridge and its new approach roads would have disrupted the appearance and character of one of the holiest places in industrial archaeology. There was uproar. A public inquiry was held: the Secretary of State refused planning permission.

The inquiry inspector accepted the need for the new bridge, and recommended that it should go alongside the Free Bridge. During the inquiry a consensus had been reached that the Free Bridge was incapable of repair to take vehicular traffic.

In 1991 discussions between the County Council and English Heritage were resumed. Design studies explored options for bridges either upstream or downstream from the Free Bridge, which would remain as a footbridge. However it soon became clear that very little of the bridge's fabric would survive repair even to take pedestrian loadings, and that the continuing decay of the early fabric could not be arrested. It also became clear that the alterations to the approach roads would themselves be visually and archaeologically disruptive to this part of the gorge, which would thereby become far more dominated by tarmac than if the new bridge were on the site of the old.

After thorough verification of these matters, discussions moved on to the possibility of demolishing the Free Bridge. English Heritage made it clear that it could only tolerate such an action if, taking a holistic view of the character and quality of the gorge, the replacement was fully worthy of the site. The County Council appointed Ron Weeks of Percy Thomas Partnership and Gordon Clark of Gifford and Partners as consultants to advise on the design of the new bridge. They proposed a cable-stayed bridge supported from a single tower, expressively overcoming the problem of bank instability by deriving all support from one bank.

In 1993 listed building consent was granted for total demolition of the Free Bridge. A part of the scheme was an agreed programme of archaeological recording, and the salvage and display nearby of a representative sample of the structure, with interpretive material. In coming to the decision not to oppose demolition English Heritage had taken into account a combination of factors, no single one of which would have justified demolition in its own right.

The extent of necessary replacement was a powerful argument, but the case can be made that over a long period many historic buildings and artefacts require repairs that make them little more than replicas of their former selves. Loss of early fabric diminishes the special interest of an historic building, but it does not necessarily extinguish it. The reconstructed building may lose much of its ability to tell future generations about its own technology, but it still carries forward messages about the taste that formed its design, and about the economic and social circumstances that caused its construction.

Taking into account the quality and importance of the gorge as a heritage entity, the inevitable clumsiness of the two parallel bridges with their elaborate approaches was another negative factor in heritage terms. So was the potential loss of archaeological deposits in the course of these works, as the banks of the river are particularly rich in the evidence of earlier industry. Another consideration was the effect of further delay on the Coalport Bridge, itself an ancient monument, subject to excessive use by heavy traffic in the absence of an alternative.

Another consideration for any public body involved in conservation is the retention of public support. English Heritage had retained a large measure of public support for its opposition to the Ladywood proposal. Not only would it have been most unlikely to win the argument for retaining the Free Bridge, it would have lost a great deal of local public goodwill for the whole process of heritage conservation. This statutory process is, after all, only justifiable because it is protecting a cultural resource for the community as a whole. We forget that at our peril.

This political dimension of heritage lies at the heart of our other example, Oldbury Wells School, Bridgnorth, seven miles south of Jackfield. In the late 1950s there was a general expansion of secondary education to accommodate the post-war baby boom. Salop County Council (as it was then called) appointed the London firm of Lyons, Israel and Ellis to design separate secondary modern schools for boys and girls on adjacent sites at Oldbury Wells, on the outskirts of Bridgnorth. The boys' school, on the east side of the road, was completed in 1958, and the girls' school, on the west side, followed in 1959.

Both schools have an exposed structural frame of board-marked concrete, lightweight infill panels and flat roofs. Both are mainly two storeys high, with strong architectural emphasis on their chimneys and tank housings. The boys' school has a relatively organic and informal plan, with its main hall at the rear gaining top light from a butterfly roof, a range of single-storey labs and workshops and an open courtyard lighting the small assembly and dining hall. The girls' school, by contrast, has a rigidly regular plan, controlled by the structural module of this long rectangular building. The structural system is strongly expressed in elevation by the columns running through both storeys, with infill and first floor kept back behind them. The entrance bays are more deeply recessed, with a boldly displayed staircase. The original intention was apparently that the girls' school could be extended by adding to each end of the building on the same system and module.

In practice, extension has been informal and pragmatic. Both schools expanded considerably in the 1960s. Lyons, Israel and Ellis designed a large matching extension to the rear of the boys' school in 1960, although it appears not to have been built until 1964. In 1966 the girls' school lost its architectural clarity when a large classroom block on the Scola system was added to one side of its front entrance, a kitchen block was added to the other side of the entrance and two further blocks were attached at the rear.

In 1972 the two schools amalgamated to form the present single comprehensive school, with some adjustment to internal arrangements. Relatively minor alterations have since continued, as the patterns and needs of education have changed. For example, there is no longer the need for the whole school to assemble every day, so the former boys' hall is used for larger teaching projects. Meanwhile its stage has been amalgamated with the former small hall to make a larger library, as school libraries now need more space for private study and there is less pressure for dining space.

While the accommodation continues to work well, the construction gives increasing cause for concern. Again the main problem is the exposed concrete, where carbonation and inadequate cover has caused spalling of the surface and corrosion of the reinforcement. The 1964 extension of the boys' school is the worst, as the original buildings seem to have better cover, which more than compensates for their more variable quality of concreting. The problem started to appear in the 1980s, and was tackled unsuccessfully by patching with sand and cement. In 1990 a specialist survey was commissioned and a programme of repairs subsequently specified. The procedure was an orthodox one of power hosing, hammer testing, breaking out, treating reinforcement then applying Fosroc, a proprietory system of repair mortars, by trowel. This was followed by a thin render, in which efforts were made to reproduce the board marking (which is not very pronounced) without complete success. On the early phases of repair, the frame was then coated with a masonry paint, but since the buildings were listed that specification has been changed to a clear silicone treatment.

When the school buildings were listed grade II in 1993, the users were astonished and horrified. As the notice of listing arrived on 1 April, they were not at first sure whether to believe it. This being a local authority building, applications for listed building consent are made to the Secretary of State for the Environment. The head teacher and governors expected this to be an entirely negative and obscure procedure. Early exploratory meetings with the county conservation officer and English Heritage started in an atmosphere of suspicion, if not actual hostility. The users were reassured to find that listing does not freeze all change, but that it does require an extra mental discipline in assessing what is special about their building. Like many owners of listed buildings, they have looked with fresh interest at their surroundings. They now understand that there are compensations for having to go through an extra process, in that they have buildings that are themselves a cultural and educational resource. On my last visit to the school, I was proudly shown the latest display in the school reception area. It tells of the history and importance of their buildings.

CHAPTER 9
THE WINDOWS OF CHURCHILL GARDENS

Elain Harwood

Churchill Gardens was the first major housing project undertaken in Britain after the Second World War. In 1943 the Ministry of Health had asked London authorities to produce a one-year plan for housing that could begin as soon as the war ended, a project soon incorporated within the County of London Plan. Westminster councillors chose to take a longer view. They identified a single large site in Pimlico where there were some houses capable, with repair, of lasting another ten years, next to land already cleared by bombing which could be redeveloped with housing in the meantime. The result was that though Churchill Gardens was planned as a single entity, it was built piecemeal over nearly 20 years.

In 1946 Powell and Moya won a competition for the site. The fact that so prestigious a competition had been won by men aged respectively only 25 and 26 seemed symbolic of the new era. The generous flats and carefully laid-out gardens and amenities set model standards for post-war housing at the maximum permitted density of 200 persons per acre. Work began in 1947, and the first block, Chaucer House, was completed in June 1950. Four distinctively designed blocks were officially opened in 1951 and won an RIBA Bronze Medal and Festival of Britain Merit Award. These are large flats, built to a high specification. They exemplify the best of the work begun before July 1947, when Stafford Cripps introduced a cost ceiling as part of a package of austerity measures. Most distinctive are the large number of projecting staircases, each serving just two flats per floor. Their full-height glazing makes a bold contrast with the expanses of plain brickwork (hiding a monolithic concrete shell) across the blocks themselves. In 1951 they were followed by a series of lower blocks, with rendered fronts and the more conventional (and cheaper) gallery access. There was gallery access, too, for the last block in this phase. This was the first tall block of maisonettes in Britain, with shops on the ground floor and named De Quincey House.

In 1990 there was some consternation in the architectural press when new PVCu-coated aluminium windows were installed, replacing Williams and Williams' standard metal frames which are so characteristic of the period. On the lower blocks the installation of new, repetitive glazing was the subject of a damning article in *Building Design* (August 1990 supplement) that criticized the introduction of extra glazing bars and top opening lights. 'Glazed areas are clearly much reduced and illogical sitings of some units mean impossible to reach catches can only be released by long arm rods. Flats and maisonettes with private balconies have multi-unit replacements where large fixed lights and end casements previously provided better visibility and ventilation.'[1]

This work at Churchill Gardens was compared unfavourably with a similar replacement scheme at the Alton Estate, the model development of the London County Council, largely built in 1953-9 and now managed by the London Borough of Wandsworth. There the original window pattern was repeated almost exactly, so that although double glazing has made the new frames thicker they are comparatively less intrusive.

However, on the larger blocks at Churchill Gardens the window replacement had little impact, because of the relatively small size of the flats' windows in proportion to the scale of the buildings (Figure 9.1). The replacements have the problem of being thicker, but on the large blocks they largely respected the pattern of the earlier windows. The dramatic fenestration in these blocks was in the staircase, where a like-for-like replacement of the metal windows was made easier as double glazing was not asked for. Here at least the reglazing programme was successful. It also had the effect of emphasizing the quality of these very first blocks over those erected in the later part of phase I after cost controls had been imposed.

'Churchill Gardens remains a major landmark which is clearly much loved and is respected by the majority of its residents. The same "pride of place" feeling is also evident when one walks round the Alton Estate. But given the cost and complexity of the Westminster refurbishment, it is regrettable that more attention was not given to the need to respect and preserve the visual purity of this classic.'[1] So wrote *Building Design* in 1990. But later the same year, it was Churchill Gardens which was designated a

Figure 9.1   One of the earliest blocks, Coleridge House, after restoration. The window replacement to the large blocks has been more successful than that to the smaller blocks behind (English Heritage)

Conservation Area in its own right just as this first phase of restoration and window replacement was completed. Churchill Gardens, Hallfield (1947-55, for the former Paddington Metropolitan Borough) and Lillington Gardens (designed 1961, built 1964-79) were the first post-war estates in England to be designated as Conservation Areas and Westminster City Council is to be congratulated on this initiative, itself a tribute to the exceptional quality of the housing erected by its precursors between 1945 and 1965.

Window replacement has continued at Churchill Gardens, and attention has turned to the large number of flats built in the 1950s. When work on phase II of Churchill Gardens began in 1951, cuts in subsidies and the findings of a new census caused Westminster to ask for more small flats. These could only be provided by means of access decks or galleries, reducing the need for the large and expensive numbers of stairs and lifts found in Chaucer House and its siblings. The strong horizontals of these galleries, in the large blocks usually set in two banks across the facade, are contrasted with strips of glazing in the centres and at either end, whose vertical mullions set up a strong counter-rhythm (Figures 9.2 and 9.3). The pattern of horizontals and verticals is carefully balanced, and is the principal composition of blocks ranging from Gilbert and Sullivan Houses, completed in 1954, to Littleton House, finished in 1962. Timber windows were used on these blocks, with galvanized metal opening casements. The softwood frames have deteriorated, for as the replacement programme got underway maintenance was not carried out.

In 1993-4 Lutyens House and Bramwell House were refurbished with PVCu-coated aluminium windows, with a continuous transom of toplights, thicker frames and a more

Figure 9.2   *De Quincey House in the 1950s (English Heritage)*

Figure 9.3   De Quincey House in 1995 after window replacement. The change from a vertical pattern of glazing to one with strong horizontals has been most disfiguring (English Heritage)

regular pattern of fenestration. The first English Heritage learned of this was when they were alerted in May 1994 by concerned residents, architects and amenity societies, demanding that the estate be listed immediately. But a contract had just been let for a similar replacement scheme at Blackstone, Littleton and Langdale Houses. The listing of post-war buildings, with a new minister at the Department of National Heritage then just developing the idea of public consultation, was, as it remains, a slow and often controversial procedure. English Heritage were reluctant to hold up the work, given that a solution had to be found whether the buildings were listed or not. The blocks where work was due to start lie in the centre of the estate, one of the last parts to be developed. Littleton House looks north over Lupus Street, and has a line of shops and a small library on its ground floor. Although contributing powerfully to the quality of the Conservation Area by their very central position, the blocks were not obvious candidates for listing in their own right.

A reason for the new window pattern with top lights is a need for easier cleaning, in line with British Standard 8213 issued in 1991. This states that if you have to lean out to clean a window above the ground floor you should not need to stand on a chair to do so. New windows in unlisted buildings must meet this requirement. The architects reported that the residents preferred small opening toplights to give night ventilation, while they did not

Figure 9.4   Lutyens House. Replacement windows in 1994, with continuous toplights, prompted a request that the whole estate be listed (English Heritage)

welcome the swivel-opening windows employed at the Alton Estate and elsewhere where English Heritage has been involved in refurbishing modern buildings. The elderly and vocal population of Churchill Gardens liked the new-style Lutyens House and could not see why English Heritage did not (Figure 9.4).

As the contract had been let, a solution had to be found quickly. English Heritage and Westminster planners accepted that for this reason there was no alternative to using PVCu-coated aluminium and opening casements. What could be done was to try to reduce the number of toplights, and restore the irregular rhythm which had enlivened the old facades. English Heritage was very fortunate indeed in being able to call upon the help of the original architect, Sir Philip Powell. In the middle of a walkabout with the residents, Sir Philip devised a new pattern. The bands of toplights which were so obtrusive on Lutyens, Bramwell and De Quincey Houses were broken up with an alternating pattern of full-height fixed lights, while the windows were made of varying widths to give something of their previous staccato pattern. As he had designed the original, and his new design satisfied residents' needs, Sir Philip's proposals were adopted.

The three blocks are just emerging from the netting covering the builders' scaffolding, so it is possible only to give a first impression of the result. But Sir Philip's solution is clearly a very considerable improvement on what was done before. The frames are only a little thicker than those originally employed, and the alternating pattern is lighter and more lively than that on blocks refurbished hitherto. Yet its effect is clearly different from that of the originals. The question now is, will it 'do' for the large number of blocks still to be refurbished, or should English Heritage continue to press for a solution closer to the originals? Sir Philip thinks they should. But Westminster are anxious to commit funds this financial year, and are again pressing for English Heritage to agree a solution.

The area remaining to be refurbished is potentially the most difficult, with a large number of blocks, closely spaced, which gain their visual impact from the large areas of glazing employed. Whereas phase III, the area not completed until the early 1960s, is broken up by an earlier school, a community centre and a large square, phase II, built in two contracts from 1951, is entirely homogeneous. Particularly prominent are the two blocks at the edge of the estate, Gilbert and Sullivan Houses, which were the first to be built according to the revised pattern of gallery-accessed small flats with big windows. English Heritage have proposed these blocks for listing, in part because they were the first of these flats to be built and have slightly more generous standards than the others, but also because of the visual impact made by these two great walls of brick and glass, emphasized by being the only blocks placed side by side. The dramatic balance between the horizontal galleries and vertical window pattern is powerful, whether seen from Lupus Street or from the nearby viaduct into Victoria Station. Top lights would destroy this balance. How much does this matter? Can English Heritage justify seeking a different solution here, perhaps ignoring residents' preferences and introducing 'tip and tilt' windows with a swivel? Or should they try to find an acceptable solution for all the blocks?

An encouraging development is that Westminster are now looking at a range of options. It has been suggested that they approach the Steel Windows Federation for an alternative to PVCu-coated aluminium. In 1994 the Steel Windows Federation proposed that Crittall's W20 windows, double-glazed, in PVCu subframes would give a slimmer finish at comparable cost. English Heritage and Westminster have agreed that any solution should be double-glazed and meet the standards of BS 8213, as the residents have come to expect. As the estate has a celebrated district heating system, Britain's first and largest, and originally fuelled from Battersea Power Station, the problems of condensation and cold-bridging, regularly raised with steel windows, are reduced. Indeed the adequate heating may be a reason why the estate has worn so well.

Double glazing and modern frames are more reflective than the original windows, and many white plastic panels have been installed under the windows of the refurbished blocks, particularly the lower blocks like Martineau House. Yet originally the blocks were richly and distinctively coloured, De Quincey House in particular being celebrated for its bold tones. It originally had dark green panels below the windows, not the repetitive white seen now, while there were crimson doors and the balcony backs were dark 'madder red'. Sir Philip has been approached about the colour schemes for the blocks nearing completion, and has given advice. It is hoped that he can become a formal consultant to the scheme, and that a policy of restoring the building's original colours become a part of the continuing management programme, both for those blocks not yet refurbished and for those already restored and refenestrated.

Churchill Gardens is the only case study in this selection not to involve a listed building. The story of Alexandra Road makes an interesting comparison. English Heritage first met Camden's Building Design Services in December 1992, but Alexandra Road was not listed until August 1993. I had been on site and approved a matching colour mix for the concrete repair, but had no control or right to be consulted when that mix was changed with disastrous results for the appearance of the buildings. Although Churchill Gardens is a Conservation Area, English Heritage has no formal role in its management and its involvement rests on its excellent relationship with Westminster City Council. The fact that the buildings are not listed limits the estate's access to professional advice from experienced buildings officers, architects and engineers.

What is the effect of the Conservation Area protection? Hitherto it has served as a recognition of the estate's importance and perhaps as some justification for the huge amount of money Westminster have committed to its refurbishment programme. With the exception of just two terraces of single-occupancy houses, the much mutilated Telford Terrace and the well-preserved Paxton Terrace, the blocks have no permitted development rights. Article Four directions are thus irrelevant. There is nothing to stop Westminster, as owner and planning officer, or its management agents, doing as they please. English Heritage would like to draw up management guidelines for the maintenance and preservation of the estate's finest features, but its role would continue to be merely advisory unless elements of the estate were listed.

There is no doubt that Churchill Gardens is one of the most important post-war housing developments in England. It was also among the most ambitious, a remarkable fact given its very early conception. The high internal standards, the prominence and elegance of its design and the sophisticated overall layout set it well above the other estates of the time, and above all others entirely composed of *zeilenbau* blocks. 'The tall early blocks are a striking example of the simplification of tall building design by minimizing the expression of the horizontal layers of the section and accenting the continuity of such features as stair and lift towers which use the full height', wrote Henry Russell Hitchcock in praise of the estate as early as September 1953.[3] It has been celebrated since the first block, Chaucer House, opened: in 1952 the *Architects' Journal* considered that it was 'deservedly becoming the most highly praised example of high density development in the country'[4], while in 1981 Lord Esher called it 'the most successful high density project in London'.[5] It is worth remembering, too, that English public housing was widely admitted in the 1950s as amongst the best in the world. While the American critic G.E. Kidder Smith reserved his highest praise for the Alton Estate, he said of Churchill Gardens that 'architecturally the buildings range from good to very good' and that 'nothing in New York can touch it'.[6]

In 1987 English Heritage recommended the whole estate for listing. That recommendation was rejected by the Department of the Environment, but time and the thematic project set up in 1991 under the auspices of the then Minister's Heritage Forum have enabled us to study public housing in greater detail and to form a more sophisticated policy for its preservation. Because the best of our public housing is among the most internationally and critically significant of our entire post-war building programme, it cannot be disregarded. The policy of closely studying an estate identifies the most successful or characterful elements for listing rather than seeking to impose a blanket protection. These carefully selected listings would be accompanied by a management agreement to ensure that residents were free to do as they wished inside their flats, while setting out policies for the continued maintenance of the estate. Where this is appropriate English Heritage will recommend that a Conservation Area is declared. Churchill Gardens is one step ahead of all but one of our seventeen other recommendations, in that it is already a Conservation Area and that English Heritage's advice is already being sought by the local authority. As the discussions on window replacement continue in the next few months it will be a test case for English Heritage listing policy on public housing.

References

1   Jones, N. (1990), 'Pride of Place', *Building Design*, (1001, supplement), vi-vii.

2   Jones, N. (1990), 'Pride of Place', *Building Design*, (1001, supplement), vi-vii.

3   Russell Hitchcock, H. (1953), 'Pimlico', *Architectural Review*, **cxiv**, (681), 176-84.

4   anon (1952), 'Housing at Churchill Gardens', *Architects Journal*, **116**, (3005), 406-1.

5   Lord Esher, (1981), *A Broken Wave*, London: Allen Lane, 105.

6   Kidder Smith, G. E., (1961), *The new architecture of Europe*, New York: Meridian, 46.

CHAPTER 10
THE UNIVERSITY OF SUSSEX
Richard Morrice

By the post-war years there were broadly two groups of universities in England, the ancient foundations of Oxford and Cambridge, and the Victorian and Edwardian universities of the cities, including the colleges of London University, Birmingham, Liverpool and Manchester. Later foundations were few, only Reading between the wars and Keele just after the war. The Macmillan government began a new wave of university foundations dedicated to broadening the curriculum and breaking down traditional subject boundaries. The first six were all in similar locations, outside larger historic and county towns: Sussex outside Brighton, East Anglia at Norwich, Essex outside Colchester, York, Kent at Canterbury and Lancaster.

Although a university had been mooted for Brighton as early as 1911, the University Grants Committee only gave the go-ahead for a new university at Falmer in 1958. The site chosen was Stanmer Park, formerly the seat of the Earls of Chichester but now the property of Brighton Borough Council. The site gives the University, like so many post-war foundations, a parkland setting, here in the midst of the South Downs. The eighteenth-century Stanmer House stands on the other side of a low rise to the south-west, close but remarkably unaffected by the presence of such a large institution nearby. The University has been expanding fast, from 6000 students during the 1980s to about 10,500 in 1995. This has put great pressure on the buildings.

Planning the University began in 1959 and the architect chosen was Basil, later Sir Basil, Spence. The first building to be begun was Falmer House (1960–2), intended to operate as a collegiate university centre during the first years. It was followed by Mathematics and Physical Sciences I (1960–2), the Library (1962–4, later extended further), Arts A and B (1962–8, again extended later), Molecular Sciences I (1963–5), the Meeting House (1963–5), the Gardner Arts Centre (opened 1969) and Engineering and Applied Sciences I (late 1960s). Later expansion has been to the north of the site.

Character

The buildings have many design features in common, including the use of a good-quality red brick set in a yellowy-buff, slightly cementitious mortar, board-marked concrete, segmental arches, particularly in concrete, both internally and externally, and internal fittings, such as laboratory fittings in science buildings and shelving units in Arts A, crafted in oak to match chairs and tables also designed by Spence.

The buildings are set around Fulton Court in a defile in the South Downs and in the eastern part of the park of Stanmer House. Spence always saw views out from the buildings as important, of grass from the buildings themselves, of trees through and between the buildings and of the surrounding Downs.

Significance

The choice of Spence as architect and master-planner of the new University was an interesting one, for, although a fully-fledged Modernist, he had spent some time during the 1930s in the office of Sir Edwin Lutyens. Thus, although these buildings reflect works of the mid-1950s by Le Corbusier (including the Jaoul houses of 1954 in France and his work in India, including the Villa Sarabhai at Ahmedabad of 1955 and the Palais de Justice at Chandigarh of 1956), and though neither the buildings, nor the layout, are 'classical' in the strict sense that Lutyens would have understood, the symmetry and monumentality of many of the buildings and their use of arches and brickwork recall some of Lutyens's later works rather than British Modernism. Spence had first become well-known with his design for Coventry Cathedral and he went on to build up a large practice based on a Modernism where monumentality was combined with a picturesqueness, particularly in materials. Indeed his work has been described as combining the monumentality of Denys Lasdun with the feeling for picturesque layout which is so important for Sir Hugh Casson. For this reason Spence's work at the University of Sussex is among his most important work and among the most important architecture of the 1960s.

Eight buildings at the University of Sussex were listed in 1992, Falmer House at grade I and the other seven mentioned above at grade II*. The only other contemporary university buildings to be listed grade I are at St Catherine's College, Oxford, by Arne Jacobsen.

Planning and listed building issues

Apart from the Meeting House (Figure 10.1, a kind of ecumenical religious building) and the Gardner Arts Centre (which includes a theatre and various galleries), these buildings were intended, like so many post-war buildings, to be used more flexibly than earlier ones. As the University has a large estates and building staff who regularly altered the buildings as the need arose, English Heritage suggested two means to ease potential planning problems. These were to have a meeting every two months between staff from English Heritage, the University estates department and Brighton Borough Council to discuss proposed alterations and extensions to the buildings, and to draw up guidelines on listed building consent, in order to ensure that care of historic buildings does not inhibit works of alteration and at the same time ensuring that due regard is given to the architectural and historic interest of the buildings. The guidelines are divided into eight sections and define the character of the buildings and list

Figure 10.1   The Meeting House, Sussex University (English Heritage)

those parts which do not contribute to that character. Applications for listed building consent on alterations for these will not be required.

1.   an introduction, giving their parameters
2.   a discussion of the character of the buildings which it is considered important to preserve
3.   a list of the works for which listed building consent will usually be required. This includes all works to Falmer House and the Meeting House. Throughout the rest of the buildings works affecting exteriors should also be referred to the local planning authority, for consideration of whether listed building consent is necessary, as should all internal works affecting staircases, floors of wood block, quarry tile and brick, walls with exposed brick and board-marked concrete, all original fixtures and fittings, where attached to the building, and ceilings with segmental arches.
4.   a list of the works for which listed building consent will not usually be required. English Heritage and Brighton Borough Council agree that the following works in these areas are unlikely to affect the character of the building, provided that they do not have any

effect on the exterior or structural stability of the building: the Gardner Arts centre understage area, removal and insertion of partitions in the phase 3 part of the Library, and in Arts A and B, Engineering and Applied Sciences I, Molecular Sciences I and Mathematics and Physical Sciences I, alterations to offices on all floors (and which, in Arts A only, do not affect built-in shelving units) and removal of no more than four adjacent partitions. Although the cumulative effect of minor alterations is recognised and accepted, major alterations to the layout of offices involving sub-division or incorporation of more than five offices should be referred to Brighton Borough Council or English Heritage. Proposals which lead to the removal of partitions in any listed building in such a way as to render that building liable to be seen through from one side to another should also be referred.

5.   a list of works for which local authority guidance should be sought
6.   curtilage issues
7.   the setting of the buildings. This is not easy to define but includes the complete complex of the listed buildings, and so intervisibility may prove an important consideration. The University should seek the guidance of the local planning authority when considering development which would be intervisible with or affect the setting of the listed buildings. The immediate context of the listed buildings is equally important and signs, lamp-posts and other furniture should follow historically appropriate models. The landscape setting of the buildings will also be included.
8.   terms of the guidelines

By and large, while works to the exteriors of the buildings as well as to the interiors of both Falmer House and the Meeting House, and to certain staircases, lecture theatres and other interior spaces of the other buildings, will require listed building consent, others, including works to the interior of a large part of the Library, for instance, would not need listed building consent.

Some significant issues have been raised in the course of the regular meetings.

The infilling of the gaps in Falmer House

Falmer House (grade I) is the centrepiece of the University and the most prominent building on the site (Figure 10.2). Spence wrote that he designed Falmer House with gaps which could be infilled in future, but this contradicts his avowed intention to allow the landscape setting to be seen through the buildings. It has been mostly used as the Student's Union for some years while proposals for a new Union are developed. These are coming to fruition and English Heritage and Brighton Borough Council were asked for views on proposals to infill gaps in the structure of the building to provide further space. English Heritage's view was that it would oppose such proposals as the gaps are so important to the character of the building. The University has not pursued the matter but with growing pressure on its available space it may revive the argument in the future.

Figure 10.2   Falmer House, Sussex University (English Heritage)

The extension of the Library

The Library was originally relatively small and has been extended twice, latterly in the 1970s across its west side, away from the University. To cope with pressure on library space the University brought forward proposals for its extension further to the west. English Heritage and Brighton Borough Council attended the selection panel for the architectural practice as specialist advisors.

Concrete repairs

The most worrying proposals have been for concrete repair. A combination of faulty concrete construction, poor supervision during the works and a maritime climate has meant that the concrete, and particularly the steel reinforcement within, is, in many cases, in poor repair. English Heritage sympathizes with the University but finds its proposals for concrete repair very worrying because they include painting the concrete with a shiny plasticized coating. This hides the patch repairs to the concrete and gives it extra protection, particularly the steel reinforcements which have insufficient covering of concrete to prevent rusting and thus bursting and spalling. It does, however, greatly change the character of buildings thus coated from a natural appearance to one much more mechanical and uniform without the capacity to change with alterations in light and weather.

The Meeting House was the first building to be repaired in this way, before the buildings were listed. Next was Mathematics and Physical Sciences I in the summer of 1995. English Heritage's concerns were swallowed after it was proved to their satisfaction that there was no known alternative. They are now considering an application to repair the concrete of a section of Falmer House. It is likely that it will be opposed, unless reasons of cost prove persuasive, to enable Falmer House to be coated in one go when full repairs are begun in about two years time. This will allow English Heritage and the University to consider again possible alternative methods of concrete repair.

The need for planning permission and listed building consent are not the only constraints as the University is also within the South Downs Area of Outstanding Natural Beauty. Brighton Borough Council has also been discussing with the University a proposal to designate a Conservation Area over a rather wider part on the site. This has not met with approval from the University which considers that it would inhibit development and tree surgery within the area. A management agreement is currently being considered.

Grant aid

The University has applied for English Heritage Historic Buildings and Monuments grant aid towards the cost of repairs to a part of the Library. This is an unusual case because as University buildings they are eligible, but English Heritage will need to know how the University and the Higher Education Funding Council for England consider that the extra costs which might, however rarely, derive from listing should be paid for. It is understood that extra costs arising from other parts of the planning legislation are ineligible for grant from other sources.

Conclusion

When the buildings were listed, appaarently out of the blue, the requirements of the listed building legislation appeared to be onerous. With patience and a pragmatic approach to the legislation during the early days English Heritage and Brighton Borough Council have strived to help, rather than hinder, the University in its search for a solution to its problems.

PART TWO

PRACTICAL
SOLUTIONS
TO
CONSERVATION
PROBLEMS

CHAPTER 11

RECONCILING AUTHENTICITY AND REPAIR IN THE CONSERVATION OF MODERN ARCHITECTURE

Susan Macdonald

'Modern architecture is dead; long live modern architecture'[1]

This century has been one of tremendous change. The nineteenth century introduced industrialization to the world and the twentieth century used the possibilities it offered to reshape our environment and change the way we live. As the history of the twentieth century is studied and its artistic expression examined, people will begin to recognize the value of its architecture and will become more interested in conserving it. As yet, the conservation of buildings from the modern era is a relatively new concept and highlights new aspects of contemporary conservation thought.

Moral dilemmas

It is important that we consider these problems if we wish to conserve our recent cultural heritage. At the same time, there is a need for a more comprehensive historical study of twentieth-century architecture. At the moment there is much criticism of Modernism and its failure to fulfil its ambitious intentions. Just how and why Modernism is perceived to have created the physical and social problems that are laid at its door is not fully understood. We need to examine the conservation of modern buildings, urban planning and landscapes, particularly when these constitute a major part of the built environment. A more thorough understanding of this century's contribution can also provide options for future building technology and help to achieve current aims of sustainable development.

The Sydney Opera House, designed by Joern Utzon as a result of the 1957 international competition, is a national symbol indicative of its place, time and its country's culture. It is one of the most powerful and enduring symbols of Australia, one of the icons of modern architecture and testament to the fact that a modern building can hold a place in the hearts and minds of the general public, not just an informed minority. Countries like the United States and Australia, whose built traditions do not carry the same cultural load as in Europe, rest easier with a notion of a twentieth-century heritage, and have come to terms with a number of the issues Europe is still beginning to tackle. It is useful to examine the main issues relating to the

Figure 11.1 Notre Dame du Raincy, outside Paris, Auguste Perret 1923 (Susan Macdonald)

conservation of modern architecture on an international level, as we are beginning to be more global in our approach to conservation.

The architecture of the twentieth century, particularly Modernism, was conceived with the aim of expressing the opportunities and optimism of the new age. Architecture, which was to be the highest form of artistic expression, was based on a new vision of artistic abstraction, a new understanding of spatial qualities, utilized new technology, structural innovations and new materials. It enabled mass production through prefabrication and was to provide the infrastructure of the new society, to raise levels of hygiene, amenity and standards of living. Architecture was to be a powerful tool in social reform.

Modern architecture instigated a complete break with traditional architectural forms, planning and use of materials. Architects such as Auguste Perret at Notre Dame du Raincy (1923), (Figure 11.1) exuberantly utilized new materials, which were not fully understood at the time. Traditional construction methods were largely abandoned to create the new architectural aesthetic of the functional machine, the streamlined, minimalist modern building. The misapprehension that modern buildings were low-maintenance compounded many of the material and construction problems such as ungalvanized windows, internal drainage and thin concrete walling with its minimal cover to reinforcement and poor thermal quality. Many twentieth-century buildings have not stood the test of time well and their perceived inability to age gracefully has questioned some fundamental conservation principles such as the aims of minimal intervention, maximum retention of original fabric, conserve as found and reversibility.

Global exports

By 1931 *The International Style* by Henry Russell Hitchcock and Philip Johnson had been published and the influence of the Modern Movement began to be felt across the globe.[2] There was not only an emergent aesthetic language, but also a universality in the use of new, untried and developing materials such as concrete, metals like aluminium, plastics and so on, with fewer regional characteristics in comparison to traditional building. Different architects utilized materials in different ways in response to climatic conditions and the availability of construction techniques and materials. However, one of the characteristics of Modernism is its attempt to standardize construction for prefabrication to provide a new infrastructure on a large scale. Prefabrication tends to enlarge the construction industry market and thus globalize rather than regionalize the resulting architectural expressions. Thus many of the physical problems faced in the UK appear to be gradations of what are essentially universal problems. This has a great advantage in conservation terms by enabling us to deal with the philosophical and physical conservation problems on an international level, helped by improved communications systems which allow us to access international information networks.

Theories and principles

In principle the philosophy and methodology adopted in the conservation of twentieth-century structures should be no different to that utilized for buildings from our more distant past. However, when we begin to examine specific cases a number of issues need reconsideration. This encourages the re-examination and clarification of those principles when they are applied to work on more recent buildings. It is worth reminding ourselves what the process of conservation involves and the definition provided by the Burra Charter is a particularly useful reference point.

> Conservation means all the processes of looking after a place so as to retain its cultural significance. It includes maintenance and may according to circumstances include preservation, restoration, reconstruction and adaptation and will commonly be a combination of more than one of these.[3]

So how does all this relate to conserving modern buildings, and what are these so-called problems in reconciling authenticity and repair? Rather than suggest solutions to such theoretical issues it is perhaps more useful to outline the main conflicts which cause difficulties and pinpoint other issues which make achieving general conservation aims problematic.

Authenticity – a catch phrase for the 90s?

The most difficult issue seems to relate to the concept of authenticity. The Venice Charter, which is still the most important international reference for conservation policy, states as one of its aims the handing down of our cultural heritage to future generations in 'the full richness of their authenticity'.[4] When we begin to examine authenticity in relation to the conservation of many twentieth-century buildings we run into a number of problems. These are directly related to the fundamental characteristics of modern architecture, new technology and construction techniques, new materials and prefabrication and new disciplines of planning and functionalism.

What exactly do we mean by authenticity? It is a much-discussed term at present and has been the subject of at least three international meetings over the last few years. Jukka Jokihleto, the director of architectural conservation at ICCROM, and Herb Stovel of ICOMOS International have defined authenticity in relation to conserving cultural heritage as 'a measure of truthfulness of the internal unity of the creative process and the physical realisation of the work, and the effects of its passage through time'.[5]

Perhaps this is a rather cumbersome definition, but the direct dictionary definition of authentic, 'real' or 'genuine', does not describe the concept adequately for our purposes, and Jokihleto and Stovel's definition introduces artistic intention into the discussion.[6] It seems that what we are interested in conserving is truth to the materials from which a building was constructed, truth to the architect's design and its resulting aesthetic integrity and acknowledgement of the building's past. This works quite well for many traditional building projects but how can it be applied to the Modern building types, and where do the perceived conflicts lie?

The most difficult area to reconcile can be described as material versus aesthetic or design authenticity, or, preserving or prolonging the life of the building at the expense of the original fabric and/or design. In order to identify where authenticity becomes problematic it is simplest to examine some of the principal deterioration problems of modern architecture.

Material failures

One of the characteristics of modern architecture is the use of new materials or the use of traditional materials in new ways. Using new materials which did not have a proven performance record or traditional materials used in new ways often built problems into the building fabric which resulted in premature failure. A lack of understanding of the projected performance of these modern materials and a lack of maintenance inevitably caused failure. Many of the new materials were erroneously believed to be low-maintenance or maintenance-free. Concrete, for instance, was thought to last indefinitely. These factors create considerable problems when we come to conserve the structures.

The development of new materials and prefabrication systems was conceived as a solution to providing quick, cheap construction, and often poor workmanship and quality control are important contributors to early failures. The Metropolitan Cathedral of Christ the King, Liverpool, completed in 1967 by Sir Frederick Gibberd (built to last 500 years) is a good example. It is now being overclad where the original glass mosaic surface treatment has failed, a short-term solution to ensure that deterioration is abated while solutions are found to the problem of the material failure. At present there are no economically viable means by which the architect's intention of a surface of smooth glistening ribs can be achieved, and the result is not only loss of original fabric but loss of the design intention and aesthetic integrity. The authenticity in material and design terms is thus reduced significantly by the lack of knowledge to deal with the material failures. This is the subject of an English Heritage research project to identify and define suitable repair options in order to retain and conserve the large-scale mosaic cladding (see also John Streeter's paper elsewhere in this volume).

Concrete deterioration is one of the most common problems faced by anyone involved in the care of twentieth-century buildings. There are difficulties enough in matching patch repairs to cement render, including the precursors of modern concrete, Roman Cement and stucco, or originally painted concrete, but these pale in comparison to those faced when we are dealing with structural bare-faced concrete, which became much more popular in the second half of this century. Auguste Perret's Notre Dame du Raincy of 1923 understandably earned the name the 'Sainte Chapelle of reinforced concrete', utilizing the material in an exuberant and expressive manner which was not realised again for decades. The conservation works to the church include repairs to the two-foot square, reinforced prefabricated pierced panels which make up the upper walls of the church. All the repaired sections of the concrete fenestration panels are complete replacements. Thus in order to retain the design authenticity the material authenticity has been substantially reduced. It is unfortunate that such important early examples of such a monumental use of concrete in its most expressive form should be lost on such a large scale, but there may not be an alternative solution at present. Much of the importance of the building is in its revolutionary use of the material, and yet the material is sacrificed to retain aesthetic authenticity.

Figure 11.2   High Cross House, the Dartington Estate, designed by the Frenchman William Lescaze in 1932. Lescaze was then living in the United States and the construction of the house was supervised by a local architect in England (Susan Macdonald)

The difficulties presently faced at Sir Basil Spence's University of Sussex is typical of the problems many brutalist buildings of the 1960s and 70s pose (see Richard Morrice's paper elsewhere in this volume). Here the bare-faced concrete of a number of the buildings is suffering from carbonation causing deterioration of the reinforcement and resulting in spalling of the concrete in many areas.[7] Due to the extremely shallow cover to the reinforcement, almost nothing in some areas, the repairs to date have used a traditional method of cutting out and replacement to the spalled and at-risk areas of concrete. This is followed by the application of a very thin concrete layer to fill small voids and provide a base for the anti-carbonation paint which assists in slowing the rate of deterioration. The expressive use of board-marked bare-faced concrete contrasting with the brick walling is a fundamental part of the architectural language of the buildings, and it is over the protective coatings where authenticity becomes an issue. An opaque coating or even a transparent version (which deepens the colour and appears shiny when wet) is at odds with conservation aims. The coatings, which are a fundamental part of the guaranteed repair system, also cover the repair mortars which do not match the existing colour and texture of the original concrete, thus necessitating a covering vehicle in any case. The effect of painting the concrete not only changes the colour of the building but eventually obliterates the decorative textural finish as well as building-in a new maintenance task which will need attention every ten to twelve years.

Detailing failures

Another common cause of premature failure was the lack of knowledge of the best way to detail new materials to ensure the fabric's long-term survival. The abandonment of traditional weathering details to achieve the streamlined aesthetic is a frequent cause of problems. Altering or improving proven detailing failures depends on the severity of the problem and the client's required performance criteria, as well as the usual budgeting constraints. Sometimes it is possible to carry out such improvements with minimal alteration to the fabric without destroying the aesthetic or material authenticity. The detailing around the external opening at High Cross House, Dartington, was one of the problems faced by the architect John Winter during the works carried out in 1993. Here Winter reluctantly sought to carry out minimal alterations to the openings to provide some weathering profiles and ensure problems did not reoccur (see Figure 11.2).

At Villa Roche (1923–5) by Le Corbusier, now the head office of the Foundation Le Corbusier in Paris, the influence of the client determined the outcome. The architect in charge of the conservation, Christian Gimonet, chose to maintain the original methods for repainting the interior of the building. Le Corbusier's original window details had proven unsuccessful, providing a cold bridge which contributed to the accelerated degradation of the interior walls and paint scheme. Rather than improve or alter the original detail, or replace the delicate matt paints of the interior with less fragile surfaces, the architect decided that the interior should be repainted in accordance with Le Corbusier's original intention. This called for frequent repainting, but it was decided that this was one of the duties of the foundation.[8]

Outmoded production

The tremendous expansion in the production and variety of building materials this century has meant that many products had short-lived production periods and are no longer available. The development of modern plastics, metals and paints has moved so rapidly that many materials were superseded relatively quickly. Replacing a damaged section may have required expensive hand-crafting of what was intended to be a mass-produced item. Salvage is the alternative, although the salvage industry for twentieth-century building materials is tiny compared to that for other periods of architectural history. The replacement problem is not unique to buildings from this century but is exacerbated by the importance of the idea of mass production in the architectural concept of many buildings and is an ethical rather than a physical problem.

The Rose Seidler House in Sydney (designed in 1948 by Harry Seidler for his parents) underwent a programme of conservation in the late 1980s before its opening as a house museum and resource centre for mid-century modern architecture. Much of the flooring was extensively damaged and needed attention during the conservation works, but the materials were simply no longer available. The Historic Houses Trust of NSW decided to provide temporary replacement materials approximating the originals until enough salvage material could be collected. Like the Foundation Le Corbusier, the management accepted that conservation is a process, not restricted to a moment in time, and that solutions unavailable now may be found in the future. This attitude is more likely to be adopted by organizations whose role is to care for heritage and who have different requirements in terms of use and finance than the building owner who needs the building to function efficiently for their needs and is less able to compromise. Another common problem today is that some materials were removed from production due to their toxicity. In this case, not only was the original fabric not available but the existing materials were now considered dangerous.

Maintenance failures

Built-in material problems and the lack of maintenance inevitably exacerbates deterioration. New materials were often, naively, believed to be low-maintenance or maintenance-free. We often find that regular maintenance programmes were originally designed as part of the architect's brief, but it is often the failure to take on board such recommendations which have substantially contributed to decay problems. The architect for the National Theatre in London (completed in 1977), Sir Denys Lasdun, included a five-year cleaning cycle for the concrete in his maintenance plan for the building. This has never been carried out and recent consultations on the cleaning of the concrete examined the possibilities of protective coatings. However it is still uncertain whether such coatings would have any long-term detrimental effect to the extremely high-quality finish of the concrete, which is one of the important characteristics of the building. In any case the application of such a coating with its 12-year guarantee introduces a maintenance cost to the care of the building comparable to that of cleaning.

The importance of maintenance in the conservation and care of any building is paramount. Modern buildings do require the same levels of care as buildings from any other historic period and it is only by acknowledging this and incorporating maintenance programmes into post-conservation care that we can ensure their continued performance. The importance of maintenance in order to retain the aesthetic and material authenticity of these structures must not be underestimated.

The patina of age

The perceived inability of modern structures to age gracefully appears in arguments against the conservation of and in arguments for the conjectural restorations of modern buildings. Ungainly and accelerated ageing is brought about principally by the materials or the details adopted which do not guarantee the lifespan expected. The patina of age we so often attempt to save and see as an important part of a traditional building is not recognized with the same romanticism with modern buildings. In this case the patina is likely to be seen as an ugly blot on what is intended to be a pristine image, and detracts from the original aesthetic concept. Did modernity, which advocated the new, clean streamlined expression leave room for a patina of age? Is it perhaps that we simply do not recognize age and deterioration as part of the language of modern architecture? Is the language so precise for there to be no room for the changing aesthetic, or is it that many of the architects responsible for the buildings are still alive and naturally seek to continue the building's image as built, clouding our view? We acknowledge that the softening effect provided by organic growth to many old buildings is detrimental to their material well-being. In this case the romantic patina is more important than the potential loss of material authenticity and is thereby retained. Is this attitude any different to the attempts to reinstate the streamlined pristine image of the modern building ? The repair methods often adopted for traditional building types, such as the tile method of masonry repair advocated by the SPAB, takes on board the philosophy of acknowledging conservation as part of the building's history at the expense of material authenticity and aesthetic integrity and no doubt would appal the original architect. This method is also at odds with Jokihleto's arguments acknowledging the creational aspect of the architectural composition.

Functionalism

Functionalism was mentioned earlier as another of the characteristics of modern architecture which may be a perceived difficulty in conservation terms. The highly specific design solution for a building's function should, in theory, make such buildings difficult to adapt to another purpose, if this is required in order to continue the life of the building. In reality the aesthetic of modern architecture meant that the anonymous nature of such structures, with their skeletal frames and openness of plan, finds them more easily adapted for other uses than more traditional building types. (The integration of now redundant services with the structure may inhibit this.)

The principal conservation problems which arise out of this can be summarized as:

- difficulties of adaptation to new use in spatial and planning terms. For example, open planning and large expanses of glazing makes subdivision of spaces difficult for reuse and also make it difficult to achieve fire regulation and building control requirements without altering the spatial qualities of the building.
- difficulties in upgrading to modern service requirements. For example, changing technology means that functionalist features which are an important part of the building aesthetic may become redundant.
- the adaptation for today's environmental performance requirements may be problematic. For example, lower energy use conflicts with large expanses of glazing, and low thermal-resistant thin concrete walls may require improvements to insulation to achieve such aims.

The Qantas building in the heart of Sydney's central business district is a case in point. Designed in the 1960s to facilitate the complete computerization of the organization, it has one-metre voids between each floor to accommodate the computer equipment. But by the time it was complete nearly ten years later technology had developed so rapidly that such huge service spaces rendered the building uneconomical in space/ratio terms, as it was located in the most commercially competitive part of the city.

The D10 building of the Boots Factory, Nottingham, designed by Owen Williams in 1931, was restored recently and is an example of the difficulties in planning and energy terms (Figure 11.3). As part of the restoration all the glazing to the principal elevation was replaced. This decision was based on the extensive deterioration of the original metal frames, the performance requirements of the building which had to meet very high EC hygiene standards and an attempt to improve energy efficiency and reduce thermal gain. This required double glazing and thermal glass. The opening lights were now no longer required to function as the building needed to be hermetically sealed to comply with hygiene regulations. The result has ensured the continued usefulness of the building, but the glazing sections have very subtly altered and the tinted effect of the glass detracts from the original transparence and lightness of the structure.

Windows are causing significant problems right across Europe. One of the characteristics of modern architecture is the volumetric role of the horizontal openings of light, simple frames which provide light to the interior. 'Windows constitute a more important element in modern architecture than they have in any architecture since that of Gothic cathedrals'.[9] Metal (ungalvanized until well after the Second World War) and timber (often softwood) were used with an emphasis on prefabrication and economy of construction. Often the material failure is problematic in conservation terms, but the large expanses of glazing with implications for low-energy aims, and material failure, together frequently determined that replacement rather than repair is deemed necessary. As has been the case with traditional windows from other periods the PVCu window seems to have provided the preferred alternative based on arguments of cost and low maintenance. As yet international studies have not been coordinated to provide

Figure 11.3   D10 building at the Boots Factory in Nottingham, designed by Sir Owen Williams in 1931 before restoration (British Architectural Library)

convincing arguments for repair. A study of the long-term performance of PVCu versus the maintenance of timber, or metal versions is needed to measure the economics of replacement versus repair.

Health and safety regulations are the final straw for many high-rise buildings with threatened windows. Recent health and safety legislation which requires easy access for cleaning purposes has caused alterations in the fenestration pattern and thus impacts significantly on the building's architectural composition. Solutions and compromises which accommodate minimal impact in conservation terms need to be identified.

Services are another area of conflict faced by the conservationist. Many modern buildings used innovative service technology to provide higher levels of amenity, which may be significant in their own right. Buildings such as the Pompidou Centre in Paris rely on building services for their aesthetic. While these services continue to function adequately there is no problem, but once they become obsolete how are the subsequent difficulties coped with? Services in historic buildings have long been a neglected area, and their obsolescence usually results in replacement. But when they are an important part of the functionalist aesthetic their fate requires rethinking.

At the Lubetkin Bungalow of 1933 the present owner recognized the value of the services of the house and attempted to work with the existing system. It is believed to be one of the first all-electric houses in the UK. As part of the gradual conservation of the building all the wiring was gradually rethreaded though existing conduits, including the flush wall-mounted heating panels. Where light fittings were lost, replacements were found in the United States and reinstated in their original positions in the door frames. It is an interesting case and indicative of what can be achieved with patience and on a limited budget.[10]

Lifespan

Ever since modern architecture began to be protected by law there has been a continuous cry from critics who feel that modern architecture was intentionally designed for a short life span.[11] Certainly Modern architects spoke of the building as a machine, as a functional tool, but it is arguable that they deliberately set out to make their buildings unable to endure the effects of time and decay.

When we refer to the manifestos and philosophies of the Modern Movement, disposability is not mentioned as one of the stated aims of the architects, with the exception of the Futurist manifesto of 1914 written by Antonio Sant' Elia and Filippo Tommaso Marinetti: 'the fundamental characteristics of Futurist architecture will be obsolescence and transience. "Houses will last less long than we. Each generation will have to build its own city" '.[12] However, other key figures in the Modern Movement cite longevity as one of the functions of new materials.[13]

The development of concrete, modern metals and plastics as solutions to an economic use of materials and labour sometimes resulted in a cheap fabrication of the buildings which did not endure time well. However, was it a conscious decision of early modern architects, or was the concept of the 'throwaway society' something that developed later after the early failures when the material and constructional problems became apparent? The objects around us which we now see as an essential part of modern life, such as the car, have shorter and shorter periods of use, due to a conscious economic decision by the manufacturers to ensure that continuous replacement is necessary. It is arguable that this is a trend which developed during the second half of this century and was not in the original concept. Certainly in recent UK cases where the architect is still alive and can be consulted it is more common for architects to wish to extend the life of their buildings within the bounds of the original architectural concepts rather than wish the building to be demolished. Although Renzo Piano is rumoured to have said of the Pompidou Centre that when it ceases to serve its function he hopes they get rid of it.[14]

If it is symptomatic of our society that longevity plays only a minor role in the way in which we intend to construct then perhaps we must acknowledge 'throwaway architecture'. The role of the conservationist in this case would be to ensure that thorough documentation of the structure is carried out, ensuring that it is recorded for prosperity. But how does this tally with the increasing emphasis on sustainable development and green architecture?

If we choose to keep buildings which are of limited material lifespan then we must accept either higher maintenance responsibilities and/or higher incidences of material replacement if the buildings are to continue to function. As is the case in the development of any conservation policy understanding the history of the building and the architect's intention will affect conservation decisions.

New problems, new solutions

Another difficulty in the conservation process is the recent nature of the work. Lack of specific guidelines, inexperience, lack of knowledge of the materials and their performance over time, lack of knowledge of repair systems in the longer term, undeveloped repair methods to meet conservation aims and a lack of understanding of the value of many modern buildings means we are still working unaided. This must be acknowledged if we are to move forward.

One final point to note relating to the recent nature of this type of conservation activity is the availability of resources. Conservation of more traditional architecture has built up a network in terms of professional knowledge, craftsmen, antique dealers, suppliers of materials and so on. No such network yet exists for Modern architecture. Those in charge of the restoration of the Gropius' Lincoln House (1938) concluded that 'it is far easier to restore, accurately, a house built in the seventeenth century using historic building crafts than it is to restore a house built in the twentieth century using the products of industrial production'.[15] Not only is the 'network' unestablished, but as yet no complete histories of the period have been published. To date literature on the topic is limited to particular, famous, architects, and individual strains of Modernism, such as the Modern Movement and De Stijl.

Future options

The conservation of twentieth-century heritage offers the opportunity to reassess approaches used in the past and rethink some of the ways we deal with buildings generally. At the same time we need to determine whether these buildings are so different. The fact that we have not yet developed economically justifiable and still sympathetic repair methods may cause much of the problem, rather than the inappropriateness of existing conservation methodology. There are still conflicts and uncertainties in contemporary philosophy for historic buildings generally and it should be remembered that these are not a set of rules, merely guiding principles.

The extent we intervene to conserve a structure is dependent on the extent of decay and how the decay is likely to continue, the future role of the building and the finance and knowledge available to carry out the intervention. Generally in contemporary conservation we subscribe to the idea that the less intervention there is the better for the structure. However when dealing, without intervention, with modern buildings and problems with material with a limited life span we may need to reconsider. Characteristics of Modernism such as functionalism should be recognized as being both negative and positive in conservation terms and the balance weighed up with other issues under consideration. Arguments concerning authenticity will subside as less intrusive repair methods are developed, and acceptance of loss of material authenticity may be warranted. The principle of approaching a project by carefully analysing the historical and physical evidence in order to evaluate the building's significance and then develop the appropriate conservation strategy is still valid.

As yet there is little written information specifically dealing with the technical problems. We need to push forward technical barriers which limit what is achievable in conservation terms and to enable the aims of minimum intervention and retention of authenticity to be realised. We need to appeal to industry to work with us to achieve these aims and develop financially-viable solutions if we are going to secure the future of buildings like Sir Denys Lasdun's Keeling House, whose future is now in question after the National Heritage Memorial Fund's recent decision not to recommend it for funding, or the Bryn Mawr rubber factory of 1947, whose fate is now uncertain following the recommendations of the local authority planners for its demolition.

The establishment of knowledge networks already underway will enable us to learn from each other. We need to carry out further research into the history of twentieth-century architecture, develop our understanding of the materials and their deterioration mechanisms and experiment with repair methods. Lastly, we must accept that conservation is a process, not a finite act. If we are confronted with a problem which appears insurmountable today, it must be remembered that a solution may be found in the future, thus reversibility should be observed. Conservation is a broad term and we may need to expand our understanding of it to cope with new problems we are now encountering.

References

1   Banham, R. (1975), *The age of modern masters*, London: Architectural Press.

2   Russell Hitchcock, H. and Johnson, P. (1932), *The International Style: architecture since 1922*, New York: W.W. Norton & Co.

3   ICOMOS (Australia) (1981), *The Australia ICOMOS Charter of the conservation of places of cultural significance* (The Burra Charter), Sydney: ICOMOS.

4   ICOMOS (1966), *International Charter for the Conservation and Restoration of Monuments and Sites* (The Venice Charter), Venice: ICOMOS.

5   Jokihleto, J. (1995), 'The debate on authenticity', *ICCROM newsletter*, **21**, (July), 6–8.

6   Brandi, C. (1963), *Teoria del Restauro*, Rome: Ediz. Storia e Letteratura, 34. Brandi's theories of conservation stressed the importance of the creation of the artistic work as fundamental to the object. He argued that the artistic quality, and hence the aesthetic, should be given precedence over the historic passage or the patina.

7   Reinforcement corrosion is one of the most common causes of damage to reinforced concrete. Corrosion is usally caused by the presence of chlorides or carbonation, which occurs when atmospheric carbon dioxide penetrates the concrete and in the presence of moisture forms carbonic acid. This reduces the alkalinity of the concrete and breaks down the naturally-forming passivating layer to the reinforcement. The cement content and permeability of the concrete as well as the depth of cover all affect the rate of carbonation. Well-compacted high-quality concrete will retain the alkaline-rich environment needed to protect the reinforcement for a long period. Where chlorides are present in the concrete the protective layer of the steel will begin to break down at a higher pH level.

8   Gimonet, C. (1991), 'Restoration of buildings of Le Corbusier', in *Proceedings of the First DOCOMOMO International Conference*, Eindhoven, The Netherlands: DOCOMOMO.

9   Russell Hitchcock, H. and Johnson, P. (1932), *The International Style: architecture since 1922*, New York: W.W. Norton & Co., 46.

10   from an interview with the owner, Mike Davies, in September 1995

11   Pawley, M. (1991), 'A Modern Morituri', *Proceedings of*

the First DOCOMOMO International Conference, Eindhoven, The Netherlands: DOCOMOMO, 64.

12   Conrads, U. (1991), *Programs and manifestos on twentieth-century architecture*, Massachusetts, USA: MIT Press, 34–8.

13   Conrads, U. (1991), *Programs and manifestos on*

twentieth-century architecture, Cambridge, Massachusetts: MIT Press, 133.

14   Pawley, M. (1991), A Modern Morituri, *Proceedings of the First DOCOMOMO International Conference*, Eindhoven, The Netherlands: DOCOMOMO, 64.

15   Lingel, T. (1987), 'The Gropius House in Lincoln, Massachusetts', *Ottagono*, **iv**, (22 December), 59.

CHAPTER 12

REINFORCED CONCRETE: PRINCIPLES OF ITS DETERIORATION AND REPAIR

Gareth Glass and **Nick Buenfeld**

Introduction

The practice of embedding steel bars in a mixture of ordinary Portland cement, graded aggregate and water to form reinforced concrete was introduced during the second half of the nineteenth century. Initially the material was employed for projects of modest scale but it is now one of the most important structural materials available and its usage by mankind is second only to that of water.[1] Reinforced concrete is exposed to many different types of environment, and there are several degradative processes which may lead to loss of serviceability (Figure 12.1). These include both the physical deterioration of the concrete itself as well as corrosion-induced deterioration.

The maintenance and repair of reinforced concrete is becoming a major problem. It is estimated that as much money is spent on repairing old structures as is spent on building new structures in Europe. The extent of the problem is also demonstrated by the rapid growth of the concrete repair industry and the many new materials and systems designed specifically for this.

Concrete repair covers a range of disciplines including engineering, materials science and electrochemistry. This paper introduces the deterioration mechanisms and principles behind the repair options.

Concrete deterioration

Background

It is important to differentiate between the problems of steel corrosion in concrete and the problems associated with the deterioration of concrete itself. Direct concrete deterioration may be either physical or chemical in nature. Thus, for example, weathering, the occurrence of extreme temperatures, attack by natural or industrial liquids and alkali-aggregate reaction may lead to deterioration.[2] The action of many of the chemicals is to destroy the cement paste thus weakening the concrete. Acid attack may occur when concrete is exposed to acidic gases or water and sea water attack partly results from the chemical action of sulphates in the water as

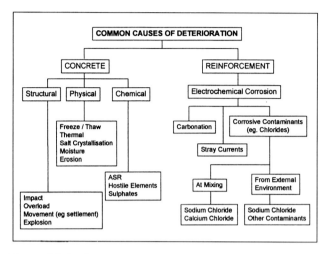

Figure 12.1   Causes of deterioration of reinforced concrete (prEN 1504-9: 1995)

well as the crystallization of salts in the pores. In many cases the resistance of concrete to these forms of attack is determined primarily by its penetrability. The type of cement used may also have an effect. Two more important forms of chemical attack, namely sulphate attack and alkali silicate reaction, are covered in greater detail below. Examples of physical deterioration include the effects of freeze/thaw (covered in greater detail below), fire damage and wave impact occurring in the tidal zone. The main effect of fire is to cause a large temperature gradient through the concrete with the differences in thermal expansion causing spalling of the surface layers. Deterioration may also be caused by poor design and physical damage. Examples of these include inadequate allowance for thermal expansion and overloading.

Sulphate attack

Sulphate attack results from the deleterious chemical reaction between soluble sulphates which may arise from an external source and the constituents of cement. The binder (cement paste) is destroyed. Furthermore, the reaction products produced occupy greater volume than the compounds they replace, thus expansion and disruption of the concrete may result.[3]

Hydrated cement paste can be attacked by sulphates which may be present in ground water, canals and sewers. The deterioration starts from the surface where sulphate contamination first occurs. Edges and corners are particularly vulnerable and these are followed by progressive surface cracking and spalling which reduces the concrete to a friable or even soft state.[4] Factors affecting the rate of sulphate attack include the concentration of sulphate ions in solution, the sulphate salt type, the penetrability of the concrete, the rate of sulphate ion replenishment and the rate at which products are removed. The resistance of concrete to sulphate attack is improved by lowering the tricalcium aluminate phase in the cement thus reducing the quantity of the calcium aluminate hydrate. This forms the basis for producing sulphate-resisting cements in which the C_3A content is below 7%. Improved resistance to sulphate attack is also obtained by the addition or partial replacement of the cement by pozzolanas which results in a reduction in free $Ca(OH)_2$.[5] Existing damage may be repaired using conventional patch-repair techniques which may be complemented with a barrier coating to prevent further sulphate contamination.[6]

Freeze/thaw attack

Freezing of water held in capillary pores at temperatures below zero results in expansion as ice occupies a greater volume than water. Subsequent thawing and refreezing allows further expansion to take place and repeated cycles will ultimately result in the disruption of the surrounding pore walls.[7] The extent of the damage varies from surface scaling to complete disintegration as layers of ice are formed. In temperate climates, the most aggressive conditions occur in areas such as road kerbs and slabs which remain wet for long periods. In colder climates damage due to freezing is more general and more serious if suitable precautions are not taken.

The main factors affecting frost resistance are the degree of saturation and the pore structure of the cement paste. For a closed container the critical degree of saturation is 91.7%. If water occupies a greater volume than this it will, on freezing, become filled with ice and be subjected to a bursting pressure. For a porous body such as concrete the situation is more complicated. Critical saturation depends on the size of the body, its homogeneity and the rate of freezing. Below a critical value of saturation (91%), concrete is highly resistant to freeze/thaw damage. Dry concrete is totally unaffected.[8] Frost damage may be prevented by air entrainment. Air-entrained concrete has air intentionally incorporated using a suitable agent to provide space for water expelled from capillaries in which the ice is formed. The air bubbles, typically 0.05mm in diameter, are clearly distinguished from larger, accidentally trapped air bubbles. Air entrainment does not usually affect the permeability of the concrete as the air bubbles are discrete, but the strength of air-entrained concrete will be reduced.[9]

Conventional patch-repair techniques may be used to replace frost-damaged concrete. Frost-resistant repair materials should be used.[10, 11] In addition further treatment may be applied to minimize moisture ingress into the concrete so minimizing the risk of future frost damage.

Alkali-silica reaction

Alkali-silica reaction was first encountered in the UK in 1978 in several structures between ten and 30 years old. This is the deleterious chemical reaction between some siliceous minerals in the aggregate and the alkalinity of the concrete which results in a gel causing internal pressure leading to expansion and cracking of the concrete.[12] Factors which control the reaction rate and degree of expansion include the alkali content, the quantity of reactive aggregate and its particle size, the moisture content of the concrete and moisture content variations, temperature and the permeability of the concrete. The quantity of alkali (a measure of the sodium and potassium content which may result in high solution pH's within the concrete pores) depends on the type and quantity of cement. Expansion is seldom observed if the alkali content ($Na_2O + 0.658\ K_2O$) is below 0.6% and generally increases with an increase in alkalinity.[13]

Visual indications of the existence of alkali-silica reaction in an advanced stage are provided by the characteristic cracking associated with internal swelling. Detection of the reaction at an early stage involves the removal of concrete samples for petrographic analysis which can identify the presence of the gel.[14] The repair of the deterioration caused is still the subject of much research. At present the best approach is to keep the concrete dry, thus inhibiting the reaction. Possible methods include the use of surface treatments and cladding. A more recent, but as yet unproven, method involves the use of an electrochemical treatment to impregnate the concrete with lithium which inhibits the reaction.[15]

Reinforcement corrosion

Concrete normally provides a non-aggressive environment to reinforcing steel. However, the deterioration described above may lead to the loss of this protection as the result of the loss of effective concrete cover. In addition changes to the concrete environment itself may render it corrosive. Subsequent corrosion of steel produces products which have two to three times the volume of the original metal. This generates the stresses causing cracking and spalling of the concrete cover.[16] Very often the first indication of the problem is the appearance of a crack following the line of reinforcement, or the development of rust stains in porous concrete.

The mechanism of corrosion

It is well known that the corrosion process is electrochemical, that is, the chemical reactions occur in conjunction with the flow of an electric current. Metal oxidation occurs at one site, called an anode, leaving free electrons in the metal. For example iron dissolves (is oxidized) to form positive iron ions. The electrons produced are then consumed at another site, called the cathode, as the result of the reduction of species in the environment (for example oxygen is reduced to negative hydroxyl ions).[17] If there is no external electrical source of electrons, the anodic reaction must generate electrons at exactly the same rate as the cathodic reaction consumes them, with the flow of electrons in the metal and ions in the environment between the anode and cathode preventing any accumulation of electric charge. The cathodic reaction results in the generation of alkalinity (a measure of hydroxyl ion concentration).

This is true for most common cathodic reactions. By contrast the iron ions produced at the anode may react with water (hydrolysis) to produce hydrogen ions which will lead to acidification of the local environment at the anodes. The processes involved in the formation of rust include the precipitation of iron ions as iron hydroxide and the oxidation of the iron hydroxide by further reaction with oxygen to form $FeOOH$.

Potential may be viewed as one of the driving forces affecting an electrochemical reaction. More positive potentials result in the production of higher oxidation states which release more electrons. Thus iron will dissolve as positive ions as the potential is raised (like charges repel). Likewise more negative potentials will attract positive ions back to the metal surface and stimulate the reduction reactions. Metal potentials can be measured relative to a stable standard reference electrode.

The stability of compounds in a given environment and potential range is determined by chemical thermodynamics. In the case of iron a number of possible electrochemical reactions exist. By examination of the possible products and influence of the local environment, an indication of the corrosion risk may be obtained.[18]

Corrosion of steel in concrete

The hydraulic binder in concrete, usually Portland cement, reacts with water to form a porous matrix of hydration products between the aggregate particles and around the reinforcement. Thus the reinforcing steel is usually in contact with moisture containing dissolved oxygen and the necessary reactants are present to permit corrosion. However a significant feature of cement hydration is that the aqueous phase rapidly acquires a high pH. Furthermore, the material contains a substantial portion of reserve basicity in the form of sparingly soluble $Ca(OH)_2$ and the system is therefore buffered to resist downward pH changes at a value of 12.6.[19]

When steel is in contact with an alkaline solution of pH values in this range it is normally passive. This condition arises because the corrosion products are insoluble in these conditions. A thin oxide film covers the surface presenting a barrier to further metal dissolution. Passivation is thus the primary mechanism of corrosion protection for steel in concrete and no significant corrosion will occur if this environment remains intact and free of contamination.[20]

The two most important causes of passive film breakdown, and therefore corrosion of steel in concrete, are a reduction in the local pH resulting from carbonation, and the disruption of the passive film by aggressive contaminants such as chlorides.[21] These are considered in greater detail below. Other factors, which include acidic gases such as sulphur dioxide, and aggressive ions such as sulphates, fluorides and bromides, may also render the passive film unstable by reducing the concrete pH, or promoting film breakdown. In addition stray electrical currents may cause corrosion by forcing some areas of the steel to become anodic. These causes of corrosion-induced deterioration are however not common and are restricted to environments such as concrete chimney stacks.

Carbonation

Carbonation of concrete results when atmospheric carbon dioxide (CO_2) dissolves in the cement pore solution to form carbonic acid. This reacts with some of the products of cement hydration as well as neutralizing the calcium hydroxide ($Ca(OH)_2$) present. As the reserve levels of $Ca(OH)_2$ are depleted a zone of low pH (the carbonated zone) extends from the surface of the concrete. This fall in pH may render the passive film unstable.[22] The most important factors affecting the carbonation rate are the type of cement used, the quantity of cement used, the penetrability of the concrete and the environmental conditions of the concrete.

The moisture content of the concrete has a marked effect on both the carbonation rate and the corrosion rate. If the pores are dry, carbon dioxide diffuses inwards but the lack of water reduces the rate of the carbonation reaction. If the pores are completely filled with water there is hardly any carbonation because of the low diffusion rate of carbon dioxide through the water-filled matrix. Significant rates of corrosion are however not automatic when the depth of carbonation reaches the reinforcing steel as the resistance of the environment to the flow of ionic current may be high. Corrosion requires the presence of sufficient moisture and the risk is further enhanced in the presence of low levels of chlorides.

Chlorides

A more serious cause of the corrosion of steel in concrete is chloride ion contamination which renders the passive film unstable. Local breakdown of the passive film results in reinforcement corrosion even though it is surrounded by a highly alkaline environment. The corrosion risk generally increases with an increasing chloride content.

Chloride contamination may arise from internal or external sources. Internal sources include contamination of the mix materials and the use of calcium chloride as a set accelerator in construction. Limitations are placed by current codes of practice on the acceptable levels of chloride contamination resulting from the use of contaminated mix materials, while the use of chloride containing admixtures for reinforced concrete is generally not permitted.[23] External sources of chlorides include de-icing salts and sea water.

Penetration of chlorides can occur by a number of mechanisms which include diffusion and absorption by capillary suction. Wetting and drying of the concrete promotes the movement of chlorides to areas of greater moisture content. A proportion of the chloride ions are also bound by the concrete which will slow down the rate of ingress.[24] A number of other factors will also affect the rate of penetration. Thus, for example, the openness of the pore structure will be partly determined by the cement type, and blended cement concretes, which have a very fine pore structure, exhibit a considerable resistance to chloride penetration.

Once passive film breakdown has occurred, a local corrosion cell is established. This results in the production of acid at the anode together with an increase in chloride concentration there, as chlorides are carried to the anode by the ionic corrosion current between the anodic and cathodic sites. Thus the process is accelerated and further disruption of the adjacent passive film may occur resulting in an increase in the attacked area.[25]

Macro-corrosion cells

The mechanism of corrosion results in the development of corrosion cells which will be present on both a macroscopic and microscopic scale in concrete. Micro-corrosion cells result when the anodic and cathodic reactions occur essentially at the same location. However a reinforcing bar embedded in concrete of varying properties along its length will in time develop different electrochemical potentials at different areas. The potential difference between two points becomes the driving force for the corrosion reaction occurring in a macro-corrosion cell where corrosion at an anodic area is accelerated by being coupled to a passive cathode.[26]

The passive area immediately adjacent to the active anode is subject to a form of cathodic protection. This results from the stimulation of the cathodic reaction there which in turn maintains the high pH and removes chloride ions. However the chloride contamination which has occurred may render these cathodic sites potential anodes if this local form of cathodic protection is removed. This may occur when the corrosion-induced deterioration at the active anode is repaired by replacing the chloride-contaminated concrete with a chloride-free, highly alkaline aerated repair material. The embedded steel in this repair becomes cathodic to the adjacent passive areas and stimulates an anodic reaction there. The former passive cathode may therefore be termed an incipient anode. Thus when conventional patch repairs are used to inhibit chloride-induced corrosion deterioration all contaminated concrete should be removed if further deterioration is to be avoided.[27]

Factors affecting corrosion rate

It was noted previously that the essential elements of a corrosion cell are an anodic reaction (metal dissolution), a cathodic reaction (oxygen reduction), the movement of electrons through the metal between the anodic and cathodic sites (electronic current flow) and the movement of ions through the environment between the anodic and cathodic site (ionic current flow). The rate at which corrosion can occur may be controlled by a restriction in any one of these processes. However the resistance to electronic current flow within a rebar is usually very small. Thus in practice the rate at which a metal is consumed can be controlled by the kinetics (speed) of either the anodic or cathodic reactions, or by the resistance to current flow between the anodic and cathodic sites through the concrete. The associated controlling mechanisms are termed anodic control, cathodic control or resistive control.[28] Reinforced concrete is exposed to a wide variety of environments and any one of these three mechanisms may dominate depending on the exposure conditions.

In above-ground structures the presence of a passive film often restricts the overall rate, the corrosion rate effectively being under anodic control. To increase the corrosion rate further passive film breakdown must occur. In this environment one of the factors affecting the corrosion rate is therefore aggressive ion contamination. In very resistive environments the corrosion rate may be controlled by the resistance to ionic current flow. Such a situation may occur with dry carbonated concrete, although in this case the main effect of ionic resistance is on the anodic reaction kinetics (anodic resistance control). Factors affecting the corrosion rate would therefore include the moisture content of the concrete as higher moisture contents would be associated with lower resistivities.

In submerged marine environments, access of chloride to the bar is not necessarily rate-limiting. However, access of oxygen is severely restricted due to its low concentration in solution and its slow transport rate through waterlogged concrete. Thus the rate of corrosion may well depend on the rate at which oxygen can reach the steel. Since oxygen concentration affects the cathodic reaction, the corrosion rate is under cathodic control.[29]

Repair of corrosion-damaged concrete

There are many stages leading to a successful repair. These include:

- assessing the cause and extent of the damage

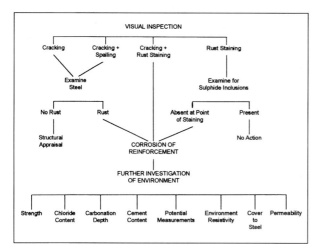

*Figure 12.2   Techniques which may be used to
identify the cause of the deterioration (Gareth Glass)*

- identifying functional requirements of the repair and the repair options
- designing, specifying and installing the selected option
- monitoring the performance

Diagnostic approach to repair

The choice of a successful repair system depends on an accurate identification of the cause of the problem. Thus, for example, if carbonation is the cause of corrosion-induced deterioration, an anti-carbonation coating may be considered when specifying the repairs. A number of inspection methods are available. These include visual examination, chemical analysis of samples removed from site and NDT tests for corrosion-induced problems. Figure 12.2 shows a flow chart of various techniques which may be used to identify corrosion problems and the order in which they may be used.[30]

The assessment of the current condition is aimed at identifying whether repairs are needed, what repair options are excluded and providing quantities for contract documentation. Thus, for example, one may need to determine whether a paint coating can be applied to the concrete surface and which surface preparation would be most appropriate to obtain the durability required. In this case trials may be undertaken to provide the relevant data. Visual examination is the most common method used to determine the extent of the deterioration and provide a measure of the associated quantities. However other methods such as a delamination survey or a potential survey may also be appropriate.

The rate of deterioration will also be useful in assessing the future serviceable life and maintenance requirements of the structure as well as the current need for and cost-effectiveness of repairs. Methods which may be used include modelling the rate of penetration of aggressive species and the determination of corrosion rates.

Functional requirements of a repair

The functional requirement of the repair system will depend on the rate and extent of the deterioration together with the maintenance costs and design life of the structure. Repairs may be considered to be part of the maintenance required to achieve the design life. Factors which may affect its function include its compatibility with the existing structure and its durability in the service environment. As an example of compatibility, a coating system may not be applied to an existing friable concrete surface which may have resulted from some form of acid attack. Besides adhesion other factors which may affect compatibility include thermal expansion and shrinkage.

The durability of the repair system depends on both its own ability to resist deterioration in the environment to which it is exposed and on its ability to prevent further deterioration to the neighbouring or underlying concrete. Thus, for example, while conventional patch repairs may prevent further corrosion-induced deterioration in the repaired area, they may not be able to prevent further corrosion in adjacent chloride-contaminated concrete. The expansive forces resulting from this subsequent corrosion may cause the bond between the patch repair and the original concrete to break, or induce cracks within the repair material.

Repair options

A number of repair options are available for deteriorated structures. These include:

- do nothing and monitor
- patching
- concrete replacement
- crack injection
- surface treatment of concrete
- cathodic protection
- chloride removal
- re-alkalization

These may be divided into those in which active steps are taken to improve the environment within the concrete by removal of aggressive species, those in which the aim is to exclude any further contamination from the environment and those in which the effects of the deterioration are minimized. Various repair principles and examples of methods based on the principle are given in Figure 12.3.

Methods which improve the environment include concrete replacement together with the electrochemical methods of cathodic protection, chloride removal and re-alkalization. Such methods may be appropriate when the aggressive species are contained within the concrete and any further deterioration must be minimized.

Exclusion of the environment is primarily achieved through surface treatment of the concrete. The aim in this case is to prevent further ingress of aggressive species which may cause future deterioration. However some coatings also allow the concrete to dry out while greatly reducing further moisture ingress. Thus this may also be viewed as improving the internal environment. In some cases the aim may be to do the minimum necessary to maintain the function of the structure until the end of its useful life determined by other factors. Methods which can then be considered include simply monitoring the structure and installing holding repairs.

Communicating technical requirements

The design, specification, drawings and bills of quantities contain the technical requirements of the repair system and are the basis for discussions between the consultants, owners and

PRINCIPLE AND ITS DEFINITION	SOME EXAMPLES OF METHODS BASED ON THE PRINCIPLE
Restoring passivity Creating conditions in which the reinforcement is protected by a film of ferric oxide	**Replacing contaminated or carbonated concrete** Physically removing contaminated or carbonated concrete and replacing it with uncontaminated uncarbonated concrete **Restoring alkalinity to carbonated concrete** Re-alkalising carbonated concrete in-situ *May cause hydrogen embrittlement and force discontinuous steel to corrode. **Chloride extraction** Removing chloride contamination from concrete in-situ. *May cause hydrogen embrittlement, bond strength reduction, alkali aggregate reaction and force discontinuous steel to corrode **Cathodic protection** Moving the potential of the steel into the passive region *May force discontinuous steel to corrode
Control of anodic areas Creating conditions in which potentially anodic areas of the reinforcement are unable to take part in the corrosion reaction	**Applying a barrier (chemical or sacrificial coating) to the reinforcement** **Applying anodic inhibitors to the concrete by impregnation or diffusion** Anodic inhibitors are chemical agents which discourage the formation of anodic regions on the reinforcement
Increasing resistivity Increasing the electrical resistivity of the concrete	**Limiting moisture content with surface treatments, coatings or by sheltering** *Reducing moisture content may increase the rate of carbonation
Cathodic contro Creating conditions in which potentially cathodic areas of reinforcement are unable to take part in the corrosion reaction	**Limiting oxygen content (at the cathode) by saturating the concrete** **Applying cathodic protection to remove oxygen at the steel surface** *All electrically connected potentially cathodic areas must be included in the saturated area

*denotes a warning

Figure 12.3 Repair principles for reinforcement corrosion-induced deterioration (prEN 1505–9: 1995)

installers. The specification may be in the form of a simple method statement, or be related to the performance required. In the latter case a specialist contractor may be required to interpret the specification in terms of a method statement which may be submitted during the tender process. The design contains the basis for all the decisions and choices made concerning a particular repair system. This includes any calculations that may be required. The aim of the specification and drawings is to translate the design requirements into an understandable document. Within the specification, a bill of quantities is usually provided to give the units by which the work may be measured.[31, 32]

Performance monitoring

The performance of repaired structures is becoming increasingly important due to the long service lives required by concrete structures and the high cost of building and maintaining the infrastructure. Performance monitoring may provide early identification of future potential problems which will facilitate planned cost-effective maintenance. In addition it also provides data for predicting the service life of repair systems enabling an improved choice to be made in the future.

References

1   Sedgwick, J. (1991), 'Strong but sensitive', *The Atlantic*, **267**, (4), 70–82.

2   Creegan, P.J., Graham, J.R., Tatro, S.R., Herreryherrera, A.E., Kaden, R.A., McDonald, J.E., and Schrader, E.K. (1994), 'Abstract of compendium of case-histories on repair of erosion-damaged concrete structures', *ACI Materials Journal*, **91**, (4), 408–409.

3   Lea, F.M. (1970), *The chemistry of cement and concrete*, London: Edward Arnold, 338–59.

4   Lawrence, C.D. (1990), 'Sulfate attack on concrete', *Magazine of Concrete Research*, **42**, (153), 249–64.

5   Lawrence, C.D. (1990), 'Sulfate attack on concrete', *Magazine of Concrete Research*, **42**, (153), 249–64.

6   BRE Digest 363, (1991) *Sulphate and acid resistance of concrete in the ground*, Watford: Building Research Establishment.

7   Pigeon, M., and Regourd, M. (1986), 'The effects of freeze-thaw cycles on the microstructure of hydration products', *Durability of building materials*, **4**, (1), 1–19.

8   Neville, A.M. (1981), *Properties of concrete*, Harlow: Longman Scientific, 461–87.

9   Pigeon, M., and Lachance, M. (1981), 'Critical air void spacing factors for concretes submitted to slow freeze-thaw cycles', *Journal of the American Concrete Institute*, **78**, (4), 282–91.

10   Setzer, M.J. (1995), 'Draft recommendations for test methods for the freeze-thaw resistance of concrete slab test and cube test', *Materials and structures*, **28**, (180), 366–71.

11   CEN TC 51, WG 12, TG 4 (1995), 'Draft recommendation for test method for the freeze-thaw resistance of concrete – Tests with water (CF) or with sodium-chloride solution (CDF)', *Materials and structures*, **28**, (177), 175–82.

12   BRE Digest 330 (1988), *Alkali aggregate reactions in concrete*, Watford: Building Research Establishment.

13   Concrete Society (1987), *Alkali-silica reaction – minimising the risk of damage to concrete*, Technical Report (30), London: The Concrete Society.

14   British Cement Association (1988), The diagnosis of alkali-silica reaction, Slough: British Cement Association.

15   Page, C.L. (1995), *Improvements in and related to treatments for concrete*, UK Patent GB 2 275 265 B.

16   Dagher, H.J., and Kulendran, S. (1992), 'Finite-element modeling of corrosion damage in concrete structures', *ACI Structural Journal*, **89**, (6), 699–708.

17   Shreir, L.L. (1982), *Electrochemical Principles of Corrosion – A Guide for Engineers*, Teddington: National Corrosion Service.

18   Pourbaix, M. (1966), *Atlas of electrochemical equilibria in aqueous solutions*, Houston, Texas: NACE, 312.

19   Page, C.L. and Treadaway, K.W.J. (1982), 'Aspects of the electrochemistry of steel in concrete', *Nature*, **297**, (5862), 109–15.

20   Leek, D.S. (1991), 'The passivity of steel in concrete', *Quarterly Journal of Engineering Geology*, 24 , (1), 55–66.

21   Treadaway, K.W.J. (1988), 'Corrosion Period', in P. Schiessl (ed), *Corrosion of steel in concrete*, London: Chapman and Hall, 56–69.

22   Parrott, L.J. (1987), *A review of carbonation in reinforced concrete*, Report C/1-0987, Slough: Cement and Concrete Association.

23   BS 1881 : Part 124 : 1988, (1988), *The testing of* *hardened concrete*, London: British Standards Institution.

24 Sergi, G., Yu, S.W. and Page, C.L. (1992), 'Diffusion of chloride and hydroxyl ions in cementitious materials exposed to a saline environment', *Magazine of Concrete Research*, **44**, (158), 63–9.

25 Shreir, L.L. (1982), *Electrochemical Principles of Corrosion – A Guide for Engineers*, Teddington: National Corrosion Service.

26 Arya, C. and Vassie, P.R.W. (1995), 'Influence of cathode-to-anode area ratio and separation distance on galvanic corrosion currents of steel in concrete containing chlorides', *Cement and concrete research*, **25**, (5), 989–98.

27 Cavalier, P.G., Vassie, P.R.W., Safier, A.S., Papworth, F., Bratchell, G.E., Geoghegan, M.P., Brook, K.M., Murray, A.R., Leeming, M.B., Mackie, K.P., Manning, D.G. and Smith, P. (1982), 'Investigation and repair of reinforcement corrosion in a bridge deck', *Proceedings of the Institution of Civil Engineers*, Part 1, **72**, (August), 401–419.

28 Evans, U.R. (1971), *The corrosion and oxidation of metals*, London: Arnold.

29 Arup, H. (1983), 'The mechanism of protection of steel by concrete', in A.P. Crane (ed), *Proceedings of the First International Symposium on Corrosion of reinforcement in concrete construction*, Chichester: Ellis Horwood, 151–7.

30 Everett, L.H. and Treadaway, K.W.J. (1980), *Deterioration due to corrosion in reinforced concrete*, Watford: Building Research Establishment.

31 Concrete Society Technical Report No. 37, (1991), *Model specification for cathodic protection of reinforced concrete*, Slough, The Concrete Society.

32 Concrete Society (1991), *Patch repair of reinforced concrete*, Technical Report (38), Slough: The Concrete Society.

CHAPTER 13

CORROSION-DAMAGED CONCRETE: PRACTICAL ASSESSMENT, PROTECTION AND REPAIR

Peter Pullar-Strecker

Quite unexceptional reinforced concrete should be able to survive intact for a thousand years or more, but much of it is already damaged at less than fifty years old. During the last 20 years experience of reinforcement corrosion caused by the use of salt-contaminated aggregates during the Arabian Gulf building boom of the 70s and the rapid carbonation of concrete in many of our own poorly-constructed framed buildings of the 60s has taught us more about the deterioration of reinforced concrete than we could ever have imagined we would want to know. Gareth Glass has outlined elsewhere in this volume the current state of knowledge of concrete deterioration and the principles of protection and repair: this paper looks at the significance of that knowledge for the owner to help understanding the options for effective protection or repair strategies.

Carbonation

All reinforced structures are affected by carbonation which sooner or later reaches the reinforcement and leaves it unprotected from rusting. Designers cope with this by trying to ensure that the penetration rate will be slow enough and the cover thick enough to protect the reinforcement for sixty, or a hundred, or however many years they think the structure ought to last. Things do not always work out that way in practice.

Depth of cover can be measured with the careful use of a cover-meter and the depth of carbonation by spraying a broken surface with phenolphthalein. The hallmark for concrete quality is the 'carbonation coefficient' K which indicates the resistance of concrete to carbon dioxide penetration. It is calculated from the equation $K = d\sqrt{t}$ where d is the depth of carbonated concrete in millimetres and t the years since construction.

Even today providing good cover gets too little attention on site. The depth of cover often varies over different parts of buildings and structures but experience has shown where cover depth is likely to be less than average (Figure 13.1). The quality of cover will also vary. Testing the surface with the Schmidt rebound hammer can be useful for identifying locally-poor concrete. Especially vulnerable places are suggested in Figure 13.2.

Parts of buildings or structures	Likely cause
Thin sections	Reinforcement not located centrally
Beam-to-column T connections	Insufficient cover over end of reinforcement
Floor-to-beam connections	Insufficient cover over end of floor reinforcement
Near edges of beams	Tilted reinforcement cage giving low cover along one edge
Near edges of columns	Reinforcement cage skewed, not central, or not vertical
Inside joints in concrete	Insufficient end cover
Near joints in formwork	Misplaced or displaced formwork

Figure 13.1   Places where cover depth is likely to be less than average (Peter Pullar-Strecker)

Chloride contamination

Chloride contamination is not very common, but it is difficult to treat because any concentration of chloride exceeding about 0.2% (by cement weight) remaining in concrete can destroy the protection given to reinforcement. Figure 13.3 shows where chloride contamination should be suspected. Chloride concentration is expensive to measure because many samples of concrete have to be taken for chemical analysis. A way of pinpointing where samples are most likely to be needed is by using surface electrode potential mapping to show up places of potentially high corrosion activity.

Parts of buildings or structures	Likely cause
Near tops of deep lifts	Locally high water/cement ratios due to bleeding and settlement
Where reinforcement is likely to be congested	Poor compaction
Near the bottoms of members where there are signs of badly-fitting formwork	Grout leakage

Figure 13.2   Places where cover quality is likely to be poorer than average (Peter Pullar-Strecker)

Locations of buildings or structures	Likely cause
Near the sea	Salt water or wind-blown spray penetrating hardened concrete
Near, or part of a highway	Salt run-off, salt spray, possibly wind-blown, penetrating hardened concrete
In an area where sea-dredged aggregates were available at time of construction	Salt-contamination of concrete when mixed
Areas where fire-mains are supplied with sea-water	Salt penetrating into hardened concrete if structure has been damaged by fire, (or if fire-practice has been carried out)
Parts of buildings or structures	
Precast elements made before 1978	Use of calcium chloride accelerator (including "extra-rapid-hardening" cement) in the concrete when mixed
Parts constructed in frosty weather before 1978 (weather records may show an unusually cold winter at the time of construction)	Use of calcium chloride accelerator (including "extra-rapid-hardening" cement) in the concrete when mixed
Parts adjacent to wood-wool formwork (especially flat roofs)	Leaching of calcium chloride (which was used to pre-treat the shredded wood during manufacture) into the hardened concrete
Decorative exposed-aggregate finishes	Chloride from hydrochloric acid (often used to "freshen-up" the surface during construction) penetrating the hardened concrete

Figure 13.3   Places where chloride contamination should be suspected (Peter Pullar-Strecker)

Protection, repair and restoration strategies

Between the extremes of taking no action at all and demolition or reconstruction, owners have a range of options, as does the repair designer (shown in brackets). Owners can do as little as possible other than maintaining safety (and repair designers can do nothing, downgrade structural and service requirements or erect and maintain protection and support). Owners can maintain performance (and repair designers can protect the fabric from the environment or repair where necessary), owners can improve performance (where repair designers have the option of protecting the fabric from the environment, repairing and upgrading, reconstructing parts or adding new elements), or rebuild (or demolish and reconstruct) or abandon the structure (or do nothing, erect and maintain protection or demolish the structure).

The designer's objectives can be summarized in terms of the repair options. In order to downgrade structural requirements the designer can reduce and restrict live loading or partially demolish to reduce dead loading and live loading. To downgrade service requirements the

Protection or repair option	Advantages (+) and disadvantages (-)	
Surface impregnation	(+)	Reduces ingress of salty water;
	(+)	Reduces corrosion rate by increasing electrical resistivity;
	(-)	Reduction of moisture content may increase carbon dioxide penetration;
	(+)	Has little effect on appearance;
	(-)	Does not improve appearance;
	(-)	Needs regular renewal;
	(+)	Low first cost
Surface coating	(+)	Reduces ingress of salty water;
	(+)	Reduces carbon dioxide penetration;
	(+)	May reduce corrosion rate by increasing electrical resistivity;
	(-)	May increase corrosion by reducing evaporation;
	(+)	Can improve appearance;
	(+)	Hides repair patches;
	(-)	Changes appearance;
	(-)	Needs regular renewal;
	(+)	Low first cost
Overcladding	(+)	Reduces ingress of salty water;
	(+)	Reduces carbon dioxide penetration;
	(+)	May reduce corrosion rate by increasing electrical resistivity;
	(+)	Can provide thermal insulation, better windows, etc;
	(-)	May increase corrosion by reducing evaporation;
	(-)	May increase corrosion rate by increasing temperature;
	(+)	Hides repair patches;
	(+)	Can improve appearance;
	(-)	Changes appearance;
	(+)	Long-lasting;
	(-)	Needs some maintenance;
	(-)	High first cost
Cathodic protection	(+)	Controls corrosion rate even if chlorides are present and even if alkalinity has been lost;
	(-)	Needs to be working continuously;
	(-)	Needs periodic maintenance;
	(-)	May cause alkali reaction with sensitive aggregates;
	(-)	May cause embrittlement of pre-stressing steel;
	(-)	Need for an external anode affects appearance;
	(+)	Relatively long-lasting;
	(+)	Moderate first cost;
Patch repair	(+)	Permanent if properly done;
	(-)	Difficult to do properly where chloride contamination has to be removed;
	(-)	May not carry full share of structural loads;
	(-)	Affects appearance;
	(-)	High first costs;

Protection or repair option	Advantages (+) and disadvantages (-)	
Electro-chemical re-alkalization	(-)	May cause alkali reaction with sensitive aggregates;
	(-)	Longevity at present unknown;
	(+)	Does not in itself affect appearance;
	(-)	Affects appearance if over-coated as is normal;
	(+)	Coating can improve appearance;
	(+)	Moderate cost;
Electrochemical chloride extraction	(-)	May cause alkali reaction with sensitive aggregates;
	(-)	May cause embrittlement of pre-stressing steel;
	(+)	Does not in itself affect appearance;
	(-)	Longevity at present unknown;
	(+)	Moderate cost;
Replacement of elements	(+)	Permanent and maintenance-free if properly done;
	(+)	Can carry full share of structural loads;
	(+)	Need not affect appearance detrimentally;
	(-)	High first cost;

Figure 13.4 Advantages and disadvantages of protection and repair options (Peter Pullar-Strecker)

designer can change or restrict the type of use. To erect and maintain protection propping, scaffold 'fans' and access barriers can be provided. To protect the structure's fabric from the environment the designer can apply a surface coating or impregnation or construct over-cladding or sheltering. To passivate reinforcement cathodic protection can be installed. To repair and restore the structure the designer can patch repair, re-alkalize electrochemically, remove chlorides electrochemically or replace elements where necessary.

The cost, long-term prospects and effect on appearance of the different options vary a lot. A hasty decision to repair can either lock the owner into uncontrollable expenditure as the full horror of the deterioration is revealed during the repair process, or result in a budget-controlled patch-up job which has no prospect of having any lasting value. Careful inspection and expert independent advice can give the owner time to examine other options before he has a tiger by the tail.

Concrete deterioration and repair are subjects where controversy reigns and research is intensive. Opinions about the best courses of action often appear to differ widely, though mainly because the most appropriate repair strategy is highly specific to the exact circumstances of the structure and its environment.

Figure 13.4 is not intended to give answers which can be applied in individual specific cases, but they are an attempt to inform owners about their options and the questions which they should be discussing with their expert advisers. In concrete repair, as in medicine, failing to consider carefully alternatives can be more dangerous than the lack of ready remedies.

CHAPTER 14

METAL WINDOWS: TECHNOLOGY AND OPTIONS FOR REPAIR

Peter Johnson

Metal windows in the twentieth century are principally made of iron, steel, bronze and aluminium (Figure 14.1). Steel windows are the main consideration of this paper, and for this it is important to understand how these windows are made from basic hot-rolled steel sections.

The suites (sets) of sections used are common to all manufacturers, in contrast to windows made from other materials where each manufacturer has their own design and section profile. From a conservationist's point of view this means that in a domestic context windows available today are identical to those produced from 1920 onwards. This applies particularly to those types and designs which dominated the pre- and post-war housing scene.

In commercial buildings, including factories and warehouses, pre-1965 windows were mainly fabricated from the Medium Universal suite of sections. These were replaced in 1965 by the W20 suite, so named because it originally included 20 sections. Windows made from the earlier sections are easily replicated in W20 and can provide a very close visual similarity. Although there are some current developments in the steel window industry in producing a further updated suite of sections for commercial use, the ability to be able to match exactly, or closely replicate, windows installed during much of this century, will remain.

The virtues of steel as a window material lie in its high strength-to-weight ratio, enabling large glazed openings to be created with slim sight lines, virtues that were particularly appropriate in buildings featured in the Modern Movement where the fashionable provision of ample ventilation and daylight were important considerations. Earlier in the century the fact that metal windows had much better fire resistance compared to those made of wood was also important, a virtue that remains important, as does that of the security of steel as a window material.

However, there are two negative aspects to steel as a medium for window frame construction, one of which has been eliminated and one which can be minimized by design. Since 1945, all steel windows complying with the British Standard have been galvanized, eliminating the rust that is often a feature of poorly maintained pre-war windows. The other factor is the cold-bridging effect of steel at its junction with the facade's opening. This is an area that careful design in a replacement scheme can minimize, particularly in the use of sealed-

20TH CENTURY METAL WINDOWS

- **IRON:**   **PRE 1914**

- **STEEL:**   **MEDIUM UNIVERSAL (TO 1965)**
             W20 (FROM 1965 - DATE)
             DOMESTIC (F SERIES)(1920-DATE)
             GALVANISED & UN-GALVANISED

- **BRONZE:**   **SIMILAR TO W20 (TO 1980)**

- **ALUMINIUM:**   **FROM 1950**
                MILL FINISHED
                ANODISED

Figure 14.1 Twentieth-century metal windows (OCS Group)

unit double glazing and suitable jamb linings. Careful consideration should always be given to the likelihood of condensation and how to deal with it. This is rarely a problem in commercial buildings but must always be considered in domestic situations, indeed, some authorities suggest that the window is the most likely place for condensation to collect, and the windows should be designed accordingly.

Given that a building owner or other advisors can readily specify steel windows for a replacement or renovation scheme, what factors face them in making the appropriate decisions?

To illustrate this, the matrix shown in Figure 14.2 gives an idea of the trade-off or compromise that is often struck between the desires of the end user and the strict conservationist. The end user will be looking for a window system with a high level of comfort factors, whereas the conservationist may well be seeking windows that are as identical as possible to the originals: the two may or may not be incompatible. It is probable that the building owner, if not the end user, will also be seeking the cheapest option.

As the provision of enhanced comfort factors rises, so does the window specification and cost. However, neither the owner, end user nor the conservationist has a free choice in any of these areas since current legislation (much of it new in 1995) now has to be considered where windows are being replaced in a commercial building, and, in certain circumstances, in buildings intended for domestic use.

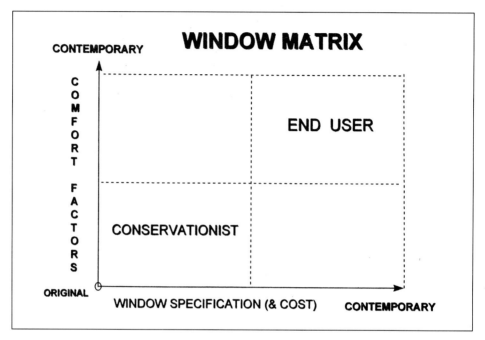

Figure 14.2   Window matrix (OCS Group)

In respect of Part L1 of the Building Regulations and the Construction, Design and Management Regulations it should be noted that W20 steel windows can meet the U values now specified, but for domestic window units, sealed-unit double glazing incorporated in special inserts is required. The traditional triangulated putty glazing system cannot then be used, another example of a compromise between end user and conservationist. This is a complex area and reference should be made to newly-published information from either the manufacturers or the Steel Window Association.

The Construction, Design and Management Regulations impose duties on both the professional team involved in building and construction and on the contractor. For windows the area for principal consideration is the provision of safe, practical access for window cleaning. In many cases this will be achieved by the incorporation anchorages (eye bolts) for attaching a safety harness. However, it should be particularly noted that codes of practice established under the UK enactment of the EC Workplace Directive limit window cleaning by ladder to 10 metres, effectively ground and first floor only (see OCS/ROSPA's *The ultimate guide to safe window cleaning*).

Although replacement windows are often the first thought of a person restoring a building, repair of existing windows is also often a viable proposition. Rust is the most evident form of decay of steel windows but is usually confined only to the sill bar of the frame and may look much worse than it actually is. The surface build-up caused by continual over-painting since installation also causes distortion of steel frames but after removal of both paint and rust the inherent strength of steel means that in the hands of specialists the window can be effectively restored.

In some instances it may be viable to remove the frames from the building, de-glaze them and shot-blast entire frames, subsequently zinc-spraying the cleaned metal surface for future rust prevention. However, the cost of doing this begins to approach the cost of the provision of new frames, incorporating improvements in window technology. Each case should be considered in its merits in conjunction with a company specializing in this area. However, firms largely involved in mass-marketed domestic replacement windows are unlikely to be interested in repair and renovation work and tend to have little or no knowledge of steel windows.

Window fittings such as coxspurs and peg stays are often the only individual item of design to be found on the steel window. Indeed, many architects, particularly in the 1930s, took pride in designing their own window fittings. When these are required today they can be recast or, if standard mass-produced fittings of the period were used, these are again readily obtainable, either as an exact or close match from specialist window repair companies.

Turning now to other metal window materials, bronze has been used for windows for many years. Often to be found in ground-floor treatments of prestigious commercial buildings, bronze windows were fabricated from sections very similar to both Medium Universal and W20 steel. Although bronze does not deteriorate through corrosion in the same way as steel over-painted frames can often be found which require mechanical overhauling. Overhaul involves similar skills to those used on steel windows but surface-finish restoration requires highly specialized techniques. This will often involve either chemical cleaning or a light sand-blasting to remove surface corrosion. The surface can then be chemically toned to renew the patina to any one of a large number of finishes of which 'coinage bronze' is the most common. This restored finish is often protected by waxing or spraying with lacquer and regular specialist maintenance is recommended.

If bronze windows are to be replaced, or there is a requirement to match existing bronze windows, steel W20 windows can provide a very close match and can be spray-finished to the same tones as that obtained in finishing natural bronze.

Aluminium windows present different sets of problems in both replacement and repair. Aluminium became established as a window material from 1950 onwards. Early production was mainly in mill-finish aluminium, frames fabricated from aluminium extrusions that received no further treatment after leaving the extrusion mill. This material corroded rapidly but in a self-limiting fashion. The grey pitted and scaly surface can be removed chemically and the metal brought back to a bright finish. However, unless regularly cleaned, or further protected by spraying, it will corrode again.

Many early aluminium windows also suffered from being gravely under-designed in structural strength and it is quite likely that replacement rather than repair is the most viable option. However with no common sections available, the exact matching of window designs will present a problem.

Later aluminium windows and most of those used in commercial buildings used anodized material where the surface was electro-chemically oxidized and coloured. However, early anodizating was not as successful as its modern counterpart and, where coloured finishes were incorporated, considerable loss of original colour could occur. Structural weakness is not usually a factor of commercial window and curtain walling design and cleaning and restoration of existing facades is usually a viable proposition. Colour restoration can be achieved by spray finishing with modern paint systems, giving a potential ten to fifteenyears of life before refinishing will be required again, given adequate specialist maintenance of the paint finish in the intervening period.

CHAPTER 15

CONSERVATION OF MODERN BUILDINGS: A PRACTITIONER'S VIEW

John Allan

I am a practising architect for whom rescuing modern buildings in trouble is only one part (and a relatively minor part) of a practice workload that consists predominantly of new-build projects. My experiences in conservation originated not in theory or research but in circumstances where a building owner needs answers to real problems, problems to which theory and research and a good deal of practical ingenuity must then be applied. The process is one of moving from the particular to the general and then back again, from the close-up to the overview rather than the other way round. Or, to borrow Andrew Saint's phraseology, a continuous oscillation between the Charybdis of empiricism and the Scylla of principle.

This approach has influenced my stance towards the subject of conservation as a whole, which I see as a sort of negotiation between the past, the present and the future, in which the present has the casting vote. Because formulating theory is so fraught with difficulty there is a tendency to arrive at large rhetorical questions like 'should we preserve the past in aspic, or at all?', or 'shouldn't we demolish buildings in disrepair with no other use?' or 'if modern architecture was predicated on the idea of transitoriness, isn't it quite legitimate for us to change it however necessary to suit changed circumstances?'.

What intrigues me about such questions is that they are invariably posed in the first person plural, as if they could be settled by us, assuming we all agreed, whereas the main constituency to whom they are addressed is not represented here. But while buildings may or may not be architecture they are always property, and since this confers certain extremely powerful rights and presumptions in favour of the owner it is actually only in the context of a proprietor's dominion over his assets (or liabilities) that any realistic discussion about conservation can begin. In other words, architects who depend on finding and keeping clients as a precondition of doing any work at all see conservation not so much as an application of theory as practising the art of the possible.

The projects I discuss here have been undertaken for a variety of reasons that may or may not include conservation. In cases where that motivation was weak or non-existent, conservation has become a condition of the job only by virtue of the building's listed status. Figure 15.1 illustrates this variability of motives, indicating the principal objectives in the client's agenda in each instance.

PROJECT	CLIENT	LISTING GRADE	FUNDING	LISTED BUILDING CONSENT FOR WORK	CHANGE OF USE	CLIENT OBJECTIVES (OTHER THAN CONSERVATION)	NATURE OF AVANTI'S CONSERVATION WORK	SURVIVING ORIGINAL FABRIC
PENGUIN POOL	London Zoo (charity)	I	Zoo/Private benefactor/EH	Required	No	Backlog maintenance Improve facility	Restoring the concept Sympathetic adaptation Repair	Armature mainly, limited finish
DUDLEY ZOO	Local authority	II* (5) II (7)	Private	Required	Required for conversion options	Demolish if possible/ redevelop site	Propaganda for repair and adaptive reuse	Partial armature Partial surface texture (no surface finish)
LUBETKIN BUNGALOW	London Zoo (charity)	II* and II	TBA	TBA	No	Sell off land	Repair estimate for rehabilitation and reuse	Armature and some components
FINSBURY HEALTH CENTRE	NHS Trust	II to I	FHSA DoH Grant(s)	Required	No	Clear surplus off capital account before financial year end Improve facility	Restoring the concept and repair of selected fabric Improve performance	Armature and some components
HIGHPOINT (LIFTS)	Private	II* and II	Private Residential	Required	No	Overcome intolerable unreliability of 60-year old lifts	Saving maximum fabric Restoring the concept	Some components
THE WHITE HOUSE	Private	II to II*	Private Local grant	Not required	No	Increased comfort and protecting property value	Repair, sympathetic replacement and improving performance	Armature and some components
WILLOW ROAD	National Trust (charity)	II	National Trust Donation	Required	House to museum (and cinema)	Heritage, education and revenue	Saving maximum fabric Repair/re-service Sympathetic adaptation	Almost complete, with authentic later additions
THE HOMEWOOD	National Trust (charity)	II	TBA	TBA	TBA	Heritage & education (Revenue, TBA)	Repair maximum fabric Repair/re-surface Sympathetic adaptation	Almost complete, with authentic later additions
GORILLA HOUSE	London Zoo (charity)	I	Zoo and fundraising	Required	No (change of exhibit)	Annual conservation, increased attendance	Repairing selected original fabric. Sympathetic adaptation	Armature and some components
BRISTOL GOODS SHED	City Council	II	Developer?	Required	Required for conversion	Demolish if possible	Propaganda for survival (Feasibility Study for Preservation Trust)	Partial
45 UNDERGROUND STATIONS	London Underground Ltd.	II	LUL	Required	No	Contraventions 'audit'. Set priorities for 95/96 spend	Rectify contraventions	Fairly complete

Figure 15.1   Recent projects from Avanti Architects (Avanti Architects)

As you can see, even in a list containing three grade I buildings and eight grade II* from a total of 77 buildings, there is not a single conservation project which has not or will not have required some sort of intervention in the fabric, even if there were one or two that have not required listed building consent. This is why I am inclined to regard conservation not as a matter of keeping something as it is, but more as a specialized way of changing it. Dealing with such interventions is always more difficult than straight repair, if indeed there is such a thing, but is correspondingly more interesting because it calls for architectural judgement. In other words conservation is ultimately about priorities. And this is why, when confronted by the sort of universal questions mentioned above, I have found that the only answer which is always correct is 'It depends . . . '.

To sum up this introduction I would refer to an observation of Arthur Drexler which might perhaps be considered a suitable motto for conservationists: 'The problem of deciding what is important is a function of human intelligence, and to suppose that its difficulties can be avoided is to advocate that we make ourselves stupid'.[1]

The Penguin Pool (grade I)

The modern conservation movement seems to have become associated with the Penguin Pool but I only want to consider two aspects of this project which still seem relevant to our discussion (though it is nearly ten years now since the job was completed). The first concerns the problem of sympathetic adaptation. An important aim in the pool's rehabilitation was the reinstatement of the deep diving tank at the top of the south ramp which had fallen into disuse. We were told by the Zoo that if this facility was to be any use it must be made larger.

So Lubetkin and I set about exploring the possible ways this might be achieved. Figure 15.1 shows a few of the options we considered. Obviously the alteration would require listed building consent (the pool is grade I) as there was clearly no way of enlarging the tank within the existing envelope. I remember vividly the meeting that took place between Westminster City Council, English Heritage, Lubetkin and myself when Lubetkin's preferred proposal was rejected by the Heritage officer as 'not being in the spirit of the original design'! But the point I want to make is I that think the officer was right. It was suggested that Lubetkin's solution had slight 50s overtones that seemed foreign to the classic lines of the original pool, though it could well be argued that what the Heritage officer read as a 50s motif (the canted cheeks of the tank) was only what Lubetkin himself had invented in the 30s at Finsbury Health Centre.

I think the eventual solution, which emerged after I had made models of the preferred options, was better for being less assertive and adopting the purer geometry of the original. The moral being that even when the original designer is available for guidance the best adaptation may be derived from the original design rather than from its author.

The second point has to do with restoration vis-a-vis conservation. 'Restoration' has had a bad reputation since the SPAB promulgated the conservation creed we now all take virtually for granted. Yet, as has already been pointed out, the sort of buildings that provoked and informed that creed, buildings more often made of stone, brick, tiles and timber, are not the sort we are addressing here, namely, ones made of concrete, glass, steel and plastic. If you compare a

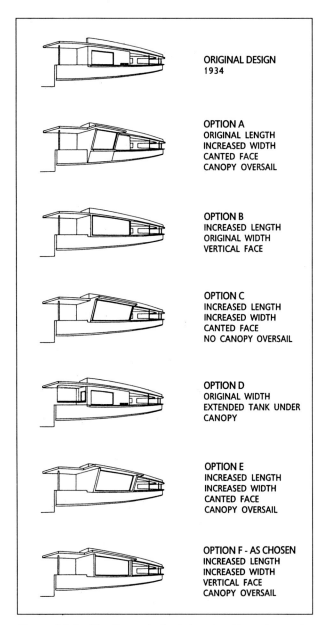

ORIGINAL DESIGN
1934

OPTION A
ORIGINAL LENGTH
INCREASED WIDTH
CANTED FACE
CANOPY OVERSAIL

OPTION B
INCREASED LENGTH
ORIGINAL WIDTH
VERTICAL FACE

OPTION C
INCREASED LENGTH
INCREASED WIDTH
CANTED FACE
NO CANOPY OVERSAIL

OPTION D
ORIGINAL WIDTH
EXTENDED TANK UNDER
CANOPY

OPTION E
INCREASED LENGTH
INCREASED WIDTH
CANTED FACE
CANOPY OVERSAIL

OPTION F - AS CHOSEN
INCREASED LENGTH
INCREASED WIDTH
VERTICAL FACE
CANOPY OVERSAIL

Figure 15.2 The Penguin Pool, London Zoo: alternative proposals for the enlargement of the diving tank (Avanti Architects)

traditional classic with a modern classic the different sort of problems one is likely to confront become clear. One is deep, thick, heavy, rough, soft, permeable and approximate. The other is shallow, thin, light, smooth, hard, impervious and precise. It is evident that if and when these buildings fail they are going to fail in different ways, and accordingly that they will require different types of rescue operation.

The received wisdom of defending and retaining the culturally significant fabric is as good a starting point as any, given that it leaves wide open the interpretation of what *is* culturally significant. But what if the culturally significant fabric is no longer visible, as, for example, in the case of the Penguin Pool, obliterated by 13 subsequent overcoats of paint, bituminous compound, render and other miscellaneous formless coverings? The exemplar is not William Morris and his woody, bricky, stoney churches, but with an earlier generation of architecture altogether, the classical period which, like the early moderns, also relied on formal armatures with formless coverings, rather than composite assemblies of differentiated materials. A comparison of the Penguin Pool with Kenwood House might seem improbable, yet what they have in common is that not a single square inch of the wall surface of either of these buildings is original. In the case of reinforced concrete, where the concrete needs the reinforcement, and the reinforcement needs the concrete, structural repair to remedy or arrest carbonation starts and ends with the surface.

It soon became clear to us in rescuing the Penguin Pool that we were not repairing the authentic architectural fabric so much as restoring the culturally significant design, that is, the concept. Only by using some of the specialized products referred to elsewhere by David

Heath could the concept, in which I include the key attribute of *thinness*, be maintained at the same time as effecting a repair of reasonable quality. The concrete repair of the Penguin Pool involved removal of all the umpteen inauthentic coatings down to a sound (or repairable) substrate and re-establishing an alkaline-rich surface with no appreciable thickening of structural sections, in a way which, as far as we could tell, resembled the high state of finish of the original. I readily admit that what has been restored is the concept, an ideal proposition, an affirmation of the deeply unfashionable precept that man dominates nature, and reason dominates man.

Even if it had been technically possible to retrieve the structural integrity of the building without disturbing the surface I doubt if such a result would have been acceptable operationally to the Zoo, or indeed aesthetically to the benefactor Lord Palumbo, in the absence of whose assistance the project is unlikely to have happened at all. That it did happen is due to the convergence of sufficient need, sufficient will and sufficient money at a moment when Lubetkin and Palumbo's friendship kindled the first spark. As I suggested at the beginning, conservation in practice is the art of the possible.

The White House 1932 (grade II*)

This problem of authenticity in modern surfaces reappeared at the White House, or New Farm,

Figure 15.3 The White House, London: not a modern house just built, but a 60-year old monument just repaired (Avanti Architects)

by the architect Amyas Connell, where we undertook a similar repair contract. Here the original concrete was considerably more primitive than at the Penguin Pool but its repair still involved removal of defective subsequent coatings, which in this instance were also contributing to the fabric decay by retaining interstitial moisture. However, apart from using a brush-applied 1mm fairing mortar coat to close blow-holes in the concrete we decided against including levelling renders between the repaired substrate and the protective coatings. This had the effect of leaving a more clearly discernable record of the irregular character of the original building. The appearance we sought was not that of a modernist house that had just been built, but that of a 60-year old building that had just been repaired (Figure 15.2).

The other main item of work involved replacement of the staircase window. The original was literally on its last legs and nearly twenty five per cent of the glass panels (which had fractured through corrosion induced stresses) had been replaced by polythene bags from a well-known supermarket chain. Neither I nor Crittalls, the original installers, who were asked to report on the feasibility of repair, considered that there was any economical prospect of saving the original screen (which was ungalvanized painted mild steel).

The replacement in W20 galvanized powder-coated section maintained all the fenestration details and almost all the profile characteristics of the original while incorporating 14mm double-glazed low-emissivity units, reducing the U value from 5.4 to 2.6. I know this departs from the original, but is it ethically reprehensible? I would still contend that it was a legitimate reconciliation of the client's desire for improved performance and the conservation requirement for a sympathetic response.

There is one last point of interest about the White House, which I think reinforces my earlier observation about proprietorial rights and illustrates another common feature of conservation, namely that the architect often finds he is joining the game after play has already started. Apart from the large staircase enclosure we were only asked to deal with one other defective window. All the others had only just been repainted white by the owner. I am well aware that the original colour scheme was black windows and sugar almond pink walls, but the owner, not unreasonably, was not prepared to re-repaint the windows he had just done or change the colour (and consequently name) of the whole house. We had to choose between installing two black windows and leaving a mixture, or matching the replacements to the existing adjacent. We chose the latter as the less unacceptable of two compromises.

Finsbury Health Centre 1938 (Grade I)

The issue of legitimate intervention, or seeking to reconcile conservation criteria with improved performance, again runs all through the project we did at Finsbury Health Centre.

The Finsbury Health Centre was designed by Berthold Lubetkin and Tecton and opened in 1938. Since then it has continuously provided primary health care facilities for the local community. It is internationally recognized as a pioneering example of social architecture and a masterpiece of twentieth-century modern design. In 1988 Avanti Architects prepared a report on the scope of works required for the restoration of the outside of the building. Funds were allocated by the Camden and Islington NHS Trust and Family Health Service Authority in the autumn of 1993 for the first phase of the exterior restoration, which comprised the following works.

Re-roofing works

The original roof finish was rock asphalt generally laid over screed on 25mm cork slab insulation. On the curved roof the build-up was 25mm rock asphalt on e.m.l. on 25mm rock asphalt on 25mm cork slab on concrete. In the central area of the building the rock asphalt, a naturally-occurring material no longer commercially available, was dressed over verges and projecting copes and was therefore an integral feature of the building's appearance.

Research into alternative roofing systems, particularly single-ply membranes, found no material that could achieve the jointless monolithic quality of the original asphalt. It was therefore decided to use a polymer-modified asphalt, which, unlike the traditional product, maintains its performance when subject to naturally-occurring temperature extremes, together with 50mm or 70mm cork slab insulation in a warm roof system (Figure 15.3). This approach had the advantage of using known materials and technology and maintaining the authentic appearance. Cork insulation, as well as replicating an original element of the specification, is

Figure 15.4 Finsbury Health Centre, London: the roof terrace as refurbished with original colours and seamless asphalt coping (Avanti Architects)

also a CFC- and HCFC-free renewable resource. The barrel roof insulation was lined with three layers of 6mm ply, felt and e.m.l. to reduce the surface temperature variation within the asphalt on the inclined surface.

Concrete and render repairs

Extensive concrete repairs were required. Initial repairs were carried out using traditional techniques. These involved grit-blasting the surface of the concrete and render, testing for physical soundness and then removing all loose and defective material. Corrosion was removed from rebars before application of proprietary coatings and polymer-modified concrete repair compounds to re-establish the original profile.

Following further tests the decision was taken to exploit the recently developed technique of re-alkalization. Flat tanks of sodium carbonate solution were clamped to the prepared concrete surface and an electrical charge established between the reinforcement and the electrolyte. This induces alkalinity into the concrete by ionization so that further corrosion to steel reinforcement and consequent concrete damage is arrested.

Re-alkalization offered two advantages, as a less invasive and therefore quieter process it would cause less disruption to building users, and as a pre-quantifiable process the specialist contractor was able to offer a fixed-price quotation. Tests confirmed the suitability of the structure for re-alkalization and this process was used on all the parapet walls. The concrete and render repair process was completed by the application of proprietary decorative coatings to preserve the integrity of the repaired concrete.

All render and concrete surfaces above basement level had been overpainted white during subsequent maintenance. By studying contemporary black and white photographs and removing later applications of paint and render it has been possible to retrieve a picture of the original surface tones and colours. A typical Tecton palette of colours was discovered: intense red-brown applied to selected surfaces on the terrace, pale blue to the reveals of the glass block entrance screen, terrace canopy soffit and lecture theatre block, a dark French navy-grey to basement and undercroft areas, and a honey colour elsewhere. On completion of concrete and render repairs, surfaces were re-coated with closely matching colours from the Sika and SBD concrete repair systems.

Steel windows and curtain walling

The curtain walling on the face of the wings, the most innovative feature of the building but damaged in the war and marred by subsequent modifications which themselves were in an advanced state of decay, needed to be repaired and restored to its original appearance. Phase 1 funds only allowed the south-east-facing entrance wing to be tackled.

Perhaps ironically, perhaps not, the most 'traditional' component of the curtain wall, the teak frame, was the best preserved of all, and only required cleaning and some minor local renovation. However, its mild steel fixings to the concrete structure had largely corroded and were all replaced in stainless steel.

The replication of the original window details was governed by the range of W20 steel sections currently available and the decision to introduce double glazing. Paint scrapes revealed that the windows were originally painted an olive grey colour. New steelwork was galvanized and polyester powder-coated. The original silver bronze lever handles and distinctive friction pivot levers were salvaged and reused on the replacement windows.

One of the biggest challenges of the restoration was the treatment of the spandrel panels. These were access panels for the external service ducts running along the face of the building, and were originally composed of 'Thermolux', two sheets of clear glass with a coloured spun-glass silk interlayer. Although we discovered that 'Thermolux' was still made in Germany, it is now only available in white.

None of the original panels survived to give an indication of colour. Until the contractor had started on site and subsequent replacement spandrels were removed, the only clues to these consisted of black and white photographs, published drawings, written accounts and the recollections of Lubetkin (according to whom they 'shone like a girlfriend's hair'), Francis Skinner, sole surviving partner of Tecton, and David Medd, who visited the building as a student during construction. No-one could produce evidence that was wholly conclusive.

Fortunately fragments of the original panels were discovered at the base of the ducts, and these were sent to a materials laboratory for forensic analysis and colour matching. The eventual solution for the replacement replicates the original colouration of the curtain walling with a laminated glass panel, comprising tinted glass and a clear PVD interlayer, and retrieves the original textured reflective character by placing plain white Thermolux behind it. The solution will have the additional benefits of protecting the Thermolux, improving insulation values and providing a more durable outer skin by virtue of the BS 6206 class A lamination standard.

Meanwhile the original steel flashings framing the curtain wall areas had corroded or deteriorated beyond repair. They were all replaced with matching galvanized powder-coated equivalents. However, the glazed steel doors to the terrace and a small number of steel windows in sheltered locations were in salvageable condition. These were renovated and not replaced.

Ceramic tiles and faience copings

The original and highly distinctive cream-coloured ceramic tiles were manufactured using a dust-pressed process. This allowed greater dimensional accuracy and resulted in the narrow joints (0-2mm) characteristic of the building. Unfortunately, the original tiles were not fully vitrified and therefore not reliably frost-resistant. In addition there was no effective provision of movement joints. No UK manufacturer was prepared to produce the close glaze match and range of specials required in a vitrified dust-pressed tile. The eventual solution was achieved with the help of a tile factor who procured 'biscuit' (the raw tile base) from various sources to be glazed in a factory in northern France.

A number of technical issues still had to be resolved: the original tile, not being vitrified, absorbed more of the glaze, giving an appearance of greater depth and translucence than modern tiles which have a more refined body. Also current glazes tend to be more uniform than the original, with the attendant risk that the final effect would lose the pleasing original variegation and look too mechanical. Thus the biscuit, which was brown, had to be coated with white slip or engobe prior to glazing to achieve the correct colour and surface quality.

The tiles were bonded to a new unreinforced polymer-modified render coat with a 3mm-6mm thin/thick bed adhesive. Movement joints of various types were introduced in accordance with current British Standards, including wider joints at inconspicuous locations such as at changes of profile or at the abutments of the tiled surface with steel flashing strips, and narrow joints at critical visual points on the facade, achieved by a bridging detail with a narrow tile joint over a wider render joint.

The carved crest and metal sign

The white marble crest above the entrance is carved with the coat of arms of Finsbury Council. The surface had lost much of its definition and the stone, a statuary marble weakened by vents, was on the point of total disintegration. It is proposed to provide a carved replacement. This will be in Whitbed Portland Stone, rather than statuary marble, for cost reasons. A grant towards this work has now been generously given by the Heritage of London Trust.

The 'Finsbury Health Centre' metal sign with *trompe l'oeil* letters on a cut-out metal backing has been remade and fixed to the original brackets. An exact copy has been achieved by working from the remnants of the original letters and using a process known as tungsten inert gas welding to achieve the fineness of the original folds.

Services works

The restoration included a variety of rationalization and improvement works to services. Some asbestos removal was also required.

Future restoration

The Phase I works were completed in early 1995. Grant assistance had previously been unavailable from English Heritage due to the public sector status of the building but a new agreement between English Heritage and Islington Council has opened the door to possible grant aid in future. Meanwhile the building owners are preparing a Business Case application for further funding for the completion of the exterior restoration and interior upgrading refurbishment. Additional funding is indeed essential both to secure the value of the investment to date and to arrest further deterioration of the remaining areas of this pivotal grade I listed building.

2 Willow Road, Hampstead (grade II)

Now unlike Finsbury, at Willow Road we have a conservation client with a whole philosophy and tradition of expertise in the repair, restoration, preservation, management and maintenance of architecturally- or historically-significant buildings and their contents. The concern for authenticity and interest in detail at The National Trust is exemplary and their resources, at least in terms of access to specialist skills, are seemingly limitless. Even half-finished bars of soap dating from Ernö Goldfinger's occupation have been saved and conserved for incorporation into the house when it is opened to the public.

As far as our own work in and on the house is concerned the criterion of our success upon completion will be if nobody realises we have been there. Our aim has been to do the minimum necessary to secure the fabric against progressive defects. A badly corroded window frame, for example, which might otherwise have been a case for replacement has been repaired as well as reasonably possible *in situ* to avoid the risk of damaging the glass during removal. This means it may have to be repaired again, but this is built into the whole philosophy of the Trust's *modus operandum*.

Some displaced areas of parapet wall, which in other circumstances and for another client might certainly have had to be rebuilt, have been secured by resin injection techniques. This will leave a reasonably visible defect on the facade, but arguably avoids introducing an even more visible remedy, that is by risking a patch of rebuilt brickwork where, because the original mortar was so strong, it seemed unlikely we would be able to salvage unbroken bricks for reuse in a matching repair.

Where we have intervened is in acting to arrest and correct the causes of the original fault, that is, the defective inner leaf of the parapet and the cavity (or rather lack of same) between it and the outer skin. This inner leaf of poor-quality brick which was saturated and had actually perished through frost action had transmitted movement pressures to the facade. We have therefore rebuilt it entirely in engineering brick, creating the necessary cavity and clearing weepholes, removing, cleaning and replacing the coping stones in the process.

I emphasize the significance of working for a 'conservation client' because it enables a more moderate approach to be taken in dealing with various problems. Because the National Trust has a well-established regime of quinquennial reviews it is possible to leave some things that do not need urgent attention in the knowledge that they can be considered and reappraised next time round. It demonstrates again how effective conservation relies not only on appropriate repair techniques but on the whole management culture in which they occur.

But there is a small paradox even in the exemplary activity of the National Trust. The very act of isolating and conserving a building as a fragment of architectural and social culture imposes the need for certain interventions which would not otherwise apply. Saving Willow Road for the nation has involved a change-of-use reclassification from private residence to public museum. This certainly avoids some of the pressure for improved performance that occurs in a building in occupation, insulation for example. But, as you can imagine, the very fact that the house is not in occupation has entailed the introduction of various installations to satisfy the need for security, health and safety and fire precautions. Obviously one tries to do this as discreetly as possible but there are performance-related requirements in the size, visibility and location of such things as passive infra-red scanners, alarm sounders, smoke detectors and break glass points that make them virtually impossible to camouflage, especially as a modern interior has none of the 'ornamental pastry' of a traditional one to hide things in.

We have considered the later incorporation of an aspirator-based smoke detection system when funds allow which will certainly give a more discreet installation.

The Homewood, Esher, Surrey (grade II)

The question of how a conserved building is going to be presented to the public really only arises in projects like Willow Road. Buildings like Finsbury or the Penguin Pool need to carry on earning their living by being health centres or housing birds. Where Conservation with a capital C is the key motive the programme of physical work cannot really get under way until the future regime is agreed.

The acquisition process for The Homewood still has some way to go, and the question as to how the house might be operated and shown is still under discussion. This has meant that the comprehensive survey of necessary remedial works which we undertook for the Trust in 1994 still awaits implementation. But, again, the very fact that it will be used to inform the Trust's overall long-term strategy makes it possible to isolate immediate or essential 'holding measures' from others which can be left until the larger questions are settled. For this purpose we produced the following criteria for the identification of 'holding measures'.

- work needed to arrest or prevent water ingress to the interior
- work needed to make good conspicuous consequential damage from active or previous water ingress defects
- work needed to prevent damage from active defects becoming further entrenched and disproportionately costly to remedy later
- work needed to arrest deterioration of significant elements of historic fabric (this can mean removal of an item at risk and safe storage for future work)
- investigations needed to ascertain the extent and severity of potentially progressive defects
- maintenance work needed to ensure or retrieve the operational viability of services installations
- works needed to ensure adequate compliance with health and safety requirements

The lesson from the two projects we are doing with the National Trust is, I think, that the opportunities for good conservation are vastly increased if it takes place within a culture of responsible maintenance. It must also be noted that in both cases the complete authenticity of the buildings 'as found' is attributable to each having been continuously inhabited by their original designer.

Highpoint (grade II and II*)

To return to Tecton, the problem of ageing services installations is also what we were confronted with at Highpoint. The original lifts are now 60 years old and at the end of their safe and viable existence. The technical and architectural problems of replacing them were not made easier by the fact that before we were invited to become involved, the contract had progressed quite some distance without listed building consent being properly obtained. The first lift was two weeks off completion when all works were ordered to stop.

The crux of the issue here was to preserve as far as possible the original architectural conception informing the lift design while observing all the technical engineering and safety standards required by current regulations in order to obtain the requisite operating insurance certificate. Our task was to develop a design strategy and details to obtain the requisite consents and to allow new procurement to begin.

The transparency of the lift shaft within the staircase enclosure with borrowed light from diagonally opposite quarters is absolutely fundamental to the planning of Highpoint. The whole sense of connectivity of the foyer space with the upper floors depends on it. With considerable support from the conservation authorities, whom it is a pleasure to acknowledge here, we were able to insist on the retention of the shaft mesh and its original fixings. The original fabric had already been removed from the framework, though fortunately not from site, when we arrived on the scene. Some matching new infill pieces had to be made.

Safety requirements were satisfied, but only just, by introducing clear perspex sheets behind the mesh at any position where less than 150mm existed between the public on the staircase and any moving part within the shaft. The lift shaft doors all had to be remade, and the portal fixing reconfigured to conform with what I normally refer to as the laws of visual hygiene. Wiring and controls are considerably more onerous than they were 60 years ago, and there was endless discussion with the contractor on details of the various mechanisms and their architectural harmonization.

Then the lift cars had to be redesigned. We were able to retrieve several important original features, namely a replication of the unique tapering car plan, floor-to-ceiling glazing of the rear wall, a close replication of the grille detail in this wall, and, most costly of all, a remanufacture of the twinned centre-opening doors. The loss of symmetry that would have resulted from side-opening doors was as repugnant to the conservation authorities as it was to me.

I won't pretend that the outcome is perfect, but it is certainly a lot happier than it might have been, and most important, the wonderful feeling of transparency in travel as you look through the glazed car wall and see the section of Highpoint pass by has been preserved. The remaining lifts are now being installed, but to the agreed model design of the first.

Gorilla House (grade I)

This discussion of service and moving parts brings me to my last example, another grade I building, the Gorilla House at Regents Park, which we are currently converting into a centre for Madagascan Lemurs for London Zoo. The original design was a wonderfully, innocently, ambitious solution to a complex brief: rotating roof, sliding glass screens and revolving walls to allow indoor and outdoor accommodation for the animals with round-the-year viewing for the public.

Our brief is hardly less complex. It too requires us to provide a variety of types of accommodation for several species of Lemur, nocturnal and diurnal. So we have external display areas for the diurnal lemurs, internal display areas for the nocturnal lemurs, internal sleeping quarters for the diurnal lemurs and separate internal off-show areas for the nocturnal lemurs. There is an internal gallery space for the public to view the nocturnal lemurs and separate service spaces for the zoo keepers. There must also be artificial lighting to the nocturnal exhibit to simulate daytime conditions during the night (Figure 15.4).

The building at present is almost but not quite derelict. It contains later, unsympathetic additions and also has lost several original elements, including most of the moving parts I referred to, the screens, the walls and the revolving roof. Only the spoked steel structure of the revolving roof remains, but it has been 'parked' in the exterior half of the shell. This gives a sense of complication and structural over-provision that would never have been evident in the original when the coverings were there. So we intend to rotate it back inside. It will be a difficult task technically and perhaps a controversial one in conservation terms, although it should be stressed that the beams will still be there inside and that the principle of reversibility will have been observed. But I cannot help thinking that Lubetkin himself, who was a compulsive and accomplished gambler, would have approved of the idea of having one more spin of the wheel.

Conclusions

To sum up, I offer the following conclusions, which I stress are not suggested as principles but at best might be useful as a baker's dozen of candid personal tips, mainly for architects, and in no particular order.

- Unless you are dealing with a conservation institution as such, an owner's motive is seldom if ever simply the pursuit of conservation objectives, even if he is sympathetic towards, or aware of the architectural significance of his property. The conservation-minded architect is thus likely to find himself engaging in a process ranging from mild propaganda to acts of stealth, The former is preferable, but at times it is vital to be able to lean on the statutory authorities' power to insist that something is done as a way of convincing a reluctant client they have no choice.
- Architects must be very clear about the project objectives and what you are doing to achieve them. You cannot pretend that it is conservation of the authentic fabric if it is really restoration of the original concept.
- If holding measures are necessary, always consider the design of the eventual permanent works before designing the temporary ones.
- If you normally do new-build work keep resisting your temptation to make conservation work look better, but always consider the possibility of improving performance *discreetly* if this can enhance the longevity of the result.
- Evidence of the original designer's errors can be just as interesting as evidence of his wisdom, provided the consequence of the error is not progressive damage.
- Allow the original design to suggest and govern future use rather than the other way round.
- Always search for options before making a choice, even if there seems initially to be only one solution to the problem at hand. And do not forget the 'Do nothing' option.

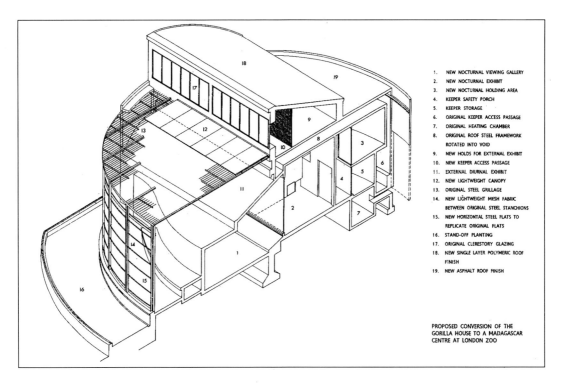

1. NEW NOCTURNAL VIEWING GALLERY
2. NEW NOCTURNAL EXHIBIT
3. NEW NOCTURNAL HOLDING AREA
4. KEEPER SAFETY PORCH
5. KEEPER STORAGE
6. ORIGINAL KEEPER ACCESS PASSAGE
7. ORIGINAL HEATING CHAMBER
8. ORIGINAL ROOF STEEL FRAMEWORK ROTATED INTO VOID
9. NEW HOLDS FOR EXTERNAL EXHIBIT
10. NEW KEEPER ACCESS PASSAGE
11. EXTERNAL DIURNAL EXHIBIT
12. NEW LIGHTWEIGHT CANOPY
13. ORIGINAL STEEL GRILLAGE
14. NEW LIGHTWEIGHT MESH FABRIC BETWEEN ORIGINAL STEEL STANCHIONS
15. NEW HORIZONTAL STEEL FLATS TO REPLICATE ORIGINAL FLATS
16. STAND-OFF PLANTING
17. ORIGINAL CLERESTORY GLAZING
18. NEW SINGLE LAYER POLYMERIC ROOF FINISH
19. NEW ASPHALT ROOF FINISH

PROPOSED CONVERSION OF THE
GORILLA HOUSE TO A MADAGASCAR
CENTRE AT LONDON ZOO

Figure 15.5   The Gorilla House, London Zoo: section showing the main features of the proposed conversion to a Madagascar Centre (Avanti Architects)

- The first priority is always to get the structure dry. There is no point in retouching details in the interior if the roof leaks.
- If you cannot finish the whole job, what is done should either be limited and exemplary or should secure enough of the significant material for someone else (preferably you) to have another shot next time.
- Never assume that something is so obvious to a contractor that it does not need to be pointed out, usually more than once.
- Specifically, a contractor's instinct, stemming from new-build culture and fear of the defects list, is always to make a tidy job of it, which while sounding admirable, is actually an easier task than the one that real conservation requires them to achieve. The contractor's attitude is crucial, because they are generally oblivious to the architectural significance of a modern building as a conservation project.
- Insist that a contractor always asks permission before removing anything from site. And ensure this regime is established on Day One, as much of your evidence may be among the 'debris' of the building you are about to conserve (for example, those Thermolux fragments at Finsbury).
- Never go on a building site without a camera.

And finally . . . despite the proverb that 'art is long and life is short', my experience is that in any battle between the two life invariably wins. This being so, it seems to me that the only lasting successes in conservation are likely to be those that are achieved through persuasion rather than conquest.

References

1   Drexler, A. (1977), 'Engineers' architecture: truth and its consequences', *The architecture of the Ecole des Beaux Arts*, London: Secker and Warburg, 43.

CHAPTER 16
MOSAIC-CLAD CONCRETE: RECENT RESEARCH

John Streeter

As a result of the extensive programme of remedial work currently being carried out at the Metropolitan Cathedral of Christ the King in Liverpool (Figure 16.1), funded in part by English Heritage, Bickerdike Allen Partners were commissioned by English Heritage to carry out a comprehensive study into the current state of knowledge regarding the performance, conservation, repair and restoration of mosaic used as external cladding to modern reinforced-concrete structures.

Much of our initial work has been to assemble and assess as wide a range of published material as possible on all aspects of the use of mosaic and techniques for its conservation, restoration and repair. This information was obtained by bibliographic searches in sources in the UK and in international conservation and materials research organizations. It is hoped that this will eventually form the basis of a comprehensive database for all concerned with mosaic matters.

Almost without exception, and perhaps inevitably, the information available concerning repair or conservation has been concerned with antiques, archaeological discoveries and other historically significant mosaics. Publications concerning modern mosaics and mosaicists unsurprisingly tend to concentrate almost exclusively on either the aesthetic issues or the artistic interpretation rather than inform the reader about materials, techniques and technical details.

For example, many sources illustrate the mosaics designed by artists with an established reputation in other mediums such as Fernand Lèger, Gustav Klimt and Marc Chagall. Alternatively authors like to dwell on the unique, such as the unclassifiable, non-traditional, multi-material work of Gaudí in Barcelona or the Watts Towers in Los Angeles, or otherwise on the spectacular reinterpretation, but on a giant scale, of mosaic derived from traditional ethnic artefacts as exemplified by the mural mosaics of Diego Rivera and Juan O'Gorman in Mexico.

Very little information has been published on the recent use of mosaic as an external cladding material where the decorative value and artistic properties of the tesserae have been largely subordinated to express the overall form of the underlying architecture. The mosaic is designed to be viewed from all but the closest positions as a homogeneous layer of minimal

thickness following the plastic form of the structure created within the architect's imagination. Individual tesserae are of uniform size, geometric shape and colour and are placed in a regular plan across the facade surface to an unvarying pattern.

Our concern in this study is primarily with mosaic used by architects in the belief that it would be a relatively inexpensive way for providing a durable, maintenance-free, weatherproof and notionally seamless skin to modernist geometric concrete forms without the attendant problem of the natural colour, texture, weathering and standing associated with bare cast concrete.

To widen our understanding of the material when applied in this context and to record as much detail about the modern use of mosaic as possible we spoke to architects and other professionals who used mosaic in their designs or have participated in repair works. Where possible we also approached contractors and craftsmen who carried out the work for details of the materials used and techniques involved. Additionally we made contact with practising mosaicists, mosaic enthusiasts and other conservation experts.

One of the difficulties of undertaking an initial study of this kind is reconciling the multiplicity of materials, both as finishes and in substrate construction which have been used as cladding but which can all be legitimately classified under the generic term mosaic. Also there are wide variations in the types of building and locations where mosaic has been installed, and consequently the

Figure 16.1   Looking up one of the main structural ribs to the stained glass drum above the altar and 'crown of thorns', Liverpool Metropolitan Cathedral of Christ the King. Mosaic cladding is used for all the exposed faces of the rib from the main podium level up to the base of the pinnacles forming the crown of thorns at the top (Bickerdike Allen Partners)

conditions of exposure to which the mosaic has been subjected. This makes comparative evaluation of performance difficult, particularly as the individual materials and craft techniques used are generally poorly recorded or apparently undocumented altogether.

Another important aspect of our study has been to identify useful parallels with the work being undertaken by conservators of historic mosaics. Most of the information that has been published on *in situ* techniques of mosaic conservation and preservation has been concerned with mosaics uncovered during archaeological discoveries, usually of Roman origin, or internal mosaics in medieval and Renaissance buildings.

We have also talked with museum conservators who have experience with smaller, often free-standing mosaic artefacts, for instance decorative panels which may have been 'liberated' in past centuries from the internal surfaces of buildings. The objective here was to consider the possible transfer for their skills and techniques to remedial work which could be carried on buildings, where the work would usually be to a much larger scale and could include many additional associated problems of decay or deterioration of substrates.

With a very few exceptions the usual approach to mosaic repair on modern buildings has been either to strip it off entirely and replace with an alternative material, or to overclad the existing surface after installing a stabilizing mesh or other restraint structure. This radically alters the appearance of the building. With buildings of major historic and architectural significance such as Liverpool Cathedral, and given the present-day views on the ethics of conservation, these are not acceptable remedial options or certainly cannot be considered appropriately permanent solutions for defects in the long term.

However because of the current state of deterioration of the mosaic and render substrates at Liverpool, which have been left untreated for some twenty years or more, it is now intended that the exposed surfaces should be 'temporarily' encapsulated with a lightweight plastic cladding. This is to ensure that no further material becomes detached with attendant safety risk, to arrest as far as possible any further decay and to enable more detailed research into the development of a long-lasting solution to the problem which respects the designer's intentions as closely as possible or practicable.

In summary we have concluded that generally mosaic cladding on all types of material used on modern buildings has fared much better than would seem to be the case from an initial overview. The perceived impression among designers and others is that mosaic cladding will inevitably fail but this is far from true when the evidence of all surviving examples of this material is examined.

There appear to be broadly three causes of failure of mosaic on concrete, the major one being failure of the substrate materials, not the mosaic itself or even its application, but primarily the failure of the concrete due to the usual defects affecting mid-twentieth century construction which are well documented. Many of these stem from poor workmanship, such as inadequate cover to embedded steel reinforcement which in combination with carbonation and water penetration has resulted in corrosion and consequent spalling and cracking of the substrate. Clearly the continuing integrity of the mosaic skin is entirely dependent on the stability of the substrate concrete (Figure 16.2).

On a smooth, relatively impervious surface material like mosaic any movement or failure of detailing in intervening sealant joints or similar features will readily permit water ingress, but the nature of the surface does not allow an equally rapid outflow or evaporation of entrapped moisture. Frost action on such water combined with the common 'splayed edge' profile of individual tesserae will tend to force off the mosaic. This debonding action is probably the

Figure 16.2 Delamination of mosaic from a free-standing rib at the main podium level. At this location all four exposed sides of the concrete were clad in mosaic (Bickerdike Allen Partners)

second most serious cause of mosaic cladding failure although it often occurs in association with concrete failure as well.

A very much less common failure of mosaic seems to be one which has unfortunately occurred at Liverpool Cathedral. This is the disintegration of the individual tesserae themselves, although this is also associated with debonding at Liverpool. Unlike the majority of case study buildings we have examined, the glass mosaic used on this building originated in Sweden and was off-white in colour, but we have been unable to obtain technical details of its constituents from the original manufacturers. To find out more about the mosaic and its performance, particularly its propensity to disintegrate, we have had a comprehensive scientific analysis carried out on a number of mosaic samples removed during the summer of 1985. The sample tesserae were taken from different representative locations on the building, at high and low levels and on different elevations, under the joint direction of Bickerdike Alan Partners and Richard Cook, a senior stone conservator at the V & A Museum.

To set this in context it should be explained that traditional Italian glass mosaic or smalti is, in very simplified terms, made from glass with metal oxides to give colour and other opacifying agents to give the required translucency. The ingredients are fused together or smelted at high temperatures, between 1200°C to 1500°C. Originally the molten glass was pressed into pancakes some 8–10mm thick, allowed to cool and then broken into tesserae. The manufacturing technique has become more and more mechanized, firstly in the late-nineteenth century by the introduction of vitreous mosaic formed by the mechanical pressing and cutting of the molten glass, and today by a more or less continuous production-line process of mixing, smelting, shaping and breaking.

The evidence from analysis of the Liverpool mosaic is that it was not made of glass in the traditional way. It appears to be made of sintered glass, most probably by pressing blanks of finely milled or powdered material which were likely to have included both raw ingredients and finely crushed recycled glass. The inclusion of recycled glass seems to be the most likely way to account for the erratically and arbitrarily varied chemical composition found in the analysis of the tesserae tested. The powdered material together with binding agents would be sintered, heated until the particles fused together but did not smelt, usually at a temperature of around 750°C to 800°C. As a result sintered solids are likely to be filled with a mass of tiny pores and the mixing process may not result in a uniform composition.

The widespread failure of individual tesserae, which appears to be almost unique to this building, may be partly attributable to poor mixing of the original ingredients, inappropriate constituents and failure to achieve adequately-fused particles in the matrix of the tesserae, possibly due to too low a furnace temperature. However, despite the discoloured appearance of the most exposed tesserae we found no evidence of permeability through the glass surface: the colouring seems to be predominantly due to a superficial deposit, most probably from atmospheric pollution.

Another problem at Liverpool results from the debonding of the mosaic together with its render substrate from the structural concrete (Figure 16.4). The concrete was originally cast with the intention of achieving

Figure 16.3 Detail of multi-layered cementitious render substrate beneath the mosaic and the keyed concrete surface of the structural concrete. Note the almost total loss of grout from all the inter-tesserae joints, which is particularly severe on the upper surface of the ribs which are more exposed to the weather and rainwater runoff
(Bickerdike Allen Partners)

an integral mechanical key on exposed surfaces, for the subsequent attachment of render finishes, which was formed by the lasting imprint on the concrete of expanded metal laths fixed

Figure 16.4 The most exposed areas of mosaic cladding in the cathedral are on the upper surfaces of the ribs above the high-level roof immediately below the crown of thorns. Here the mosaic has suffered delamination and loss of individual tesserae (Bickerdike Allen Partners)

to the face of the formwork.

In our experience this was a most unusual and perhaps unprecedented method to use to form a keyed surface and may even be unique to this structure. Normal practice to achieve a key for a subsequent render layer would be to roughen the concrete by bush-hammering or scabbling the surface after casting and washing off the resultant dust and debris. The attempt to form a mechanical key during the casting process was apparently used to speed up the construction but does not seem to have been very successful. Furthermore, up to three layers of render have been used in places, possibly to achieve the correct line and level with misaligned sections of concrete, with a final application of a strong bedding coat of 1:1 cement to sand mix. We also understand that the preparation of the concrete and application of the render coats was not carried out by the mosaic installers which in our research appears to have been a fairly unusual practice.

Regarding evidence of other failure modes there is an almost uniform loss of grout at all joints between tesserae at all levels of the building (Figure 16.3). We believe this has been a significant factor in causing the loss of tesserae when associated with measured differential thermal movement between the glass and the cementitious bedding (as the glass surface darkens with pollutants it will tend to absorb more heat). The outwardly splayed perimeter edge profile of each glass tesserae, which causes the outer surface area of the glass to be greater than the bedding surface area, tends to lift the glass outward as it expands and causes the glass to debond. This is likely to be a progressive action, leading to eventual water entry behind the tesserae, and subsequent freezing will tend to push the tesserae out of the surface altogether.

English Heritage will be publishing our findings from this research at the conclusion of the project, available by the end of 1998.

CHAPTER 17

RESTORING WRIGHT: FLORIDA SOUTHERN COLLEGE

**Adam Brown, John Figg, John McAslan,
Liam O'Hanlon** and **Kendrick White**

Introduction

Florida Southern College was established on its present site on what was then a sloping orange grove on the north shore of Lake Hollingsworth, Lakeland, Florida in 1926. At that time this Liberal Arts college, sponsored by the Methodist Church, was a small struggling institution. In those days student grants were a rarity and the college had problems in recruiting. By the 1930s the Methodist Church was considering closing it down.

In 1936 the College President, Ludd Merl Spivey, conceived the idea of an ambitious building programme, including a new church building, which would be the focus of a fundraising campaign. Having been informed that Frank Lloyd Wright was the world's greatest living architect, Spivey telegraphed him 'DESIRE CONFERENCE WITH YOU CONCERNING PLANS FOR GREAT EDUCATION TEMPLE IN FLORIDA STOP WIRE COLLECT WHEN AND WHERE I CAN SEE YOU'.

Such flowery language was just Wright's style. The go-getting College President and Frank Lloyd Wright met at Spring Green, Wisconsin and hit it off immediately. They agreed that Frank Lloyd Wright would prepare a campus master plan and detailed drawings as required for a flat fee of $15,000. Ludd Merl Spivey would pay in $200 increments as fundraising allowed.

Wright saw the project as an opportunity to put into practice his concept of 'Organic Architecture' with buildings oriented on the site with a south-north axis between the lake and the church, extended to a dramatic water feature near the top of the slope. At this time, both Wright and the college had financial problems. The former was constructing his winter school, Taliesin West, near Phoenix, Arizona and the College had to raise funds and sustain the teaching programme. In both cases the answer, long before DIY had been heard of, was self-help through student labour. The church, eventually named in 1941 as the Annie Pfeiffer Chapel, was constructed by students paying their way through college by working three days per week at a rate of 10 cents per hour, and another three days each week were spent studying. Wright provided his Clerk of Works, Wesley Peters, to oversee the work.

The Annie Pfeiffer Chapel was unlike anything seen before in Florida and even today, more than 50 years later, still has the power to surprise and shock (Figure 17.1). At the dedication ceremony Mrs Pfeiffer said simply 'They say it is finished!'.

Figure 17.1 Students in procession in front of the Annie Pfeiffer Chapel on their way to Commencement Ceremonies (John Figg)

Wright's designs for Florida Southern College placed long, low structures into the south-facing site. The buildings are characterized by wide sheltering flat roofs, often in overlapping layers with clerestory lights between, and with dramatic cantilevered eaves often perforated to give light-and-shade patterns and always with decorative patinated copper edge trim. Overall the feeling is reminiscent of his Prairie Houses, but in Florida the roofs give shelter from the unrelenting sun, not the snows and rains of Illinois.

Wright's campus plan allowed for a total of eighteen college buildings but of these only twelve were ever completed. Alterations and modifications have been carried out both during and after Wright's lifetime.

Two themes provide continuity to the various structures:

1. The use of large precast blocks, stack-bonded and reinforced in both the horizontal and vertical joints, in what Wright called his 'textile block system'. More than 50 variants of blocks were employed, all with shadow grooves and dentilated perp-ends, variously modelled and some with coloured glass inserts and glass-lensed perforations.

Figure 17.2   West facade of the Polk County Science Building (looking north) showing the tapering buttresses and cantilever roofs contiguous with the esplanade leading to the Annie Pfeiffer Chapel (John Figg)

2. Covered walkways linking the various structures with tapered triangular reinforced concrete buttresses and cantilevered roofs (Figure 17.2). Wright called these 'esplanades' and the total esplanade length on the campus is more than 1° miles.

Florida Southern College, like most Frank Lloyd Wright buildings, has problems of water penetration, particularly through the flat roofs. Some of the cantilevers have deflected significantly but the main durability concern is with the blockwork where cracking, deterioration and disintegration of blocks is coupled with corrosion of the reinforcement in the joints and consequent rust-induced spalling (Figure 17.3).

Figure 17.3   Typical spalling damage to textile blockwork caused by rusting of reinforcement in the bed-joints (John Figg)

Over the years unsympathetic changes have been made both externally and internally to the buildings, often in an ad hoc manner, and sometimes with poor advice on materials selection and building maintenance. The most recent symptom is the failure of the flat roofing system used on the Ordway Building (Figure 17.4).

This should not be taken as a criticism of the College which is immensely proud of its architectural heritage and has to juggle the competitive requirements of educational changes, health and safety legislation and building conservation, while always suffering from inadequate funding and the necessity to minimize adverse effects on the student programme. The College also has a considerable education programme about Frank Lloyd Wright and his West Campus, including extra-mural classes, a visitor centre staffed by volunteers who have completed the course and a sales office for books, leaflets and souvenirs.

Figure 17.4   Failure of elastomeric roofing after three years (Ordway Building)
(John Figg)

Initial investigations

Our first contact with the College came via John McAslan who was taking advantage of a trip to Florida to see the Frank Lloyd Wright campus. John recognized that the durability problems were related to those that Troughton McAslan had recently had to overcome with the Erich Mendelsohn De La Warr Pavilion at Bexhill-on-Sea and approached the College to see whether he could be of assistance.

The college authorities were somewhat sceptical of such an unorthodox approach but said that if he would prepare a preliminary report they would give it due attention. John managed to persuade the College to allow him to take samples and also obtained copies of relevant correspondence, reports and photographs (the College archives are extensive but largely uncatalogued).

From previous work with Ove Arup John was familiar with their research and development capability and brought the samples to London to see what could be done. This was fortuitous since the block material was immediately recognized as being similar to material studied some years previously when Ove Arup's San Francisco office made a preliminary study of the deteriorating blockwork of Wright's Samuel Freeman House (1926) in Hollywood, California. Helped by partial funding by an anonymous donor Troughton McAslan and Ove Arup prepared a preliminary report on the condition of the Frank Lloyd Wright buildings at Florida Southern College and this was presented to the College President and Faculty members in May 1994.

The College considered that the Troughton McAslan/Ove Arup report was the first positive and scientifically-based set of proposals so far put forward and wished to continue the cooperation to include more detailed investigations and comprehensive proposals which would consider the future of the West Campus as a whole but which would also concentrate on the Polk County Science Building which was in particular need of refurbishment and which it was hoped could be renovated in time for the millennium. Aided by a further anonymous donation and grant aid from the State of Florida a series of reports was compiled dealing with the structures, their condition, needs for remedial action and particular concerns. For the Polk County Science Building the urgent repair works and envisaged upgrading were tackled taking advantage of the newly-developed Building Cost Management System/Building Data Spine, the outcome of joint research by the Building Research Establishment, Strathclyde University and Ove Arup and Partners Research and Development.

No accurate as-built drawings of the College existed, especially true site-plans, and these were prepared as an integral part of the work using Global Positioning System survey data to fix the buildings. Students from Plymouth Polytechnic made measured drawings of elevations and sections of the major structures. Photographic records of all the buildings were transferred digitally to optical disc storage that could be accessed via the BCMS/Building Data Spine records system. A new architectural model was constructed of the Polk County Science Building which incorporated proposed modifications to restore the original appearance and also to meet needs for enhanced conditions for tuition and up-dated health and safety standards.

Laboratory investigations

At the same time laboratory studies were begun in order to understand the mechanisms of the blockwork's deterioration and (particularly) to prepare an improved formulation for replacement blocks that would not suffer from repeat failure (as had happened with blocks previously manufactured locally).

The structure of the existing blocks was studied by optical microscopy and measurements were made of the air and water permeability. These studies showed that the blocks had been manufactured using a single size sand (1–2mm particles), resulting in an open-textured highly-permeable material which also had a high moisture movement. Even replacement blocks made for the college containing an acrylic additive were just as permeable. All the blocks had been hand-compacted and inadequately cured and these factors exacerbated the permeability.

Enhanced-specification blocks utilized a 20mm-thick facing mix which mimicked the appearance of the original blocks but which also incorporated a styrene-butadiene rubber (SBR) emulsion to confer impermeability and to assist curing. A normal aggregate concrete 'heart' was used to give greatly reduced moisture movement. The heart concrete also incorporated SBR and could include (stainless steel) reinforcement where appropriate.

The College archives include a large number of the original block moulds, and one small and one large mould were used as patterns for manufacturing moulds for new blocks. For bulk manufacture rubber-faced moulds would be used. Prototype blocks were manufactured and some taken or shipped to Florida for evaluation and exposure trials.

Remedial possibilities

Not many blocks are so badly damaged that complete replacement is necessary but in such instances a new problem arises. Because of the interlaced reinforcement at the block edges it is not possible to remove a single block and then to replace it with a new one of identical design. In any case, even where a section of wall has to be replaced with higher specification blocks, the method originally used would soon lead to rust-induced spalling of the new work because the grouting technique does not give adequate protection to the steel. Using stainless steel for new work could also result in enhanced corrosion of original steel left in place because of the bi-metallic couple.

One approach would be to change the edge shape of the blocks so that the back-edge is castellated. This would enable the reinforcement to be placed in a 'sausage' of mortar in the groove of the lower block and then when the upper block was placed on top excess mortar would squeeze out into the cavity tray. The perp-ends could be grouted as previously since few perp-end joints have spalled and the corrosion problems are essentially at the bed joints. Inserting an individual block may require a 'single flange' edge design and will also need a revised formulation for the mortar. Practical trials of block design and replacement techniques are envisaged for the next phase of the work.

It may be possible to conserve moderately damaged blocks using a consolidation technique. Silane-based treatments have proved successful for stone masonry and silicones, siliconates and silicates have all been used to ameliorate damage in concrete structures. Various forms of polymer impregnation have been used with highway structures. Most of these treatments have adverse aesthetic effects. There is a considerable literature on conservation chemistry, including some work with Frank Lloyd Wright buildings. Conservation studies are the next most urgent need before blockwork restoration strategies can be finalized.

Building performance and cost management

In order to maximize benefit from restoration work on the Polk County Science Building (and subsequent buildings) in the restoration programme a full record must be kept of the steps carried out, and the results on a continuous basis, so that later restoration can be optimized and any unsuccessful work logged and not repeated. Over the life of a building technologies and materials evolve, others disappear from the market-place and new ones appear, and people are promoted, change employers, become ill from time to time and eventually die. The body of knowledge must be defined and held in a comprehensible and easily accessible form, and continually changed and enhanced.

The Building Performance and Cost Management system (BPCM) provides the basis for initially generating, and then holding and developing, this body of knowledge over the life of a building. The concept put to the College was to implement a paper-based version of the Building Data Spine, one of the key elements of the BPCM system.

A customized version of the Building Data Spine was prepared for the College as the basis for their long-term building asset management system. A floppy disc provided macros in Quattro Pro 6 for a five-year capital expenditure plan, plus a 30-year financial asset management program with an amortization facility. A CD-ROM was also provided containing some 80 images of the Wright buildings, the types of dilapidation, and the proposed replacement blocks.

This package provided the College with a structured approach to the overall restoration of the Wright buildings and the securing of data for ongoing management and maintenance. Demonstration discs which illustrate how the BPCM system in software form could enhance and facilitate have also been submitted to the College, and it is hoped that this computer-based version will eventually be adopted. Clearly, with the cooperation of other custodians of Frank Lloyd Wright buildings a comprehensive BPCM system/Building Data Spine could be developed to the mutual advantage of all parties concerned.

The present situation

All the work completed to date was presented to the College President and Senior Faculty in April 1995. Local architects, Lunz Associates, were also involved for computer-simulation studies. The college have now decided to proceed with the Polk County Science Building restoration to a staged programme to be finalized after preparation of a detailed specification for the works. This will entail preliminary on-site opening-up and completion of the blockwork repair and replacement techniques as well as a comprehensive programme for updating the building services.

CHAPTER 18

CONSERVATION GOES EAST: THE RESTORATION OF THE HANS SCHAROUN BUILDING ON THE WUWA HOUSING ESTATE, WROCLAW, POLAND

Jadwiga Urbanik

Introduction

Eastern Europe has a valuable legacy of buildings from the twenties and thirties which have survived relatively unchanged. One of these is the building described as a hotel designed by the German architect Hans Scharoun in 1929. It was an experimental building built to try out new materials, new technology and new tendencies in architecture. It was designed as part of the *Dwelling and Workplace* exhibition (WUWA) organized by the Silesian section of Werkbund.

Function and architectonic concept

The hotel follows contemporary modern thought on social reform by using a completely new design for an apartment block for childless couples and single people. The building consists of two accommodation wings joining 48 small split-level flats, a restaurant, a recreation hall and a rooftop garden. The right wing comprises 16 larger flats with balconies for childless couples (each with an area of 37 square metres), and the left wing consists of 32 smaller flats for single people (each with an area of 27 square metres).

The planning of the flats is particularly bold and original. The corridors are sited in between the split-level flats and serve two floors of apartments, thus eliminating the necessity for a corridor at every level. In one apartment the corridor entrance opens into an anteroom which leads, one floor below, to the living room with a kitchen niche. On the same level as the lving room, underneath the corridor, are the bedroom and bathroom. In the adjacent apartment the entrance from the corridor is downstairs, rather than in the upper level. All the bedrooms are situated in the northern part of the building, under or above the corridors, and thus every flat spans the full depth of the building, which allows cross-ventilation despite the corridor. Bathrooms are situated between the bedroom and living room and are ventilated through the roof (by means of ventilating pipes), as are the kitchen cupboards (Figures 18.1 and 18.2).

The residents of the building include doctors, students and research workers. Scharoun described his building as a dwelling place somewhere 'between the one-family house and hotel and between a shelter for settled people and nomads'.[1] The keys were left at the door-keeper's

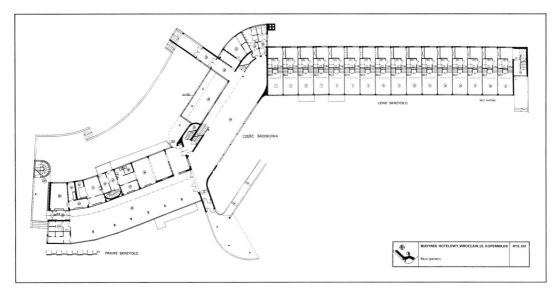

Figure 18.1   Multi-family house by Hans Scharoun, WUWA Estate. The ground floor (present situation) comprising restaurant and kitchen (left wing), the reception desk and hall (middle part) and split-level apartments for single people (right wing) (J. Urbanik and A. Gryglewska)

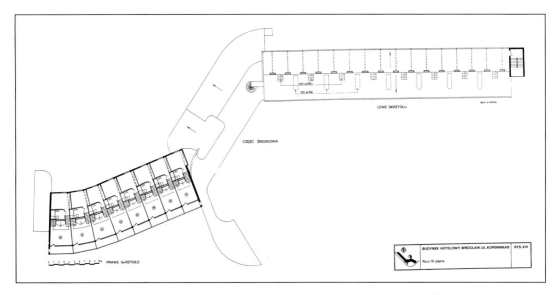

Figure 18.2   Multi-family house by Hans Scharoun, WUWA Estate. The third floor (present situation) comprising split-level apartments for couples (left wing) and a rooftop terrace (middle part and right wing) (J. Urbanik and A. Gryglewska)

lodge and all the flats were fully serviced. The kitchens were reduced to a niche where breakfasts and suppers could be made, dinners were served in the restaurant. The building had the advantages of both an individual house and a hotel. However the intention was not to design a commercial hotel, and by reducing the corridor the area of the single flats could be increased. The width of the flats across the elevation length was also affected by the need for economy of space with three metres assigned to the single flats and 3.55 metres for the double flats.

Believing that 'technology is a master of architecture'[2], and being familiar with the achievements of shipbuilding architecture, Scharoun designed an innovative building of an interesting, modern form. 'The whole composition seems to glide over the terrain, taking into the wings the surrounding area.'[3] The architectonic qualities of Scharoun's architecture were complemented by the fittings which included the light steel pipe furniture designed by Mies van der Rohe and Lilly Reich in 1927, Thonet's No. MR20, in the hall, and built-in furniture (wardrobes in the bedrooms, cupboards in the living rooms) probably designed by Scharoun himself. The rest of the furnishings were conventional.

Contemporary reactions

The building was controversial from the outset, with polarized opinions for and against. Considered to be among its virtues were the elegant proportioning, which meant that the small apartments felt spacious and comfortable, the originality and boldness in the design and layout of the dwelling units[4], the good ventilation and lighting[5], its harmonious social solution to the multi-dwelling place[6], and its appropriate solution to the provision of accommodation for single people.

The building was criticized as well as praised, the form and functional concept being described as a 'an architectonic embodiment of unrest'.[7] It was derogatively compared with a steamboat or barge. 'Does the waste, which was done in the name of art, ill from its birth, have any sense?' the traditionalists asked.[8] The opponents of 'New Building' (Neues Bauen) criticized the formal ideas which are considered the most significant aspects of the building today.

The critics were also quick to pick up on the technical shortcomings of the structure. Problems which emerged within a few years of construction included generally poor-quality workmanship with cracking of the plaster, incorrect window installation and inadequate drainage of terraces.[9] The planning and layout of the apartments were criticized on the basis of the decision to place the bedrooms above and beneath the corridor[10], the poor north-east lighting in the bedrooms[11], the lack of doors in the rooms and inadequate bathroom and kitchen niche ventilation[12], the stairways in the flats[13] and heavy windows.[14]

The critics queried the value of savings made by creating common corridors which therefore required stairs within each flat.[15] The flats, which were to be cheap, were in reality quite expensive, and the costs of the building which was to be a prototype for future mass housing escalated beyond original expectations.

Construction and materials

The building work, including the structural calculations, was carried out by the Breslau firm Huta, Hoch-u.Tiefbau, Aktiengesellschaft, Beton, Eisenbeton, Stein-u. Holzbauten, Kunst-steinfabriken. The quality of workmanship was influenced by the very short construction period (three months). The building has an *in situ* reinforced concrete frame (*Karteblatt-bauweise* type or card type) with cross frames to the main axis of the building frame. This construction freed the outer walls of their structural function which allowed the architect to design large window areas. Ceilings and floors act as connecting members of the framework.

The floors are of ribbed reinforced concrete, using Ackermann's blocks (30 $\leftrightarrow$ 25 $\leftrightarrow$ 10cm). The outer wall footings and the lower part of the walls are made of concrete while the upper walls are built of brick. Above the ground level there is a reinforced concrete framework filled with pumice concrete blocks, and the walls below the windows and lintels were also made of reinforced pumice concrete. Internally the walls are insulated with cork boards and rendered externally in a smooth cement lime plaster. The internal dividing walls are of pumice concrete blocks. Flashings were provided with galvanized sheet iron. The window joinery is of timber and fairly standard except for the restaurant and living room windows. The door joinery was individually designed in the common areas and included a variety of timber doors with large glazed surfaces (sliding-folding, sliding and swing doors). Steel doors made in a nautical style were also used in the common areas.

Technical flaws

An evaluation of the building after 60 years of use has enabled an assessment of the original workmanship and materials to be made. In 1932, three years after the building had been completed, the first cracks appeared at the junction of the reinforced concrete frame and the pumice concrete blocks infill, probably caused by concrete shrinkage or the building settling (Figure 18.3). The building design of broken-up masses, with different parts of different weights and a length of over 100 metres, did not take potential structural movement into account. Cracks occurred where there was a large differential load or structural weakness such as at the junction of the staircases, at the porch and at the chimney.

Inadequate insulation at the foundations and to the walls resulted in dampness and subsequent rust and fungal growth to the walls. The plaster at ground level is in direct contact with the earth, thus exacerbating matters. Poor maintenance and repair resulted in blocked downpipes and the partial covering of the ventilation ducts of the bathrooms (during the roof repairs) and further contributed to the dampness and fungal growth on the inside walls of the building. Insufficient roof slopes and the awkward location of downpipes encouraged dampness and fungus on the staircases and hall walls, necessitating repair of the terrace and redecoration of the interior. The connections between the gutters and sumps and downpipes were poorly jointed and caused dampness of the walls near the sumps, resulting in their complete replacement. Insufficient drainage from the right wing balconies (two balconies connected to one downpipe) and the obstruction to the gully (an excessively thick gully grating) caused loss of of plaster to the underside of the balconies.

Flashings made of galvanized sheet iron were supplemented or exchanged several times in the post-war period. In 1978 they were replaced with thin soft sheet copper which did not serve its purpose. The flashings on window-sills were carelessly made and did not provide adequate protection. The original window joinery was constructed using poor quality coniferous wood and the design has not proved functional in the long term (sliding windows in the restaurant are now stuck after being repainted many times, and the folding windows of the left wing living rooms, hung on small hinges, are collapsing). The windows were placed to the outside wall without jambs and have subsequently warped. The windows are draughty and often singly glazed, thus causing excessive heat loss. External plaster repairs and replacement, window joinery and terrace repairs have been carried out many times before and after 1945 and are indicative of the poor quality of the applied building materials, defects in finishing work and inferior subsequent repair works.

Conservation

Figure 18.3 Cracks in the plaster and damp patches (left wing) which appeared three years after the building was completed, in 1932 (Ostdeutsche Bau-Zeitung-Breslau)

Today the hotel is the only building from the WUWA estate which remains in its original form and as such is one of the exemplars of modern architecture. Its function is little changed. In 1932-43 it was a hotel (Parkhotel), after the war becoming a boarding house and the hotel of the National Labour Inspection. The technical condition of the building is however not good. Although it is recognized that it is culturally important to save the architectonic heritage of the Modern Movement and that this building deserves to be conserved with care, the lack of experience in conserving Modern Movement buildings makes this work problematic.

The building has undergone only minor changes since its inception including external repainting altering the colour scheme, additional window divisions, a change of downpipes, the construction of garages and additional entrances in the basement, rebuilding the space under the overhang (from the street side in the middle part of the building) and removal of the trellis, planter boxes and stairs on the sunny terrace of the left wing of the building. The building therefore retains much of its original aesthetic and a number of original details remain *in situ* such as window and door joinery, steel railings and door handles.

The hotel is on the national monument register in Poland, and therefore its structure and future planning is protected. The only possible changes permitted are those which restore the building to its original state. In order to determine the original appearance of the building in 1929 and identify the changes made since then a very precise and detailed historic-preservation study of the building was carried out. Photographs were often found to be the only source of evidence for the appearance of the building in 1929.

The object of the conservation was to reconstruct the original form while eliminating technical defects. One of the most important problems was to establish the original colour scheme. There were assumptions, highlighted in some theoretical studies, that the building was included among the 'white architecture' of the twenties and thirties. However during the building's evaluation it became clear that this was unlikely. Scharoun was not connected with the architects belonging to CIAM who were propagating a new 'international style', although his designs can be treated as part of this trend. The only available reference to the interior colour scheme is in an article by Edith Rischowski: 'In the background of the dark azure hall, shiny armchairs made of steel pipes shed a silver reflection. The restaurant is dominated by a different shade of red'.[16] Due to the lack of documentary evidence concerning the colouring of the building, stratigraphic examinations were made. Analysis revealed that the building was painted externally light ochre with the gray window joinery. The paint analysis was reinforced by Scharoun's water-colours painted in that period.

Financial limitations and the fact that the building remained in constant use required the conservation works to be carried out in stages. Phase I included holding works to protect the building from further deterioration and to limit ongoing expenditure. This included repairs to the rainwater disposal system, replacement of the flashings, roof repairs and resurfacing of the terrace, window repairs and replacement, plaster replacement and painting and insulation to the foundations. All work to the external fabric retains the original conception. All changes made after the war are being removed where possible.

Phase II includes the replacement of water supply and sanitary system and the reorganization of the basement level which is nowadays only partly in use. Phase III concerns the repair of the interior to reinstate the original appearance of the public common rooms (restaurant and hall) and some of the accommodation areas. The conservation programme must also take into account the funds available for adapting the building for current needs and today's building standards. It is important to ensure that the building performs its function satisfactorily as it has to, at least partially, earn its keep as a hotel.

Repair problems

Where reinstatement of original features was necessary problems arose with the supply of suitable materials (pre-war materials being generally unavailable in Poland or no longer manufactured). The use of new materials resembling original versions was justified on the grounds that the original materials were frequently used inappropriately, accelerating decay.

The dampness of the walls and subsequent fungal growth was a result of pumice concrete blocks used as infill to the reinforced concrete frame. The infill blocks, a relatively soft and porous material, had to be dried out to get rid of toxic deposits, replastered and decorated to ensure the walls were able to breathe. The cork thermal insulation to the interior wall is by today's standards technically deficient. The high heat penetration coefficient of the walls and rapid plaster deterioration necessitated upgrading by applying new external insulation. Combined with the external repairs to the windows this was not an easy process.

The concrete components required cleaning and repair, for example the spiral stairs on the roof. All the metalwork (barriers, downpipes and sumps) needed repair or replacement to match the original design, or cleaning and preservation if they were still in good condition. The galvanized sheet iron flashings which rust quickly in the Silesian climate were replaced with rust-proof sheet zinc. Obstructed gutters and downpipes (partially enclosed in the structure) necessitated large-scale repairs to stop further damp ingress, disintegration of plaster and organic growth. Before the terrace floor (post-war terrazzo) was resurfaced, the durability and condition of the moisture-proof insulation was assessed by an expert.[17] Investigations proved that the condition of both the construction and insulation layers (pressed pitch, 3.5cm) was

Figure 18.4 The rooftop terrace during repair work in 1994. Ceramic slabs replaced cement versions (A. Gryglewska)

perfect. There had however been some damage to the insulation layer during previous repair programmes which necessitated the reinforcement of the joints between the floor and walls. Unfortunately it proved impossible to preserve the original terrace floor, so ceramic slabs (40cm ↔ 40cm) approximating the original cement slabs were applied (Figure 18.4).

The inefficiency of the windows was responsible for increasing maintenance costs and excessive heat loss due to the draughtiness and single glazing. Detailed documentation of the original wooden window joinery has been carried out and used as a model for new joinery. Paint analysis revealed that the windows were gray externally, and ivory on the inside, (except for the balcony door of the right wing from the outside which was light ochre, the restaurant windows from inside which were pink and the corridor windows from inside which were light grey). Following evaluation recommendations were made to replace the joinery to the same detail with double or triple glazing retaining the previous form. Economic reasons and investors' preferences have influenced the change of the material. The cost of timber frames exceeded the cost of PVCu by two or three times, and PVCu had therefore to be considered as a replacement material. The old division of the windows was retained. The difficulty was how to accommodate the new double-glazed profiles to the old style of wooden windows and how to handle the different colouring inside and outside in the new PVCu versions. The results can be seen on the balcony windows of the right wing where the window panels have been restored. During the window replacement the external plaster which had undergone frequent repairs suffered further losses. Installing new window joinery without jambs in the thin external walls of pumice concrete blocks, in the direct vicinity of the structure of reinforced concrete, was very difficult.

Conclusion

Hans Scharoun's hotel building in the WUWA estate is unique in the European context in retaining its near-original form. The buildings remain a significant example of the new architectonic and technological trends of the twenties and deserve special interest, adequate protection and conservation policies in order to arrest the process of degradation to ensure their future is secure for the enjoyment of future generations.

References

1   Craner, J., Gutschow, N. (1984), *Bausstellungen: Eine Architeckturgeschiche des 20 Jahrhunderts*, Stuttgart.

2   Rothenberg, A. (1929), Die Werkbund-Ausstellung 1929 in Breslau, *Ostdeutsche Bau-Zeitung-Breslau*, **17**, (47), 341-9.

3   Niemczyk, E. (1978), Nowa forma w architekturze Wroclawia pierwszego trzydziestolecia XX w, in E.Swiechowski (ed) *Z dziejów sztuki slaskiej*, Warszawa, 419–67.

4   Rischowski, E. (1929), Das Wohnhaus als Einheit, Häuser and Räume des Versuch-Siedlung Breslau 1929, *Innen-Dekoration*, **40**, 400-417.

5   Harbers, G. (1929), Wohnung und Werkraum. Werkbund-Ausstellung Breslau 1929, Der Baumeister, **27**, 285-312.

6   Lampmann, G. (1929), Ausstellungssiedlung Breslau 1929, Zentrelblatt der Bauverwaltung, **49**, (29), 461-8.

7   Lampmann, G. (1929), Ausstellungssiedlung Breslau 1929, Zentrelblatt der Bauverwaltung, **49**, (29), 461-8.

8   O. (1932), Ein Spaziergang nach 3 Jahren, Ostdeutsche Bau - Zeitung - Breslau, **30**, 298-300.

9   O. (1932), Ein Spaziergang nach 3 Jahren, Ostdeutsche Bau - Zeitung - Breslau, **30**, 298-300.

10   O. (1932), Ein Spaziergang nach 3 Jahren, Ostdeutsche Bau - Zeitung - Breslau, **30**, 298-300.

11   Harbers, G. (1929), Wohnung und Werkraum. Werkbund-Ausstellung Breslau 1929, Der Baumeister, **27**, 285-312.

12   Colden-Jaenicke, E. (1929), Nachklang. Hausfrauliches zur Werkbundsiedlung Breslau 1929, Ostdeutsche Bau - Zeitung - Breslau, **27**, 613-16.

13   Colden-Jaenicke, E. (1929), Nachklang. Hausfrauliches zur Werkbundsiedlung Breslau 1929, Ostdeutsche Bau - Zeitung - Breslau, **27**, 613-16.

14   Slapeta, L. and Slapeta, V. (1979), 50 Jahre WUWA, Bauwelt, **70**, 1426-44.

15   Slapeta, L. and Slapeta, V. (1979), 50 Jahre WUWA, Bauwelt, **70**, 1426-44.

16   Rischowski, E. (1929), Das Wohnhaus als Einheit, Hüser and Rüme des Versuch-Siedlung Breslau 1929, Innen-Dekoration, **40**, 400-417.

17   Zubrzycki, M. (1993), Ekspertyza techniczna oraz PT wymiany posadzki tarasu dolnego, Wroclaw, 1993.

CHAPTER 19

HIGH TIDE FOR MODERN HERITAGE: RIETVELD'S BIENNALE PAVILION (1953-54)

Wessel de Jonge

The Netherlands Pavilion at the Venice Biennale was described by the Italian contractor in 1953 as 'exceptionally beautiful, more beautiful than all the other pavilions'.[1] A certain measure of partiality can of course be expected of a contractor, but it is true that the confident simplicity of its spatial composition made this building a very special phenomenon, evoking a striking portrait of post-war Holland. However, it is to be hoped that recent visitors did not assume that this pavilion represented Dutch architecture of the period. In the early 1990s the building was only a shadow of Rietveld's original design. Its unconcealable dry rot and the severe subsidence of the small office attached to the pavilion would have left an undesirable impression, quite different from the impression the first visitors in 1954 must have had.

In the course of time the architectural character of Rietveld's pavilion was seriously affected. The interior spatial concept was weakened by later interventions, while a number of characteristic elements had been radically altered. There were also a number of construction problems hazarding both the aesthetic appreciation of the building and its proper maintenance. Damp from the Venetian lagoon was devastating, as the inner walls showed a persistent salt-efflorescence making it necessary for the plasterwork to be repaired every other year. Due to frequent downpours serious leaks occurred and the roofboards and the casings rotted through.

Changing view

The degeneration of this national showpiece must be partly attributed to the way in which, until roughly a decade ago, its stewardship was seen almost exclusively as a problem of upkeep. Changing views on the conservation of recent architecture have resulted in a new direction for the stewardship of Rietveld's pavilion. The time had come for the structure's management to be seen not as a problem any longer, but as a challenge of an integral restoration of a special example of recent architecture.

The preservation of Modern Movement architecture is not yet a public concern. Some obvious reasons can be put forward for this. The history of this architecture still is very recent and it is not easy to recognize older examples as being particularly significant, and Modern architecture has been unpopular with the general public since the Second World War, due to the misuse of its guidelines in an effort to cope with the enormous post-war housing shortage. Yet the Modern Movement is an essential stage in architectural history and the cultural historiography of mankind would certainly be incomplete without, for example, the Bauhaus, still missing from UNESCO's World Heritage List.

In pairing the social and the technological concepts of an era, the Modern Movement has been a radical turning point in building history, equalling in importance the fundamental qualities of Roman and Gothic architecture.

Functionalism and de Stijl

With the Industrial Revolution, the function and development of buildings became more diverse and specific, as had the buildings themselves. But while the period had changed, time and transitoriness ultimately became important issues in architecture.

Paired with the unparalleled technical progress of the era, these developments ultimately led to the revolutionary ideas and pioneering works produced by the designers of the Modern Movement. At around 1920 they started to establish a direct link between design, the technical lifespan of a building and user requirements. This vision represented a revolutionary point of view in those days. In the Netherlands, the consequent translation of these ideas into practice came to be known as 'het Nieuwe Bouwen', a deliberately ambiguous notion that can be translated as 'New Building' rather than 'New Architecture'. Architect Jan Duiker was a spokesman for this avant garde group. 'Het Nieuwe Bouwen' was not referred to as a style but rather as a working method, setting great value on the connection between form, function, applied materials, construction, economy and time. User requirements and economy were seen as the causes, while appearance and form emerged as a result. Architects in the movement regarded buildings as utilities with a limited lifespan by definition, sometimes even as throwaway articles. Duiker liked to compare his works with cars and aircraft. Some famous examples of this architecture in Holland are the Van Nelle factories in Rotterdam (Brinkman and Van der Vlugt, 1925-9), and Duiker's Zonnestraal Sanatorium for diamond workers in Hilversum of 1926-8, now also a landmark of social history (Figure 19.1).

The late nineteenth century's search for a new architecture that would reflect the industrial society seemed to have been successful for the first time. Various earlier attempts had been made to achieve this but they were based on artistic features. By merely redefining aesthetic principles, as, for instance, in Art Nouveau and to a certain extent even in the de Stijl movement, some questions were not answered fully, particularly in social issues.

Although a desire to return to the essence of architecture was shared, there was a great difference in approaches to this, which elements were to play a role and what this role was to be. In this respect, the so-called 'functionalist' approach, represented in Holland by architects like Duiker and Van der Vlugt, diverged principally from the ideas of de Stijl, as expressed in the early works of Rietveld.

Figure 19.1 One of the dilapidated pavilions of the Zonnestraal Sanatorium (Tu Delft)

Spiritual economy

Duiker and his compatriots sought to build as lightly as possible, using a minimum of material. The dimensions of the concrete frame for Zonnestraal follow the moment diagram, and beams are haunched at their supports to take up the shear forces. The necessarily complicated carpentry was not uneconomic in a period with cheap labour. This striving after optimal construction is referred to by Duiker as 'spiritual economy' leading, as he wrote in 1932, 'to the ultimate construction, depending on the applied material, and develop[ing] towards the immaterial, the spiritual'.[2]

The 'art' of architecture was not in ornamentation but in technology itself. Duiker considered the search for the optimum in materials and dimensions as a process combining the artist's inspiration and the engineer's knowledge, an 'engineer's-art'. He compared this with the construction of medieval cathedrals, the composition of Bach's fugues and the 'horrifying magnitude' of Einstein's theories.[3]

Transitoriness

The application of this technology to achieve the desired imagery of modernism produced one of the most consistent building 'vocabularies' in architectural history. Much of its visual impact depended upon the impression of lightness, thinness, whiteness and geometric purity attainable in fresh concrete. The rejection of traditional embellishment in the drive for formal clarity tended to lead to the omission of conventional details such as copings, sills, drips and overhangs, weathering falls and surface relief generally. [4]

Duiker's and Rietveld's works excel in properly detailed construction. Considering plaster and mesh as suitable construction materials for external walls, as Duiker did, may not simply be attributed to ignorance or to slender financial means. Research in the field of building history has proven that, in technological terms, some of these designers were quite well aware of what they were doing. They apparently accepted a limited technical lifespan as an answer to limited financial means. The issue of transitoriness in Modern Movement architecture should be understood as part of a designer's approach and should have an impact when considering how to restore these buildings.

Preservation

The pioneers of the Modern Movement considered that a building's right to exist should be determined not by its history but by its usefulness. To them the idea of preservation was irrelevant or even contrary to the conceptions of the Modern Movement. In deciding to conserve their buildings we might be acting against their principles. However, it makes no sense for us to use the radical points of view of a group of architectural dissidents as a starting point for our attitude to conserving their buildings. Their dreams about a modern world were not wholly prophetic, but the cultural impact of their work is significant for their future, our present. The main function of Zonnestraal today is as a architectural landmark.

Authenticity

Similar to the way that the preservation of modern architecture presents particular problems in philosophical terms, the technical background of these pioneering buildings now poses special challenges to the conservator. One practical problem is the poor material quality of many of such buildings. Modern buildings weather very inelegantly and, in contrast to most older structures, a patina on their concrete or steel envelope rarely suits them.

In the case of Duiker's works the problem is how to deal with buildings where the constructions themselves are vital to the original conception. How can they be restored without their essential quality of transitoriness being obliterated by advanced restoration technology, leaving an artificial memento behind?

> It is the combination of minimalist aesthetic with young technologies, not to mention a degree of professional naivety, that lies the origin of many of early modern architecture's technical shortcomings. [5]

Obviously architects then lacked aspects of technical knowledge which we have today. More complex is the challenge of finding out exactly what they did know before we can decide whether replacing specific components or systems is appropriate or not. We should be aware that the experiments of modern engineers and architects have a historic value of their own. On the other hand we should avoid overestimating the absolute value of materials and constructions as applied in modern architecture. In view of the temporariness of function, most building materials and constructions in modern structures are short-lived, so that the authenticity of materials is difficult to maintain.

One could successfully argue that materials are not the essence when considering an architectural idea that pursued industrial building methods and the assembly of machine-produced components. The authenticity of appearance, form, detail and space-in-time seems more important in this respect. Yet the quintessence of the Modern Movement remains the idea, the conceptual starting points of the original designer. In the case of Rietveld's pavilion in Venice, these proved to be quite different from Duiker's point of view.

Restoration approach

After financial and planning issues had been resolved the commission for the pavilion's restoration was given early in 1994. A number of starting points for the restoration plan were based on previous research. The numerous interventions in the building over the course of time did not concern the architectonic aspect but rather technical measures to counter maintenance problems. In contrast to other, mostly older monuments, which allow themselves to be read as constructed history books, nothing stood in the way of a complete restoration.

Unlike the work of some of his contemporaries, Rietveld's work stands out because of its originality in aesthetic terms rather than for its ingenuity in construction. The pavilion is a clear example of this. When technically inadequate parts of the pavilion were replaced the resulting alternative often diverged from Rietveld's original, although some changes to the exterior could still have been avoided.

For the restoration non-authentic parts and details were redesigned according to the original drawings. Details that led to early damage or disproportionate cost of maintenance were improved technically, but only if this could be done without disturbing visual consequences. What could be regarded as 'disturbing' is inevitably for the restoring architect to decide. Original parts which were in good condition were kept and reused, such as most of the stucco and the terrazzo tabletop in the office. As only the walls, some parts of the roof, the concrete floor and a mezzanine floor were still of the original composition, the topical question of material authenticity was not a consideration here.

Three dimensions of modernity

The question of whether material authenticity should be a key issue when restoring Rietveld's works remains an interesting one. The three dimensions of modernity, as formulated by DOCOMOMO during our work for UNESCO's World Heritage List (1), provide a starting point to see how innovative Rietveld's works were in technological, social and aesthetic terms. It is obvious that his approach stood apart from the sometimes rigid rationality of most contemporary modern architects in Western Europe, as displayed, for example, in Gropius' Bauhaus and Van der Vlugt's Van Nelle factories, or even in a more sensitive interpretation of these principles such as Duiker's Zonnestraal sanatorium.

Perhaps the most successful de Stijl member, measured by architectural productivity, Rietveld was much more concerned with the artistic and aesthetic aspects of his profession, with its social impact and technological development. Although his Schröder House is a fascinating exploration into how people can live together in a continuous space, this social experiment was probably a result of what was primarily an artistic effort.

Industry and crafts

In comparison with some of his contemporaries Rietveld's approach was certainly directed less towards technological innovation. The industrial production of building components was part of the architectural conception, since it allowed for easy replacement, change in time and low production costs. Therefore there seems little point in attaching great value to the material authenticity of industrially-produced parts of their buildings. Rietveld however, as a carpenter and cabinet-maker by training, was much more concerned with how things were actually crafted. In particular his earlier works, before his move towards a more functionalist approach, show strong evidence of workmanship. For example the patina of some elements in the Schröder House is a valuable witness that cannot be transferred by any medium and should be respected for its material authenticity. The Venice pavilion, on the other hand, was built by an Italian contractor, and proper supervision by the architect of the construction and technical details could hardly be expected. In contrast with the Schröder House in Utrecht, the material authenticity of the pavilion in Venice is therefore not regarded as very significant, with the exception of some specific elements such as the terrazzo flooring. Here, the issue was rather to establish the spatial qualities and Rietveld's volumetric composition as well as the splendid image of early post-war Holland, as was originally reflected by this little building.

Rietveld's pavilion

Rietveld's design was developed on a grid derived from an existing foundation with the intention of reusing it (Figure 19.2). The module of 4 m taken from this was not only applied on the flat surface but was also chosen as a guideline for the entire spatial construction. The building is a daylight pavilion providing an undivided space with internal measurements of 16 m x 16 m x 6 m. Three short cross-walls somehow divide this space into three compartments. A square stuccoed ceiling of 8 m is detached from the walls on all sides. This seemingly floating surface in the middle subtly emphasizes, as it were, the space in its entirety. The interior is thus alternatively experienced both as a whole and in its parts, with both a symmetrical space accentuator and a perceptible centre.

Around the ceiling in the middle, the volume has been raised and vertical roof lights inserted through which natural light falls on the walls of the pavilion. Horizontal venetian blinds consisting of plywood slats, usually referred to by Rietveld as 'shutters', were to keep out the sun and focus the light on the walls at eye-level.

From the outside one gets the impression of a number of volumes grouped at some

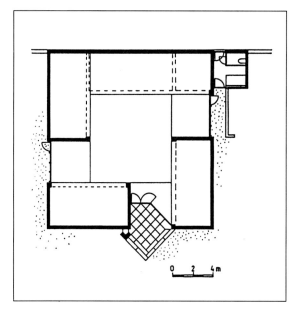

Figure 19.2   Floor plan of the Netherlands Pavilion at the Biennale in Venice, designed by Gerrit Rietveld in 1953-54 (Wessel de Jonge)

distance away from each other (Figure 19.3). The windows, which are 2 m lower, are in between. The independence of the cubical masses was further emphasized by the contrast between the black rear block and the lightly coloured volumes in the foreground. In the building as it is realized this contrasting effect was slightly toned down by finishing the rear part in smooth natural stucco, whereas the other blocks were stuccoed with a rough surface, to the right of the entrance in pale grey, and to the left in mellow yellow. The black plinth so characteristic of Rietveld's work of this period makes the masses float in the air.

At the restoration much effort was put into finding the original colour scheme again. Eventually the original shades were determined by laboratory tests on site so that the authentic textures and colours could be fully respected in the restoration. A revealing discussion arose when the colour samples of the new paints were judged 'too cool' for Italian tastes. Indeed the colours of most of the Biennale pavilions today are attuned to their Italian context. The new apricot shade of the German pavilion, for example, produces a curious and quite anachronistic reinterpretation of its rigid 1930s architecture. When the Netherland's Secretary of State inaugurated Rietveld's pavilion last June, it distinguished itself clearly from its neighbours by its brilliant and unmistakenly Dutch colouring.

Entrance

Through the large glass fronts natural light falls into the hall, admirable for the exhibition of sculptures, and, at the same time, offering some views of the park. The use of colour on the big fronts is striking: white for the transoms and black for the mullions. Choosing white for the beads at the end made a strong pattern, again emphasizing the consistently adhered-to grid. The lower half of the entrance front was moved back. Above the entrance section an ingenious coffered ceiling of diagonal latticed wooden boards was devised, with glass in between. The contrasting colour scheme between the black transoms and the white beads again produces a fascinating graphic effect.

On the steps in front of the entrance the play with the diagonal patterns is continued. Together with the base of the flagpole, which has a mosaic of the Netherland's Lion designed by Luigi de Lerma, the entrance forms the playful element in the somewhat austere design of the pavilion.

Figure 19.3 Exterior of Rietveld's pavilion after the recent restoration. The fascia boards have been restored to their original slenderness, as have the the black and white window frames (Jan Versnel)

The flat roof

The most fundamental problem of the restoration, in terms of conflicting technical and aesthetic aspects, was what to do with the lower part of the roof and its relation to the large glass fronts. Originally, the roof kerbs were designed to be very slight, so as to allow the roofboards, as the termination of the facades, to remain very slim. In the three-dimensional graduation of Rietveld's

Figure 19.4 The restored interior of Rietveld's pavilion. The terrazzo floor has been reconstructed and fitted with electric floor heating to control humidity levels. The plywood louvres have been replaced by polycarbonate to produce a more diffuse light (Jan Versnel)

overall composition, moreover, the roof was completely horizontal and so without any fall. In Venice, where it can often pour with rain, there were already serious leaks after the first season. Additionally, as there had been over-economization on the roof's construction, it sagged, allowing pools of water to form.

In the early 1970s it was rightly argued that the problem of the roof could only be solved by introducing an adequate fall and therefore a necessary lowering of the roof's perimeter. Disturbing the geometry of the windows, which followed the three-dimensional grid of Rietveld's design, would be the inevitable result. After much consideration it was decided to do this, in order to regain control over the pavilion's maintenance. Unfortunately, the roof perimeter was lowered twice as much as initially planned, and the dimensions of the roofboards themselves had to double as a result of unforeseen problems with the realization and became over-pronounced. Because of this the composition of the building as a whole was seriously affected.

Inside, the independence of the central ceiling had been encroached upon by parts of the ceiling that sloped up to the glass fronts. These had had to be pulled flush with the central part, with the resulting loss of definition of the square.

At the restoration the low roof was again replaced, this time by light corrugated steel panels with thermal insulation (Figure 19.4). A slope towards the centre of the roof allowed the roof's perimeter to be raised to its original height and, consequently, the windows as well as the interior ceiling to be restored again in accordance with Rietveld's idea. A special Swiss drainage system guarantees a speedy removal of the rainwater, essential to such a delicate technical solution. The former rainpipes along the glass fronts now serve as overflow and detector pipes in case the drainage gets blocked.

The role of DOCOMOMO

The starting point for the restoration of Rietveld's pavilion was that, wherever possible, the project should be in harmony with Italian building practice. Through the agency of DOCOMOMO Italy, we were fortunate to get in contact with the architect Maria Caterina Redini, a DOCOMOMO member, from the very beginning. With her help the work was put to tender and the contract was finally awarded to and the job finally completed by a constructing company from Venice-Marghera.

Thanks to the work of many people the 1995 Netherlands contribution to the Biennale could be presented in a pavilion that once again exuded the atmosphere that Rietveld realised in 1954. Proper stewardship and systematic maintenance planning will have to ensure that this representative building will not again be subjected to a downward spiral of decay and undervaluation.

References

1   The Italian contractor De Marchi was quoted by the Netherlands consul for Milan in his letter to Rietveld of 24 March 1953.

2   Duiker, J. (1932), 'Dr. Berlage en de "Niewe Zakelijkheid" ', De 8 en Opbouw, **5**, (March 3), 43-51.

3   Duiker, J. (1932), 'Dr. Berlage en de "Niewe Zakelijkheid" ', De 8 en Opbouw, **5**, (March 3), 43-51.

4   Allan, J. (1994), 'The conservation of modern buildings', in Edward Mills (ed) Building maintenance and preservation: a guide to design and management (2nd revised edition), Oxford, Oxford University Press, 151 (11.7.4).

5   Allan, J. (1994), 'The conservation of modern buildings', in Edward Mills (ed) Building maintenance and preservation: a guide to design and management (2nd revised edition), Oxford, Oxford University Press, 152 (11.7.7).

BIBLIOGRAPHY

The following references are intended as a basic guide to some of the most useful texts relevant to the conservation of twentieth-century buildings. As yet there are few texts on this subject and the most useful information is scattered among journal articles and chapters in more general books. Conference proceedings seem at present to provide the most comprehensive documents on the subject.

The bibliography is arranged in sections, reflecting the general themes of the conference. Like the conference the emphasis may appear biased toward the 'modern' rather than 'mainstream', but the intention was to deal with the most difficult and urgent problems first and cover more diverse themes at future events. The technology and materials sections reflect this, although bibliographical references are included for some important areas not specifically dealt with at the conference. The references are intended to reflect the international nature of our more recent architectural monuments, although the bibliography only includes items readily accessible in English-speaking countries. The editor would be grateful to hear of further documents felt to be of interest in building conservation.

Conservation theory and methodology (including charters and legislation)

Brandi, C. (1963), *Teoria del Restauro,* Rome: Ediz. Storia and Letteratura, trans (English) by Erder, C. (1986), *Our architectural heritage: from consciousness to conservation*, Paris: UNESCO.

Burns, J.A. (ed) (1989), *Recording Historic Structures: Historic American Buildings Survey/ Historic American Engineering Record,* Washington DC: The American Institute of Architects Press.

DOCOMOMO (1990), *The Eindhoven Statement,* Eindhoven, The Netherlands: DOCOMOMO International.

Department of the Environment (1994), *Draft Planning Policy Guidance Note 15: Historic Buildings and Conservation Areas,* London: HMSO.

English Heritage (1993), *Repair grants*, leaflet, London: English Heritage.

English Heritage (1995), *Agreements for the management of listed buildings,* London: English Heritage.

Fawcett, J. (1976), *The future of the past: Attitudes to conservation 1147-73,* London: Thames and Hudson.

Feilden, B., and Jokilehto, J. (1993), *Management Guidelines for World Heritage Cultural Sites,* Rome: ICCROM.

Fiorini, L. and Conti, A. (1993), *La conservazione del moderno: Teoria e practica. Bibliografia di architectture e urbanistica*, Florence: Alinea Editrice.

ICOMOS Australia (1981), *Charter for the Conservation of Places of Cultural Significance* (The Burra Charter), Sydney: Australia ICOMOS.

ICOMOS (1966), *International Charter for the Conservation and Restoration of Monuments and Sites* (The Venice Charter), Venice: ICOMOS.

Jokihleto, J. (1995), 'The debate on authenticity', *ICCROM newsletter*, 21, (July), 6-8.

Kerr, J.S. (1985), *The Conservation Plan,* National Trust of Australia (NSW).

Le Corbusier, (1941), *Recommendations del'Assemble de la Societe des Nations Adoptees le Octobre 1932* (The Athens Charter), Athens: Societe des Nations.

Ministry of Housing and Local Government (1944), *Instructions to Investigators*, London: unpublished document.

Monnier, G. (1989), A propos de la protection du patrimoine du Xxe siècle, *Les cahiers de la recherche architecture,* 24 and 25 , (1 & 2), 49-54.

Morton, W.Brown III., Hume, G.L., Weeks, K.D., and Jandl, H.W. (1992), *The Secretary of the Interior's Standards for Rehabilitation and Illustrated Guidelines for Rehabilitating Historic Buildings,* Washington DC: US Department of the Interior *et al*.

National Park Service (1975-94), *Preservation Briefs,* Washington, DC: US Department of the Interior *et al*.

National Park Service (1991), *National Register Bulletin 15: How to apply the national register criteria for evaluation,* Washington, DC: US Department of the Interior *et al*.

Planning (Listed Buildings and Conservation Areas) Act 1990, London: HMSO.

Sherfy, M. and Luce, W.R. (1989), *National Register Bulletin 22: Guidelines for evaluating and nominating properties that have achieved significance within the last fifty years,* revised edition, Washington, DC: US Department of the Interior *et al*.

History and criticism

Allan, J. (1992), *Berthold Lubetkin - Architecture and the Tradition of Progress*, London: RIBA.

anon (1952), 'Housing at Churchill Gardens', *The Architects' Journal*, 116 , (3005), 406-1.

Banham, R. (1960), *Theory Design in the First Machine Age,* London: Architectural Press.

Banham, R. (1966), *The New Brutalism*, New York: Reinhold.

Banham, R. (1975), *The Age of the Masters.* London: The Architectural Press.

Cantacuzino, S. (1978), *Wells Coates, A Monograph,* London: Gordon Fraser.

Coe, P. and Reading, M. (1992), *Lubetkin and Tecton: An Architectural Study*, London: Triangle Publishing.

Conrads, U. (1991), *Programs and manifestos on twentieth-century architecture,* Cambridge, Mass: MIT Press.

Cressy, E. (1923), *Discoveries and inventions of the twentieth century*, London: G. Routledge and Sons.

Curtis, W.J.R. (1994), *Denys Lasdun: Architecture, City, Landscape*, London: Phaidon.

Curtis, W.J.R. (1994), *Modern Architecture since 1900*, London: Phaidon.

Drexler, A. (1977), 'Engineers' architecture: truth and its consequences', *The architecture of the Ecole des Beaux Arts*, London: Secker and Warburg, 43.

Duiker, J. (1932), 'Dr. Berlage en de "Niewe Zakelijkheid"', *De 8 en Opbouw*, 5, (March 3), 43-51.

Dunnett, J. and Stamp, G. (1983), *Ernö Goldfinger, Works 1*, London: Architectural Association.

Lord Esher, (1981), *A Broken Wave*, London: Allen Lane.

Gideon, S. (1949), *Space, Time and Architecture*, Cambridge, Massachusetts: Harvard University Press.

Harwood, E. (ed) (forthcoming), *England's post-war building*, London: Yale University Press.

Hitchcock, H-R. and Drexler, A. (1952), *Built in the USA: Post-War Architecture*. New York: Simon and Schuster.

Hitchcock, H-R. (1953). 'Pimlico', *Architectural Review*, cxic, (681), 176–84.

Hitchcock, H-R, and Johnson, P. (1966), *The International Style: Architecture since 1922*, New York: W.W. Norton.

Jandl, H-W. *et al* (1991), *Yesterday's Houses of Tomorrow*, Washington, DC: The Preservation Press.

Jencks, C. (1973), *Modern Movements in Architecture,* London: Penguin Books.

Jokilehto, J. (1985), *Authenticity in Restoration Principles and Practices,* in APT Bulletin, 17, (3/4), 3-83.

Kidder Smith, G. E. (1961), *The new architecture of Europe*, New York: Meridian.

Lowenthal, D. and Binney, M. (eds) (1981). *Our past before us: why do we save it?*, London: Temple-Smith.

Morris, W. (1984), 'The manifesto of the SPAB', in N. Kelvin (ed) *The collected letters of William Morris*, I (1848-80), Boston, Mass: Princeton University Press, 359.

Overy, P., Buller, L., Oudsten, F., and Mulder, B. (1988), *The Rietveld Schroder House*, London: Butterworth Architecture.

Pearce, D. (1989), *Conservation Today.* London: Routledge.

Pevsner, N. (1936), *Pioneers of Modern Design from William Morris to Walter Gropius,* London: Faber and Faber.

Philippot, P. (1976), *Preservation and Conservation: principles and practices,* Washington D.C.: The Preservation Press.

Powers, A. (1992), *In the Line of Development, FR Yorke, E Rosenberg and CS Marshall to YRN 1930-92*, London: RIBA.

Richards, J.M. (1947), *An Introduction to Modern Architecture*. New York: Penguin Books.

Riegl, A. (1982), The Modern Cult of Monuments: Its character and its origin, *Oppositions*,

(XXV), New York: Rizzoli.

Saint, A. (1987), *Towards a social architecture. The role of school building in post war England*, London: Yale University Press.

Ward, B. (1970), 'Houses of the Thirties', *Concrete Quarterly,* (85), 11-15.

Conservation of Modern Architecture

Allan, J. (1988a), 'Landmark of the Thirties Restored', *Concrete Quarterly,* (157), 2-5.

Allan, J. (1988b), 'Tectonic Icon Restored', *RIBA Journal,* 95, (2), 30-32.

Allan, J. (1989), 'Modern Theory of Repair', *Architects Journal Renovation Supplement,* 189 , (12), pp 18-21.

Allan, J. (1990a), 'Instruments or Icons?', *Architectural Review,* 188 , (1125), 8-9.

Allan, J. (1990b), 'Renovation - Tecton's Concrete at Dudley Zoo', *Architecture Today,* (13), 91.

Allan, J. (1990c), 'Technical issues involved in the restoration of Tecton's concrete at Dudley Zoo', *Architecture Today,* (13), 91.

Allan, J. (1994), 'The conservation of modern buildings', in E Mills (ed) *Building maintenance and preservation: a guide to design and management,* Oxford: Oxford University Press, 140-80.

anon, (1937a), 'Dudley Zoo, Worcestershire II: Architects: Tecton', *Architecture and Building News,* 152 , (12 November), 201-207.

anon, (1937b), 'The Zoo at Dudley: Tecton Architects', *Architecture Review,* 82 , (October), 167-186.

anon (1939), 'House at Esher, Surrey', *Architectural Review,* 87 , (88), 103-116.

anon (1940), 'Three Houses at Willow Road, Hampstead, Ernö Goldfinger, Architect', *Architectural Review,* 88 , (89), 126-130 and 149-153.

anon (1985), 'The heritage tomorrow, A future for our past', *Council of Europe,* (26).

anon (1989), 'Cladding - Health Centre - Tecton (Finsbury Health Centre)', *The Architects' Journal,* 190 , (19), 63-5.

anon (1990), 'Listing the '60s', *The Architects' Journal,* 192 , (20), 12.

anon (1991a), 'AJ Action Saves Modern Classic', *The Architects' Journal,* 193 , (18), 11.

anon (1991b), 'Preserving what's new', *Association for Preservation Technology Bulletin,* XXIII , (2).

anon (1991c), 'When quality counts (Willis Faber, Ipswich)', *The Architects' Journal,* 193 , (18), 5.

anon (1993), 'Chip off the old block', *RIBA Journal,* 100 , (8), 40-41.

anon (1994), 'Factory with facelift (Boots Building Study: D10 Building, Nottingham, 1930)', *The Architects' Journal,* 200 , 31-42.

Astragal (1991), 'Last Memories', *The Architects' Journal,* 193 , (5), 7.

Avanti Architects Ltd (1990), *The Tecton Buildings at Dudley Zoo: A Feasibility Study for Restoration and Re-use,* London: unpublished report.

Ball, M. (1993), 'Restoring Wright's concrete campus', *The Architects' Journal,* 198, (13

October), 59.

Bell, S. (1994), 'The listing of post-1939 educational buildings: burden or blessing?', *Chartered Surveyor Monthly*, 3, (6), 16-17.

Bingham, N. (1993), 'The Homewood, Surrey', *Country Life*, 187, (29), 84-7.

Bruce, A. and Sandbank, H. (1944, reprinted 1972), *A History of Prefabrication*, New York: Arno Press.

Chablo, D. (1982), *Twentieth Century Historic Buildings*, ASCHB Transactions 12, London: ASCHB.

Chablo, D. (1988), 'Listing of post-1939 buildings', *English Heritage Conservation Bulletin*, (5), 12.

Chablo, A. (1991), 'Unfashionable Listing (Willis Faber)', *The Architects' Journal,* 193, (20), 19.

Chandler, I. (1991), *The Repair and Refurbishment of Modern Buildings,* London: Batsford.

Cherry, M. (1995), 'Protecting Industrial Buildings: The Role of Listing', in M. Palmer and P. Neaverson (eds), *Managing the Industrial Heritage*, Leicester: Leicester Archaeological Monographs.

Le Corbusier, C. (1927), *Towards A New Architecture*, trans F. Etchells, London: Architectural Press.

DOCOMOMO International (1991), *Conference Proceedings, First International Conference*, Eindhoven, The Netherlands, DOCOMOMO.

DOCOMOMO International (1993), *Conference Proceedings, Second International Conference*, Dessau, Germany, DOCOMOMO.

DOCOMOMO International (forthcoming), *Conference Proceedings, Third International Conference*, Barcelona, Spain: DOCOMOMO.

DOCOMOMO International (1996), *Conference proceedings, Curtain wall refurbishment,* Eindhoven, The Netherlands: DOCOMOMO.

DOCOMOMO Scotland (1990), *Scotland - The Brave New World: Scotland re-built 1945-70,* exhibition catalogue, Edinburgh: DOCOMOMO Scotland.

DOCOMOMO UK (1992), *Modern architecture restored*, London: DOCOMOMO UK.

Donohue, J. (1989), 'Fixing Fallingwater's Flaws', *Architecture*, (78), 99-101.

Elliot, C.D. (1992), *Technics and Architecture,* Cambridge, Mass: MIT Press.

English Heritage (1996), *Understanding listing: post-war architecture*, leaflet, London: English Heritage.

English Heritage and the Royal Institution of Chartered Surveyors with Investment Property Database, (1993) *The investment performance of listed buildings*, London: English Heritage.

Figg, J. and White. K. (1995), 'Florida Southern College', *The Arup Journal*, 30, (3), 19-21.

Fisher, T. (1995), 'Righting a Wright campus', *Building Renovation*, (Winter), 30-33.

Freiman, Z. (1995), 'Modernism's latterday heroes', *Progressive Architecture*, (9), 78-81.

Gimonet, C. (1991), 'Restoration of buildings of Le Corbusier', in *Proceedings of the First DOCOMOMO International Conference*, Eindhoven, The Netherlands: DOCOMOMO.

Greenberg, S. (1990), 'The Economist Building (1) Modernism in the Making', *The Architects'*

Journal, 192, (20), 53-58.

Hammon, F. (1988), 'Le patrimoine moderne - incertitudes et paradoxes', *Historie de l'art*, (4), 114-16.

Hammon, F. (1989), 'Architecture du Xxe siècle: naissance d'un patrimoine', *Monuments Historiques*, (161), 59-64.

Harwood, E. (1992), 'Modern architecture reappraised', *English Heritage Conservation Bulletin*, (17), 16-17.

Henket, H.-J. (1990), 'Documenting the Modern Movement', *World Architecture*, (7), 84-5.

Jackson, M. (1991), 'Preserving what's new', *APT Bulletin*, 23, (2), 7-11.

Jackson-Stops, G. (1991), '2 Willow Road, Hampstead', *Country Life*, 185, (37), 146-9.

Johnson, D.L. (1980), *Assessment of 20th Century Architecture: Notes for Conservationists*, Adelaide, Australia: Flinders University of South Australia.

Jones, N. (1990), 'Pride of Place', *Building Design*, (1001, supplement), vi-vii.

Jurow, A. (1982-3), 'The Immaculate Conception - Ageing and the Modernist Building', Part I, *Archetype*, 2, (4), 10-13, Part II, *Archetype*, 3, (2), 13-15.

Kay, D. (1993), 'Post-war listing - an update', *English Heritage Conservation Bulletin*, (20), 12-13.

Lee, Y.S. (1994), 'The dilemma of listing modern buildings', *Context: The Journal of Association of Conservation Officers*, (44), 16.

Lingel, T. (1987), 'The Gropius House in Lincoln, Massachusetts', *Ottagono*, iv, (22 December), 59.

Longstreth, R. (1991), 'The significance of the recent past', *APT Bulletin*, 23, (2), 12-24.

Lynch, M.F. (1991), 'What are we going to do with the recent past?', *APT Bulletin*, 23, (2), 6.

Mead, A. (1993), 'Restoring an early modern English house to exhibit art (High Cross House, Dartington by W. Lescaze)', *The Architects' Journal*, 198, (22 September), 32-33.

Mead, A. (1994), 'Balancing conservation with improved performance, Restoration of the White House, Haslemere, by Connell and Ward, 1993', *The Architects' Journal*, 199, (7), 18-20.

Mills, E.D. (editor) (1994), *Building maintenance and preservation: A Guide To Design and Management*, New York: Butterworth/Heinemann

Moore, R. (1991), 'Il mondo moderno invecchia', *Abitare*, (295), 252-256.

Morris, N. (1991), 'Catching up with the 20th Century', *The Architects' Journal*, 193, (15), 15.

Moubray, A. de (1984), 'Life in the Round (Chertsey House by Raymond McGrath)', *The Architects' Journal*, 180, (39), 28-31.

Overy, P., Buller, L., Oudsten, F., and Mulder, B. (1988), *The Rietveld Schroder House*, London: Butterworth Architecture.

Parent, M. (1987), *Le Corbusier: Europe and Modernity*, Council of Europe, (31).

Pawley, M. (1990), 'In the grip of museum culture', *RIBA Journal*, 97, (10), 25.

Pawley, M. (1991), 'A Modern Morituri', *Proceedings of the First DOCOMOMO International Conference*, Eindhoven, The Netherlands: DOCMOMO, 64.

Perause de Montclos J.M. (1985), 'Defining the historic monument', *Council of Europe*, (26).

Powell, K. (1994), 'The greatest of all adventures', *The Sunday Telegraph*, (27 February), 7.

Powell, K. and Schollar, T. (1994), 'Restoring a milestone of Modernism (De La Warr Pavilion by Mendelsohn and Chermayeff)', *The Architects' Journal,* 199, (7), 35-44.

Powers, A. (1990), 'Conservation Piece', *The Architects' Journal,* 192, (13), 76-77.

Powers, A. (1994), 'Industrial Buildings and Conservation', *Twentieth Century Architecture,* (1), 91.

Rappaport, N. (1992), 'Preserving the monuments of Modernism', *Historic Preservation News,* (December), 20-21.

Russell, B. (1977), 'Mending the Modern Movement (Saltings, Hayling Island by Connell Ward and Lucas)', *The Architects' Journal,* 165, (13), 582-3.

Saint, A. (1991), 'Notre Dame du Raincy', *The Architects' Journal*, 193, (7), 26-45.

Saint, A. (1994), *A change of heart*, London: RCHME.

Saint, A. (1995), *The Age of Optimism: post-war architecture in England 1945-70*, London: English Heritage.

Scanlon, K., Edge, A. and Wilmot, T (1994), *The Economy of Listed Buildings*, Discussion Paper 43, Cambridge: University of Cambridge Department of Land Economy.

Seltzer, H. (1988), 'The Dessau Bauhaus', *ICOMOS Information*, (4), 20-28.

Sharp, D. (1990), 'Preserving the Modern', *World Architecture,* (9), 84.

Shiffer, R.A. (1993), 'Cultural resources from the recent past', *Cultural Resources Management*, 16, (6), 1-11.

Slatton, D. and Shiffer, R. (1995), *Preserving the recent past*, Washington DC: Historic Preservation Education Foundation.

Spring, M. (editor) (1992), 'Restoring modern buildings', *Refurbishment* supplement to *Building,* 257, (11 December).

Striner, R. (1993), 'Preservation and the recent past', *National Trust for Historic Preservation* Information Booklet (69), 1-23.

Striner, R. (1994), *Art Deco*. New York: Abbeville Press.

Taylor, B.B. (1981), 'Restoration is not salvation', *Progressive Architecture,* (62), 116-19.

The Institute of Advanced Architectural Studies (forthcoming), *Conservation and repair of twentieth-century historic buildings, York, 4-6 May 1993*

Thorne, R. (1993), 'The right conservation policy for listed post-war buildings', *The Architects' Journal*, 198, (13 October), 21.

Trebbi, G. (1987), 'La conservazione del moderno', *Parametri*, 155, (3), 10-11.

Trieb, M. (editor) (1993), *Modern Landscape Architecture: A Critical Review*, Cambridge, Mass: MIT Press.

Von Eckardt, W. (editor) (1961), *Mid-century architecture in America*, Baltimore, Maryland: Johns Hopkins Press.

Yorke, F.R.S. (1948), *The Modern House in England*. London: Architectural Press.

Technical issues

Ambrose, J. (1994), *Construction Revisited: An illustrated Guide to Construction Details of the*

Early 20th Century, New York: John Wiley & Sons, Inc.

Arup, H. (1983), 'The mechanism of protection of steel by concrete', in A.P. Crane (ed), *Proceedings of the First International Symposium on Corrosion of reinforcement in concrete construction*, Chichester: Ellis Horwood, 151-7.

Arya, C. and Vassie, P.R.W. (1995), 'Influence of cathode-to-anode area ratio and separation distance on galvanic corrosion currents of steel in concrete containing chlorides', *Cement and concrete research*, 25, (5), 989-98.

Ashurst, N. (1994), *Cleaning historic buildings*, London: Donhead Publishing.

Association for Preservation Technology, (1989), *Historic Concrete Investigation and Repair*, Chicago: APT.

Bleekman, G.M., III, Girard, A., Link, K., Peting, D., Seaton, A., Smith, J., Teresi-Burcham, L., and Wilson, R. (editors) (1993), *Twentieth-century building materials: 1900-1950*, Washington, DC: US Department of the Interior, National Park Service, Preservation Assistance Division.

British Cement Association (1988), *The diagnosis of alkali-silica reaction*, Slough: British Cement Association.

BS 1881 : Part 124 : 1988, (1988), *The testing of hardened concrete*, London: British Standards Institute.

(British Standards Institute) prEN 1504-9, (1995), ' Products and systems for the protection and repair of concrete structures, Part 9, General principles for the use of products and systems', London: British Standards Institute, draft document.

BRE Digest 330 (1988), *Alkali aggregate reactions in concrete*, Watford: Building Research Establishment.

BRE Digest 363, (1991) *Sulphate and acid resistance of concrete in the ground*, Watford: Building Research Establishment.

CEN TC 51, WG 12, TG 4 (1995), 'Draft recommendation for test method for the freeze-thaw resistance of concrete - Tests with water (CF) or with sodium-chloride solution (CDF)', *Materials and structures*, 28, (177), 175-82.

Cather, R., Figg, J., Marsden, A.F., and O'Brien, T.P. (1984), 'Improvements to the Figg Method for determining the air-permeability of concrete', *Magazine of concrete research*, 36, (129), 241-5.

Cavalier, P.G., Vassie, P.R.W., Safier, A.S., Papworth, F., Bratchell, G.E., Geoghegan, M.P., Brook, K.M., Murray, A.R., Leeming, M.B., Mackie, K.P., Manning, D.G. and Smith, P. (1982), 'Investigation and repair of reinforcement corrosion in a bridge deck', *Proceedings of the Institution of Civil Engineers*, Part 1, 72, (August), 401-419.

Collins P. (1959), *Concrete, the vision of a new architecture,* London: Faber & Faber.

Concrete Society (1987), *Alkali-silica reaction - minimising the risk of damage to concrete*, Technical Report (30), London: Concrete Society.

Concrete Society (1991), *Patch repair of reinforced concrete*, Technical Report (38), Slough: Concrete Society.

Cowan, H. J. and Smith, P. J. (1988), *The science and technology of building materials*, New

York: Van Nostrand Reiuhold Company.

Creegan, P.J., Graham, J.R., Tatro, S.R., Herreryherrera, A.E., Kaden, R.A., McDonald, J.E., and Schrader, E.K. (1994), 'Abstract of Compendium of case-histories on repair of erosion-damaged concrete structures', *ACI Materials Journal*, 91, (4), 408-409.

Dagher, H.J., and Kulendran, S. (1992), 'Finite-element modeling of corrosion damage in concrete structures', *ACI Structural Journal*, 89, (6), 699-708.

Dietz, A.G.H. (1969), *Plastics for architects and builders,* Cambridge, Mass: MIT Press.

DuBois, J.H. (1972), *Plastics history U.S.A.*, Boston, Mass: Cahners Books.

English Heritage (1991), Supplement to *English Heritage Conservation Bulletin*, (June).

English Heritage (forthcoming) *Framing Opinions Guidance Leaflets*

Epstein, S.G. (1994), *Aluminum and its alloys*. Washington, DC: The Aluminum Association Inc.

Evans, U.R. (1971), *The corrosion and oxidation of metals*, London: Arnold.

Everett, L.H. and Treadaway, K.W.J. (1980), *Deterioration due to corrosion in reinforced concrete*, Watford: Building Research Establishment.

Figg, J. (1973), 'Methods of measuring the air and water permeability of concrete', *Magazine of Concrete Research*, 25, (85), 213-19.

Ford, E.R. (1990), *The details of modern architecture*, Cambridge, Mass: MIT Press.

Fulton, F.S. (1994), *Concrete technology: a South African handbook*, Midrand, South Africa: Portland Cement Institute.

Gayle, M., Look, D.W., and Waite, J.G. (1992), *Metals in America's historic buildings*, Washington, DC: US Department of the Interior and National Park Service.

Glass, G.K. and Chadwick, J.R. (1994), 'A investigation into the mechanisms of protection afforded by a cathodic current and the implications for advances in the field of cathodic protection', *Corrosion science*, 36, (12), 2193-2209.

Glass, G.K., Page, C.L. and Short, N.R. (1991), 'Factors affecting the corrosion rate of steel in carbonated mortars', *Corrosion science*, 32, (12), 1283-94.

Grattan, D.W. (ed) (1993), *Saving the Twentieth Century: The Conservation of Modern Materials*, Proceedings of Conference Symposium 1991, Ottawa, Canada: Canadian Conservation Institute.

Hunt, W.D., Jr. (1958), *The contemporary curtain wall: its design, fabrication, and erection*, New York: F.W. Dodge Corporation.

Hurd, M. (1993), 'The evolution of reinforced concrete', *Building Renovation*, (January/February), 51-54.

Jandl, H. W. *et al* (1991), *Yesterday's houses of tomorrow*, Washington DC: The Preservation Press.

Jester, T.C. (1993), 'Historic 20th-century building products database', *Churchill Resources Management*, 16, (6), 21-22.

Jester, T.C. (editor) (1995b), *Twentieth-century building materials: history and conservation*, New York: McGraw-Hill.

Johnson, P. J. (1993), *The restoration of bronze and aluminium windows*, London: R. Fox &

Sons.

Katz, S. (1984), *Classic plastics*. London: Thames & Hudson.

Knoblock, P.G. (1931, 1994 reprint), *Architectural details from the early twentieth century*. Washington, DC: American Institute of Architects.

Lawrence, C.D. (1990), 'Sulfate attack on concrete', *Magazine of Concrete Research*, 42, (153), 249-64.

Lea, F.M. (1970), *The chemistry of cement and concrete*, London: Edward Arnold, 338-59.

Leek, D.S. (1991), 'The passivity of steel in concrete', *Quarterly Journal of Engineering Geology*, 24, (1), 55-66.

Lewis, M.D. (1995), *Modern stone cladding: design and installation of exterior dimension stone systems, ASTM Manual 21*, Philadelphia: American Society for Testing and Materials.

Locke, C.E. and Siman, A. (1980), 'Electrochemistry of reinforcing steel in salt contaminated concrete', in D.E.Tonini and J.M.Gaidis (eds), *Corrosion of reinforcing steel in concrete*, Philadelphia, NJ: American Society for Testing Materials, 713, 3-16.

Morgan, J. (1991a), *Conservation of plastics: an introduction,* London: Museum and Galleries Commission.

Morgan, J. (1991b), *Conservation of plastics: an introduction to their history, manufacture, deterioration, identification and care*. London: Plastics Historical Society.

McGrath, R.F. (1937), *Glass in architecture and decoration*, London: Architectural Press.

Morris, A.E.J. (1978), *Pre-cast concrete in architecture*, London: George Goodwin Ltd.

Neville, A.M. (1981), *Properties of concrete*, Harlow: Longman Scientific, 461-87.

Page, C.L. (1995), *Improvements in and related to treatments for concrete*, UK Patent GB 2 275 265 B.

Page, C.L. and Treadaway, K.W.J. (1982), 'Aspects of the electrochemistry of steel in concrete', *Nature,* 297 , (5862), 109-15.

Parrott, L.J. (1987), *A review of carbonation in reinforced concrete*, Report C/1-0987, Slough: Cement and Concrete Association.

Partridge, M. F. (1993), *Why replace steel windows?*, London: West Leigh Ltd.

Pearce, C. R. (1994), *The ultimate guide to safe window cleaning*, London: OCS Group and ROSPA

Pigeon, M. and Lachance, M. (1981), 'Critical air void spacing factors for concretes submitted to slow freeze-thaw cycles', *Journal of the American Concrete Institute*, 78, (4), 282-91.

Pigeon, M. and Regourd, M. (1986), 'The effects of freeze-thaw cycles on the microstructure of hydration products', *Durability of building materials*, 4, (1), 1-19.

Pourbaix, M. (1966), *Atlas of electrochemical equilibria in aqueous solutions*, Houston, Texas: NACE, 312.

Pullar-Strecker, P. (1987), *Corrosion-damaged concrete: assessment and repair*, London: Butterworth.

Roberts, M.H. (1981), *Carbonation of concrete made with dense natural aggregates,* Watford: Building Research Establishment.

Sedgwick, J. (1991), 'Strong but sensitive', *The Atlantic*, 267, (4), 70-82.

Setzer, M.J. (1995), 'Draft recommendations for test methods for the freeze-thaw resistance of concrete slab test and cube test', *Materials and structures*, 28, (180), 366-71.

Sergi, G., Yu, S.W. and Page, C.L. (1992), 'Diffusion of chloride and hydroxyl ions in cementitious materials exposed to a saline environment', *Magazine of Concrete Research*, 44, (158), 63-9.

Shreir, L.L. (1982), *Electrochemical Principles of Corrosion - A Guide for Engineers*, Teddington: National Corrosion Service.

Simpson, W.G. (editor) (1993). *Plastics: surface and finish*, Cambridge: The Royal Society of Chemistry.

Stanley, C. (1979), *Highlights in the history of concrete*, Slough: Cement & Concrete Association.

Steel Window Association (1992), *The specifier's guide to steel windows*, London: Steel Window Association.

Steel Window Association (1995), *Guidance Notes to Part L1 of the Building Regulations*, London: Steel Window Association.

Treadaway, K.W.J. (1988), 'Corrosion Period', in P. Schiessl (ed), *Corrosion of steel in concrete*, London: Chapman and Hall, 56-69.

Vassie, P. (1984), 'Reinforcement corrosion and the durability of concrete bridges', *Proceedings of the Institution of Civil Engineers*, Part 1, 76, (August), 713-23.

Weidlinger, P. (1956), *Aluminum in modern architecture*, Louisville, Kentucky: Reynolds Metal Co.

Journals

APT Bulletin: Association for Preservation Technology International, PO Box 8178, Fredericksburg, Virginia 22404, USA

ASTM Standardization News: American Society for Testing and Materials, 1916 Race Street, Philadelphia, Pennsylvania 19103, USA

Concrete Quarterly: British Cement Association, Wexham Springs, Slough SL3 6PL

Construction Repair: Palladian Publications Ltd, The Old Forge, Elstead, Surrey GU8 6DD

DOCOMOMO Journal: DOCOMOMO International, Eindhoven University of Technology, BPU Postvak 8, 5600 MB Eindhoven, The Netherlands

English Heritage Conservation Bulletin: English Heritage, 429 Oxford Street, London W1R 2HD

Historic Preservation: National Trust for Historic Preservation, 1785 Massachusetts Avenue, NW, Washington, DC 20036, USA

Professional, amenity and trade organisations

British Cement Association, Century House, Telford Avenue, Crowthorne, Berkshire RG45 6YS.

tel: 01344 762676

The British Cement Association offers expert advice in response to enquiries on concrete and cement. It has a comprehensive library on cement and concrete including an historical section containing books on cement and concrete from the last century. The library also holds two databases on products and services and on literature. Membership of the BCA includes free literature searches, free access to product and technical information as well as access to the library.

The Concrete Society, 3 Eatongate, 112 Windsor Road, Slough. SL1 2JA.
tel: 01753 693313
The Concrete Society is an information generator and provider, specializing in practical applications and new developments of concrete for the benefit of its members. The Society has a technical development centre as well as an a concrete advisory service.

DOCOMOMO International, Eindhoven Institute of Technology, BPU Postvak 8, PO Box 513, 5600 MB Eindhoven, The Netherlands.
tel: 0031 40 47 2433; fax: 0031 40 43 4248
DOCOMOMO International (or the international working party for the documentation and conservation of buildings sites and neighbourhoods of the Modern Movement) aims to promote recognition of the Modern Movement and is actively involved in identification and promotion of distinctive Mo Mo architecture nationally and internationally, acting as advisors to ICOMOS International on 'World Heritage' listing of modern buildings. Through their specialist committees they are actively involved in development of appropriate conservation measures including protection, technical development and dissemination of knowledge. They also attempt to identify and attract funding for documentation and conservation to ensure continued exploration and development of Mo Mo architecture. There are currently some 30 member countries. A quarterly journal and biannual international conferences are some of the benefits to members.

DOCOMOMO UK, The Building Centre, 26 Store Street, London. WC1E 7BT.
tel: 0171 637 1022; fax: 0171 580 9641
DOCOMOMO UK is the British group of the international organisation and is open to all who are sympathetic to the aims of the organisation. Members include architects, engineers, art and architecture historians and administrators. Annual lecture, quarterly newsletter, exhibitions and biannual symposiums. Through the casework programme the organisation assists statutory bodies in the protection and listing of Modern architecture. Holds a national register of significant Mo Mo buildings.

DOCOMOMO Scottish National Group, 39 Partick Hill Road, Glasgow, Scotland. G11 7BY.
tel: 0141 242 5520; fax: 0141 242 5404
Modernist architecture in Scotland - largely a postwar affair - is being assessed, researched and documented by Docomomo Scottish National Group. As well as a regular newsletter, the group has also produced detailed research documents such as that on the steel buildings of the

Moredun Housing Scheme in Edinburgh and Gillespie Kidd and Coia's St Peter's Seminary at Cardross. They hold a register of fifty modern buildings as part of the drive for comprehensive coverage from all the affiliated groups of Docomomo International.

English Heritage, 23 Savile Row, London. W1 1AB.
tel: 0171 973 3000

English Heritage is an independent body sponsored by the Department of National Heritage, their aim is to protect England's architectural and archaeological heritage for the benefit of present and future generations. They are the country's principal expert adviser on the historic environment and are responsible for advising on the listing and scheduling of buildings and monuments to ensure legal protection. Historic Scotland, Cadw and DoE (Northern Ireland) are their equivalent organisations.

The Institution of Structural Engineers, 11 Upper Belgrave Street, London SW1X 8BH.
tel: 0171 235 4535

The Institution of Structural Engineers is recognised internationally as the professional body for structural engineering. Founded in 1908, and granted a royal charter in 1934, the institution now has a total membership of over 22,000. It is an authorised and nominated body of the Engineering Council and a founder member of the Construction Industry Council. The Institute publishes a yearbook of members and a directory of firms for the UK causes including concrete repair are offered on a regular basis.

The Steel Window Association, The Building Centre, 26 Store Street, London WC1E 7BT.
tel: 0171 637 3572

An association for contractors involved in the repair and maintanence of steel windows. They are able to give advice and produce guidelines for the specification of repair and replacement of steel windows.

Twentieth Century Society, 70 Cowcross Street, London. EC1H 6PP.
tel: 0171 250 3857

Originally the Thirties Society, the Twentieth Century Society was founded with the aim of promoting and protecting British Architecture and Design after 1914. Annual lecture programme, visits, newsletter and journals on 20th century design and architecture. Through their casework the Society assists statutory bodies in protection of 20th century architecture.

The Concrete Repair Association, Association House, 235 Ash Road, Aldershot, Hampshire GU12 4DD.
tel: 01252 21302; fax: 01252 333901

An association for contractors in repair concrete with aims of promoting and development best practice. CITB Courses, publications on concrete repair.